What does Jewish tradition offer as a source for healing?

"It is certain that our bodies do not last forever, and that they can't even do everything we want during their physical lifetime. This condition makes life difficult and interesting, and it is a condition that has created much of the search for healing in Jewish tradition."
　　　　　　　　　　　　　　　　　　　　—from the Introduction

Judaism has always understood the link between body, mind and spirit. When physical challenges arise, Jewish thinking provides an opportunity to gain some spiritual ground and restore a sense of comfort.

This anthology, unique in its accessible presentation, opens an engaging dialogue on the relationship between classical Jewish perspectives and contemporary health issues. Infusing the search for healing with new ideas and new ways to look at old texts, this is a vital resource for Jewish spiritual leaders, particularly those involved in Jewish pastoral care ~~ ~~~~ ~l direction, and people who work with or are ~~~~~~~~~~~~~~~~~~~~

"A remarkable collection by some of the ~~~~~~~~~~ Provocative, thoughtful, deeply infused wi~~~~~~ tions, reveals a maturity of thought and r~~~~~~~~~~ ~~~ that is highly readable and often moving for the layperson, professional, scholar, rabbi, and all who work with patients and others in need of healing."
　　　　—**Rabbi Lewis M. Barth, PhD,** professor of midrash and related literature and immediate past dean, Hebrew Union College–Jewish Institute of Religion

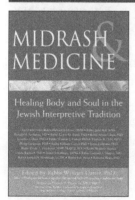

Rabbi William Cutter, PhD, is former director of the Kalsman Institute on Judaism and Health and emeritus professor of human relations at Hebrew Union College–Jewish Institute of Religion. He is editor of *Midrash & Medicine: Healing Body and Soul in the Jewish Interpretive Tradition* (Jewish Lights), and has published and lectured widely on health and healing.

Also Available

"Humane, personal and richly intellectual ... for those of us who are searching for Jewish wisdom about healing when we are not sure of cure, about hope when we know our lives are all too finite."

—Rabbi Rachel Cowan, executive director,
Institute for Jewish Spirituality

"A book that health providers, patients, rabbis, educators and all mortals—Jews and others—will want to return to again and again as age and illness affect us and those we care for and love." —*Jewish Media Review*

JEWISH LIGHTS Publishing

4507 Charlotte Avenue, Suite 100   www.jewishlights.com
Nashville, TN 37209
Tel: (615) 255-2665

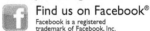

Find us on Facebook®
Facebook is a registered
trademark of Facebook, Inc.

HEALING and the JEWISH IMAGINATION

Spiritual and Practical Perspectives on Judaism and Health

Edited by
Rabbi William Cutter, PhD

JEWISH LIGHTS Publishing
Nashville, Tennessee
www.jewishlights.com

Healing and the Jewish Imagination:
Spiritual and Practical Perspectives on Judaism and Health

2012 Quality Paperback Edition

Library of Congress Cataloging-in-Publication Data
Healing and the Jewish imagination : spiritual and practical perspectives on Judaism and health / edited by William Cutter.
p. cm.
Includes bibliographical references.
ISBN-13: 978-1-58023-314-9 (hardcover)
ISBN-10: 1-58023-314-7 (hardcover)
1. Health—Religious aspects—Judaism. 2. Healing—Religious aspects—Judaism. 3. Medicine—Religious aspects—Judaism. 4. Bioethics—Religious aspects—Judaism. 5. Jewish ethics. 6. Spiritual life—Judaism. I. Cutter, William.
BM538.H43H43 2007
296.3'76—dc22

2006101447

ISBN 978-1-58023-373-6 (quality pbk.)

10 9 8 7 6 5 4 3 2

Cover design: Tim Holtz
Cover art: Inspired by I Samuel 1, *Hannah* (© 1999) was created by Michael Bogdanow, an artist, lawyer, author, and musician living in Lexington, Massachusetts. Hannah meditates, silently pouring her heart out to Adonai in her anguish. She later gives birth to Samuel. The artist's contemporary, spiritual works of art inspired by Judaic texts can be seen on MichaelBogdanow.com.

Manufactured in the United States of America

Published by Jewish Lights Publishing
An Imprint of Turner Publishing Company
4507 Charlotte Avenue, Suite 100
Nashville, TN 37209
Tel: (615) 255-2665
www.jewishlights.com

CONTENTS

ACKNOWLEDGMENTS

This anthology has involved the work of many people because so much of the thinking in our essays began as public discourse, classes, and speeches. My thanks to Lisa Kodmur and Michele Prince, who between them have guided the Kalsman Institute for seven years, and to Rabbi Don Goor, who has chaired the Kalsman advisory committee. Special thanks to Ben Cutter, superb editor and critic, and to Jessica Maxwell for her guidance in technical matters, along with Ellen Rabin and Yael Green. It's delightful to have worked with the folks at Jewish Lights Publishing, and with Karyn Slutsky, reader extraordinaire. To my wife, Georgianne, who has stayed the course in more existential ways, and who as a healer of young souls believes (properly so) that healing work must be done without calling attention to oneself.

One cannot do the kind of healing work that matters to me without the inspiration and cooperation of Rabbi Simkha Weintraub, who is missing from these pages only in the most formal sense. Wherever people care about the ill and needy, Simkha's presence hovers nearby. I dedicate this book to him and thank his colleagues at the New York and National Healing Centers who support him.

Thanks to former interns—now rabbis—Stephen Moskowitz and Mari Chernow. Thanks to Richard Address, a constant inspiration in his work for the Reform movement. The "SeRaf" group of healers was developed under the encouragement of Susie Kessler and Rachel Cowan, and elevated the healing agenda in America for many years. To the Bay Area Healing Center, a nod of appreciation for our collaborations. My former dean and still friend, Lewis Barth, encourages my plots. Bill Berk taught me what a community can do. David Freeman was the first published clinician on my path; and my friend Dr. Leslie Eber has urged me on and on! Peachy and Mark Levy, along with their Kalsman family, are behind it all. All of these people I set before me!

The Kalsman Institute began its work more than six years ago with a generous gift from Lee and Irving Kalsman. When Irving made one of his earlier journeys from illness to cure, he was assisted in healing by a young rabbinic student from the Hebrew Union College; Mr. Kalsman honored that young student with a donation to the Institute's work. From the modest beginning, his family has sponsored numerous conferences and institutes, and now—at least indirectly—has made this publication possible. We thank them profoundly as we thank the leaders of the Jewish healing movement who have urged the Jewish community to reflect more on the state of the individual spirit. And we want to express our thanks to those clinicians who cure us to the point where we can seek healing. We also thank the staff at Jewish Lights Publishing, particularly Stuart M. Matlins, Emily Wichland, and Lauren Seidman for their faith in this effort of faith, and for fostering intersections for us to write down and for you to read.

INTRODUCTION

The Intersection of Judaism and Health

Rabbi William Cutter, PhD, is Steinberg Professor of Human Relations and Professor of Hebrew Literature and Education at the Los Angeles Campus of the Hebrew Union College–Jewish Institute of Religion. He is the author of numerous articles on Hebrew literature, educational theory, and (most recently) aesthetic issues regarding health and healing. He is director of the Kalsman Institute on Judaism and Health.

HEALING AND CURING

William Cutter

It is certain that our bodies do not last forever, and that they can't even do everything we want during their physical lifetime. This condition makes life difficult and interesting, and it is a condition that has created much of the search for healing in Jewish tradition.

The authors of *Healing and the Jewish Imagination* accept the hardheaded realities that come from living with the limits imposed by Creation. Struggle with these realities is part of our human heritage and perhaps an even bigger part of Jewish tradition. There are yet other kinds of limitations—of a social and economic sort—that have direct impact on our spiritual and physical journeys. In this more socially practical domain, we want more than is available: more generosity of spirit, more promise of cure and health, more time and attention from those who try to cure us and more from those who promise healing. We want more people to benefit from whatever help is out there. But there is, after all, a difference between God and humans, and only God even qualifies for the measures of infinity. The rest of us live with a circumference around us, inspired to reach for more, in pursuit of God.

The essays in this book—in their aggregate—make the case that Jewish thinking provides an opportunity to gain some spiritual ground when we lack the things we seek. Jewish tradition ought to provide a challenge to make available more of the goods of the world to those who do not benefit from them. And it can provide comfort and proper spiritual perspectives for the inevitable sufferings with which we live. Most of our book deals with the comfort side of this ledger.

The tradition cannot solve problems; what it can do is get us started by providing the opportunity for both the comfort and the perspective that we must grasp for support. Our journey out of Eden is a fact, but accepting that fact from the biblical narrative is not enough. It takes discipline and a maturing of spirit to learn how to find consolation in our search for satisfactions that sometimes elude us because we no longer dwell in Eden. Healing is one of those ideas that "softens us up" so that we are open to inspiration; but it can also toughen us—like good scar tissue—to live with the consequences of being human.

The context of finitude, then, is where we begin as human beings. Each essay in this book bespeaks that finitude, and each author seems to have understood that healing is sometimes available even when cure is not. (Professor Arthur Green is quite explicit about that.) The authors have understood—even if only implicitly—the important difference between curing and healing. Perhaps this difference seems commonplace by now, but even so, the distinction is worth pondering. It is a difference as old as the Greeks—as old as Hippocrates. According to Michael Lee, the editor of the collection *Poems in the Waiting Room,* "the healer sees the patient as a person in trouble who needs to be made whole, while the curer sees the patient as a carrier of a disease, which must be remedied or removed." Sherwin Nuland, in his series of essays about mortality and illness (*How We Die*), has made the distinction between treating the patient as a person and treating the disease as a problem. This relatively recent publication echoes the great healing physician of an earlier generation, Ernest Cassel, who made the distinction between pain and suffering (E. S. Cassell, *The Nature of Suffering and the Goals of Medicine*). It also echoes Arthur Kleinman's distinction between disease and illness, quoted in Dr. Tamara Eskenazi's chapter here.

It is probably our personal experiences that have taught us—firsthand—this difference between curing and healing, because we have either been ill ourselves or we have cared for loved ones with permanent disabilities or particular diseases. But we have also learned about the link between healing and cure. In either case, the first thing we humans seek is cure—clinical solution as a relief from illness, whether it is something as harmless as a sore throat or an event more threatening or permanent. For good and sometimes for ill, Jewish tradition has occasionally collapsed the distinctions—mostly because of Hebrew vocabulary and its English equivalents. A limited Hebrew vocabulary has provided both enriched ambiguity and lack of clarity. In the liturgy, we may never be certain whether God as *Rofe* relates to healing, curing, or both. Our prayer language provides metaphors that can be rendered as "binding wounds" (*mazor*), "giving relief" (*leha-alot arucha*), "to overcome" (*lehitoshesh*), and "to recover" (*lehachlim*). They are all terms that can relate to physical or spiritual resolution. God is a healer and a curer; body and soul are the package in need. Classical language did not have to make a distinction between what the clinic provides and what spiritual forces may offer, that is, not until medicines and procedures actually became significantly useful. This collapsing of boundaries between cure and healing is an important spiritual legacy, but it can be an occasional source of confusion for individuals who want to hold on to hope for an eternal life that might, after all, elevate humans to divine status.

Humans—sometimes alone and sometimes in conscious partnership with God—have now made it possible to overcome remarkably difficult diseases, and we are grateful for that. But with the fostering of "cure," we humans have also fostered some alienation, and not a little hubris, which echoes another elegant Genesis narrative, that of "the Tower of Babel." Every advance in technology has added to a quantification in what constitutes health; every mechanical success, notes Lewis Thomas in his autobiographical *The Youngest Science,* has created distance between curer and the patient. And while few of us would relinquish even one of the technological, biological benefits of the age in which we live, we at least must find a way to compensate for what technology sometimes takes away from the more intimate parts of our lives. Professor Arnold Eisen comments on this through Rav Soloveitchik. In addition, we must be accountable for making all of this new technology available to all human beings and not just to the economically advantaged. For this economic imbalance, above all, has become a social sickness that cries out for healing and for cure.

In any event, we are grateful for both the curers and the healers, and we might well appreciate all those who contribute to complete health, to *refuah shlemah.* Sometimes we turn the objects of our gratitude into heroes of a kind: men and women who render a correct diagnosis, those who offer an honest but sensitive prognosis, others who accompany us more intimately in our journeys—and who provide a higher gnosis (knowledge or insight.) We may reserve a special place for those in the health drama who provide hope where there is not much hope, and even those who find that hope provides a kind of spiritual energy that might actually turn around and enhance the chance for clinical curing. Indeed, while healing and curing are two different things, science today has turned around yet again and provided some evidence that healing attitudes can actually foster cure.

The ambiguity prevails, and healing carries with it a potential controversy. It is a notion that invites pretensions and it sometimes invites false hopes. Since these spiritual energies may indeed affect cure, some spiritual healers have come to believe in their own curative powers, and some in the public like it that way. Since we humans like to embrace heroes, we also like to think about magical healers. Such was the complex theme of a recent remarkable Broadway play called *The Faith Healer* (2006), a grueling exploration of the intense and troubled relationship between curing and healing, trust and cynicism, hope and illusion. Joan Didion, too, has written eloquently of the magical thinking that sufferers sometimes engage in; her book, *The Year of Magical Thinking,* seems to be a forgiveness for our own confusion and despair.

We wish to enhance hope in this book, but not without a toughened awareness that not everyone can be cured. That is the message of Henry Samuel Levinson, American historian of ideas at the University of North Carolina in Greensboro. Professor Levinson has studied hope as a professor and has had to experience hope and its limitations as a patient. He argued in a private lecture delivered before his colleagues who invited him to reflect on his multiple sclerosis:

> As a notion, hope amounts to this: when we identify something as a hope, we are typically talking about some positive expectation we have, some chance of actualizing. The fewer my chances are to realize my possible but not inevitable fulfillment, the closer it gets to becoming a hope against hope—still an expectation but slimmer and slimmer, until nearly baseless.

We religious people walk a fine line, for hope is our business, but we mustn't foster too much hope on the end of a spectrum that is beyond "hope against hope." Our task, as Maurice Lamm once suggested, is not only to hope for realistic results, but to change, sometimes, the things we hope for. When one goal eludes us, we must shift our expectations: I may even know that I must die, but I can hope for an easy passing, for comfort for my family, for less pain tomorrow than I felt the day before (see his book, *The Power of Hope*, 1997).

So there are clinical heroes, and we prize them. This book, however, is a special tribute to those heroes who have helped us imagine hope, and who have enhanced our spiritual relationship to the task of curing and healing, the turning of curing into healing and offering healing balm when cure eludes us. (It was the Israeli poet Yehuda Amichai, in *Open Closed Open*, who said that he learned to speak from his pains.) The best of our heroes have made this distinction between cure and healing without sacrificing either, and they have done so in a way that helps brighten people's lives even when their prognosis is troubled. It would be impossible to name all of those to whom we are indebted, but their writings are in a thousand essays and books, and in references that are part of the emerging and ever-growing literature on the Jewish spirit.

There are many phases of healing activity and a corollary attention to inner spirit that have developed in recent decades. They are evidence of numerous interwoven threads that have created a fabric of healing that the Jewish community by itself may not ever have fostered to this degree. Arnold Eisen calls particular attention to this phenomenon in his essay, but in fact each of the authors in the book seems to grasp the importance of this development, and each introduces historical moments, textual innovations, or modern understandings that will now be available to the work of our healers. Herein are challenges, dissents, illuminations, and promptings. As many essays in this book demonstrate, people have long sought healing along with cure; communities that have experienced illness only vicariously (as in the biblical epoch so creatively described by Drs. Eskenazi and Leveen within) nonetheless require a kind of healing, a repair that enables them to define themselves in terms of health. Communities have always been afraid of awesome illness, and have sought either refuge or palliation.

Authors in *Healing and the Jewish Imagination* have not, for the most part, been involved in either the clinical or spiritual aspects of this work, but they do care very much about the issues of health and healing. And they enthusiastically accepted the invitation to join this anthology. Their primary attention may have been given over to various academic and professional pursuits, but they chose to contribute to this volume at a crucial time in history when many of us are trying to foster a look "inward" without giving up on the community as our outward collective of the individual spirit.

They also have the capability to push the boundaries of our Jewish knowledge, investing our search for healing with new ideas and new ways to look at old texts. We at the Kalsman Institute believe that their talents ought to touch the core of our institute: the intersection of Judaism and health. In other words, we have sought the opportunity to place some of our finest scholars into intellectual contact with some of our finest practitioners. The scholars, teachers, artists, and activists within this volume agreed to meet us, with their work in hand, on terms that have meaning to both of our communities of concern. Thus we came together on mutual terms, even if some of the terms within these pages are intended to be more scholarly than restorative, and even when the discourse may lack some of the more spiritual, delicate language of the healing professionals we all so admire.

In each of the principal essays of the book there is much autobiographical energy—either explicit discussion of the self, or implicit and nuanced consideration of the subject "I" in the conversation. The scientific-scholarly mode is not cool and analytical in these pages; it is embedded in the passion with which each subject is addressed. This intellectual encounter makes this a book of intersections.

One of the critical intersections of the healing world has to do with "stigma"—the emblem that brands people for not being what the rest of us think is the norm. It may be someone with AIDS, or it may be a disabled teenager who cannot run with his group. She may be part of the ancient biblical community and have to drink a potion, or he may be someone who just wants to look like his fellow teenagers: a girl who wants to run in a marathon, a boy who wants to throw a shot put. Stigma is weighed seriously in these pages, almost by surprise, and certainly not by design in every case. Not only are the articles by David Schulman and Rachel Adler about stigma, but the essays by Arthur Green, Elliot Dorff, and Tamara Eskenazi, along with the essay by artist Albert Winn, deal extensively with questions of Erving Goffman's "spoiled identity." Stigma even influences the way in which patients and their families make ethical decisions about their medical care, and that is what Rabbi Peter Knobel urges us to consider in his plea for "narrative ethics." Yet stigma is only one step away from generalization, and Schulman argues that even some of our well-intentioned practices may add to the spoiling of identity.

This book contains even more intersections: literature and philosophy meet up and even dispute each other a bit; history and biography join through the emergence of modern science; regret and promise are described. The idea of story, or stories, appears again and again as one of the hallmarks of this particular interpretive generation. There are texts that many of our readers will not have seen, and they sometimes point us in new directions; and—most important of all—old texts are examined in new ways.

The inspiration for this approach came from our conference, "Mining the Jewish Tradition for Its Healing Wisdom," cosponsored by the Kalsman Institute and Temple Chai of Scottsdale, Arizona. Our friend Dr. Howard Silverman was one of the guiding spirits of that meeting (along with his rabbi, Bill Berk). Much of the material in this anthology was developed at that conference, while some essays came from other Kalsman Institute happenings where leaders were invited to reflect on the intersections of their work and ours. There were other great scholars and text students who presented at the conference, but who were not able to contribute essays for us at this time; I hope that in time we can marshal their talents for a second book.

The current book shares the ideas of a scholar of *Tanach* who is also a social worker, a chaplain who teaches literary theory, and a lawyer who uses his training in anthropology to practice his advocacy. A scholar of mysticism dips into his personal past, and one of his prize students bolsters his mentor's argument with texts about spiritual and physical balance that most of us have not seen. Through all of these connections, we have discovered straight lines that can be drawn directly between varying subjects, and circles that intersect in Venn diagrams. We think that the overlapping interests replace previously separate conversations, and we hope that connecting lines help us carry hope further out and closer to infinity.

Connections, either contiguous or overlapping, tell a new kind of story. It is a story that grows out of crisis and hope and that must end in collaboration. Indeed, it was toward the goal of collaboration as a healing principle that the San Francisco Bay Area Healing Center and the Kalsman Institute sponsored a conference in the winter of 2002–2003, which yielded further encounters and intersections.

We have purposely not addressed some of the most hopeless areas of the health care scene—those issues related to social policy and the economics of health care. These were the themes of two of our conferences, and they are the subjects for another book because it is a subject essential to our communal healing. In *Healing and the Jewish Imagination* we have explored the heart of the rich Jewish tradition through the perspectives of some of our great friends who have mastered that tradition. We have mirrored the dialectical nature of our Judaism, offering up what I would suggest is a classic liberal persistence: an optimism, on the one hand, with an acceptance of the mystery of life and death that illness must remind us of, on the other; a reaching into the infinite future with acceptance of our finitude.

Dr. Howard Silverman, MD, MS, is a clinical professor of family and community medicine at the University of Arizona College of Medicine–Phoenix and a clinical professor of biomedical informatics at Arizona State University, and formerly served as the education director of the Program in Integrative Medicine at the University of Arizona College of Medicine. With five years experience in designing distance education programs for physicians and medical students, he is the Initiative's project leader. Through Temple Chai of Scottsdale, Arizona's Shalom Center, Dr. Silverman developed two programs for Jewish health care professionals to help them integrate their clinical and spiritual lives. The program resulted in increased Jewish communal participation, increased job satisfaction, and reduced feelings of burnout by participants.

A Physician's Reflection on the Jewish Healing Movement

Howard Silverman

Increasingly in clinical practice, the sacred is being supplanted by technology. While this may afford some significant breakthroughs in clinical care, the price has been a steady erosion of the soul of many clinicians as well as patients. The abundant evidence of growing stress among clinicians reflects, in my opinion, a "spiritual deficiency syndrome" endemic in clinicians, many of whom are lacking the sense of awe, mystery, and transformation that previously accompanied them into the examination room. I wonder if people in the clergy would be willing to raise the same issue.

What is the medicine for this malady? Where do clinicians (and clergy) go to renew, refresh, and recapture the sense of the sacred in their work? I believe the Jewish healing movement has the potential to open a door to rekindling an ancient partnership between clergy and clinicians in the pursuit of healing of body, emotions, mind, and spirit. I have been fortunate to experience this firsthand in a number of venues. During the conference "Mining the Jewish Tradition for Its Healing Wisdom" in May 2003, Rabbi Bill Berk and I presented a seminar titled "Prayers, Blessings, and the Mystery of Healing." To prepare for this seminar, we chose two texts related to transformation and studied them as *hevrutah* partners for more than six months. Our experience in this study reflected the ancient notion that "Whenever two people sit together and exchange words of Torah, the *Shechinah* (divine presence) hovers between them" (*Pirkei Avot* 3:3). For me, this sense of the *Shechinah* afforded an unexpected opportunity to revitalize my connection with the sacred and the mysterious. When we ultimately presented this material at the conference, we both had already experienced the healing and transformational power of our *hevrutah* relationship as we sat and exchanged words of Torah. Such is the mysterious nature and linkage of transformation and healing.

If the Jewish healing movement is to move beyond study alone, it must explore ways to engage clinicians and clergy in the kind of *hevrutah* relationship Rabbi Berk and I experienced. Experiments are already under way in many local and national venues as well as within the two sponsoring bodies of the "Mining the Jewish Tradition for Its Healing Wisdom" conference, the Kalsman Institute on Judaism and Health and the Shalom Center of Temple Chai. Ultimately, the recovery of the sacred will help clinicians to heal themselves. More importantly, however, it will revitalize the care we are able to offer our patients and their families as we integrate the sacred and science in the service of healing.

1

The Importance of the Individual in Jewish Thought and Writing

Arnold Eisen, PhD, is the Daniel E. Koshland Professor of Jewish Culture and Religion at Stanford University and chancellor-elect of the Jewish Theological Seminary of America. He is the author of numerous books and articles in the area of modern Jewish thought and practice and has long worked with synagogues and federations around the country in the effort to revitalize Jewish communities and find new meaning for Jewish texts and observances. Currently he is at work on a book entitled *Rethinking Zionism*. Eisen is married to Adriane Leveen, another contributor to this volume, and is the father of Shulie (twenty) and Nathaniel (seventeen).

CHOOSE LIFE: AMERICAN JEWS AND THE QUEST FOR HEALING

Arnold Eisen

My purpose in this essay is to reflect, as a scholar of modern Jewish thought, on the interest in health and healing that has been so pronounced among American Jews in recent years. A major problem in pursuing this task presents itself at once: the fact that the most important modern Jewish thinkers over the past two hundred years or so have had precious little to say on our subject.[1] There are of course exceptions to this rule. Rabbi Abraham Isaac Kook's voluminous and comprehensive corpus contains profound meditations about the body and its relation to personal and cosmic *teshuvah* (repentance or return.)[2] Martin Buber's insightful delineation of "I–It" and "I–You" relationships has proven extremely useful to several schools of psychology and psychotherapy as well as to many hundreds of thousands of readers in search of well-being.[3] Rabbis Abraham Joshua Heschel and Joseph B. Soloveitchik published eloquent addresses on topics such as the "patient as person" and the meaning of suffering.[4]

For the most part, however, modern Jewish thinkers from Moses Mendelssohn to Emmanuel Levinas have focused their work (and still do) on the difficult and urgent collective tasks that have marked the Jewish entry into modernity. They have reimagined Jewish community for an era of voluntary rather than coerced commitment; provided new reasons and renewed authority for the commandments; suggested new meanings for ritual observance and other aspects of Jewish tradition; responded to the Holocaust and the continuing threat of anti-Semitism; adjusted Jews and Judaism alike to the revolutionary reality of a "Jewish State"; and attempted to make the most of the equally revolutionary opportunities presented by America—not least the opportunities made possible by feminism. Other questions—more personal in nature—have usually been addressed indirectly, and in some cases have not been addressed at all.

This neglect of personal concerns, relative or absolute, led Heschel to complain with some justice (albeit with a degree of exaggeration), at a conference called by David Ben Gurion in 1957 to discuss the Jewish national agenda, that:

> Jewish thinking during the last three generations has had one central preoccupation ... the problem of the Jewish people. The group, the community and its institutions, received all our attention. The individual and his problems were ignored.... We thought about community, we forgot the person. The time has arrived to pay heed to the forgotten individual. Judaism is a personal problem ... I mean a relatedness to the center of one's being ... [to the] vital personal question which every human being is called upon to answer, day in, day out. What shall I do with my mind, my wealth, my power?[5]

Heschel exaggerated; "the individual and his [or her] problems" have not been entirely ignored, as I have just noted, and Heschel was not alone in seeking to redress the imbalance to which he pointed.[6] But there is much truth in his claim. Modern Jewish thinkers have had remarkably little to say—and virtually nothing that is systematic or rigorous—about a whole host of issues that are crucial to the well-being of Jewish selves: not only sickness and health, but also love and marriage, humor, death and what follows death, and—the corpus until recently being an all-male enterprise—the importance of gender. In this essay, therefore, I will not only seek to relate the present interest in health and healing among American Jews to what has been said on these subjects in major currents of modern Jewish thought; I will also pay attention to what has *not* been said heretofore, and speculate about why it has not been said. My aim will be to push Jewish thought along paths not yet taken very far, and in so doing to build a bridge between the volumes already on the shelves, as it were, and the expanded library of books and ideas that I hope and expect will be available in the very near future.

To that end, I will focus on two existential concerns that are receiving renewed attention of late from Jews and non-Jews alike. The first is the complex and problematic nature of the selves who need healing and who provide that healing. Modern Jewish thought, I believe, has by and large presumed a self at variance with the kind of selves whom each of us knows from our experiences of being one and relating to others. The presumed self is utterly rational, enlightened, disembodied, fully capable of exercising agency in the world, generally happy with its lot in life, and untroubled by what awaits it after death. We will examine this picture of the self with the assistance of the brief but penetrating critique of it offered by the Jewish philosopher Franz Rosenzweig. The changes that Rosenzweig suggested to our sense of self will help bring that picture of the Jewish person into line with the selves we know from experience. It should also better connect it to the images of self that we find in much Jewish thought from all eras before modernity.

The other concern on which I will focus is the *fear of death*. Rosenzweig dealt with the matter explicitly at key junctures in his work. "All cognition of the All originates in death, in the fear of death," begins his magnum opus, *The Star of Redemption*.[7] Rosenzweig's philosophy begins with dissatisfaction at the inability of the philosophers he had studied to adequately face up to the challenge death poses to being. While terror in the face of mortality is of course not new—it has given us many of the religious classics we most treasure—fear of death has arguably taken on a magnified role in Western culture in recent decades. Its presence stands front and center in existentialist and other philosophies, part and parcel of the widespread absence from secular Western culture of the hopes, the beliefs, and the integral communities that in former generations acted to contain death and the anxieties it provokes. Fear of death certainly seems to hover over a great deal of concern with both health and sickness in our day. But this subject, too—prominent in major Jewish text and tradition dating from before the modern period—appears in modern Jewish thought only rarely. We will address it with the help of a writer who is not a Jewish thinker in the conventional sense of the term but a Jewish (and Jewishly learned) novelist—Saul Bellow. Art, as both Bellow and Rosenzweig maintained, has the potential to point toward truths that cannot be stated with philosophical exactitude or conviction. The modern novel in particular—think of George Eliot or James Joyce, Franz Kafka or Marcel Proust—has proven a major vehicle for profound reflection about "boundary issues" beyond the pale of much modern philosophy and theology. Bellow's great novel *Humboldt's Gift*, I believe, has much to teach about what ails modern American Jews (and Gentiles)—and how to make us more whole.

The Sick and the Healthy

I begin with the only volume in the entire corpus of modern Jewish thought that, to my knowledge, bears a title exactly suited to our subject—Franz Rosenzweig's *Understanding the Sick and the Healthy*, written in 1921. It is, I hasten to add, a very short book—Rosenzweig himself called it a *Buchlein* (booklet)—and one that its author decided not to publish; the volume first appeared decades after his death. What is more, the book does not have much to say about actual bodily sickness and health. Rosenzweig used the terms primarily as metaphors to describe a widespread "disease" especially common, in his view, among philosophers but increasingly endangering the rest of the population as well. That "disease" is the practice of standing apart from the flow of life in the mistaken belief that you can thereby grasp hold of its essence, figure out what existence is really about, and get to the truth of things. The book makes a daring connection between the apparently abstract matter of weltanschauung—the way the world appears to us, how we view it—and our individual well-being: the way we move through life day by day and face up to death.

> No man is so healthy as to be immune from an attack of this disease. And ... the very moment a man succumbs, the instant

he believes that philosophizing is necessary, he gives up common sense ... [and enters] a state of utter paralysis.[8]

About six months after Rosenzweig finished the essay he was stricken
with Lou Gehrig's disease, ALS. He eventually became so paralyzed
that he could only work with Martin Buber on their new translation of
the Hebrew Bible by making small eye movements that signaled to his
wife whether or not he approved of Buber's proposals for particular
words. The man who argued that important truths cannot be demonstrated logically but must be verified existentially, through our living of
them, thus received the terrifying chance to enact such a verification in
response to his own illness. Rosenzweig did so for about eight years in
a way that endowed his philosophy with a degree of credibility it
might not otherwise have attained. He wrote and accomplished a great
deal. Many scholars, I among them, believe the essays he composed in
the 1920s are far wiser and deeper than the huge systematic work for
which Rosenzweig is best known, *The Star of Redemption*, begun in
the trenches of World War I and completed in 1920 before the onset of
his disease.

Rosenzweig's aim in his book on sickness and health was to con-
vince his readers to give up on the philosopher's (alleged) quest to get
behind the appearances and concealments of everyday reality in order
to grasp hold of the ultimate essence of things. We should not be trying to explain the nature of God or humanity or the world, he urged,
much less to explain away any one of these three realities or to define
it in terms of the other two. Common sense informs us, Rosenzweig
maintained, that there is a world, a real world, that cannot be reduced
to the imaginings of the human mind (or to the dreams of God). There
are real human beings in this world that likewise cannot be reduced to
mere worldly matter: biochemistry, electrons, and automatic responses
to stimuli. Finally, there is a real God in and beyond our world, a God
who cannot be explained away as a projection of human consciousness
or as a set of natural forces. Indeed, God cannot be explained in any
fashion whatever. God cannot be understood. That was a given for
Rosenzweig. We never grasp God in God's essence. But this is true of
the world and of human beings as well. We human beings remain mysterious to one another and to ourselves. But we are capable of loving

relationship. To a degree, we can be understood. The same holds true for the world, and even in some sense for God.[9]

What matters, then, is making our way through life in proper relation to all three of the independent and yet interdependent elements: God, world, and humanity. Common sense knows this, Rosenzweig argued, and should refuse to let reason persuade us otherwise. The knowledge we require for doing what we need to do has been granted us. "Man is privileged to have everything that he needs to be man. He is in possession of the moment. And as for the rest, God and the world assist him here."[10] We can and do make ourselves reasonably at home in the world, we call out God's name and are called by God, even if the message is not audible or clear. We manage somehow to love God and to love one another. "When man is in need he depends on common sense; he has no time to waste on such a luxury as sick reason. The proper time then is the present—today." We are called to live today, Rosenzweig insisted. Not tomorrow, which we cannot foresee, or yesterday, which we cannot reverse. Just today. It is such a simple matter, yet sometimes so impossibly difficult. "To avail himself of today, man must, for better or worse, put his trust in God."[11]

There are problems with this argument. Rosenzweig, a serious philosopher, at times engaged in patent hyperbole as he examined the "diseases" afflicting reason. *Understanding the Sick and the Healthy* is, when all is said and done, a philosophical essay concerning a venerable philosophical theme: the limits of philosophy.[12] In this respect it might be compared to a work of medieval Jewish philosophy that Rosenzweig very much admired: Yehuda Halevi's *Kuzari*. There is ample room to question Rosenzweig's formulations and his claims, particularly when it comes to the nature of the "common sense" that he so extolled (but never defined!) and the utter disparagement of reason—the faculty on which Rosenzweig, of course, relied in every single paragraph.

He exaggerated, perhaps, because he sought to interest and provoke readers who would not (and could not) stand up to the rigors of longer, more nuanced, and highly technical philosophical works such as *The Star of Redemption*. His readers, Rosenzweig believed, needed to be shaken out of complacency if they were to alter the course of their lives. For the same reasons, I think, Rosenzweig addressed the readers of his "little book" in second person. (I should add that he never speaks particularly to or about Jews. His work concerns, and addresses, men and women of whatever religion who participate in modern Western culture.) He thereby endowed his words with the humility and conviction of lived speech. No final word is ever pronounced; no claim is made to Truth with a capital *T*. The author rather offered what each of us brings to those whom we trust and who trust us: testimony, witness, truth hard won from experience, wisdom. He did not make the kind of truth-claims that can be proven logically or verified in the laboratory, but the kind on which each of us risks the one life we have.

Rosenzweig's essay speaks in this quiet way of the three elements (God, world, humanity) and, more important, of their three interrelations, famously identified in *The Star of Redemption*, as creation, revelation, and redemption. Understanding is a plea by Rosenzweig (perhaps addressed first of all to himself) to join in this witnessing so that we can together stand up to despair with greater confidence in the world, in God, and in one another. The book seeks to transmit Judaism's age-old empowering confidence that human beings have been created in love and that the world, likewise God's creation, is good (even "very good," as God pronounced it in Genesis). Much that is sick in us can be made healthy. The world can be made better by us. It will ultimately be redeemed by God in ways we cannot as yet even begin to imagine. Our job is not to understand the three elements but to choose life with conviction, and we can do so because we, as created beings, bear the gift and demand of revelation, and rightly hope and pray for redemption. Rosenzweig wanted to help us do that.

The Critique of Modernity

We moderns so rarely undertake the tasks needed for a healthy self, Rosenzweig believed, because modern culture has taken a wrong turn, making us particularly susceptible to the "illness" he describes and criticizes. *The Star of Redemption* attacks that problematic wrong turn in philosophical terms; understanding brings it down (or, he might have said, raises it up) to the level of the struggles of the individual person. Loyal to the dominant presuppositions of our culture, mistakenly believing that philosophical reason alone must be the standard by which all claims to truth are judged, living our lives as if we were practicing philosophers, Jews and Gentiles are led to keep a safe distance from the living God of the Bible—sometimes even while seeking God. We too often keep a safe distance from one another as well. This is not good for our health.

The claim that modern culture is "sick" in some fundamental way is commonplace in the works of leading philosophers and social theorists over the past century and a half. Think of Nietzsche, for example, or Durkheim or Freud. It is all the more striking that we rarely find a similar indictment among modern Jewish thinkers (ultra-Orthodox thinkers are a notable exception) before the midpoint of the twentieth century. Jewish thinkers from Mendelssohn onward have of course found much to complain about in their cultures. They have particularly decried anything that seems to threaten Jewish commitment or smack of revived paganism. But sustained, thoroughgoing critique of modern society and culture as a whole, of the sort that Rosenzweig hinted at in his *Buchlein*, has been rare.

This changed dramatically after World War II and the Holocaust. Abraham Joshua Heschel, in his book *The Sabbath* (1966), for example, famously criticized the modern concern with "space" rather than "time," "things" rather than the "ineffable." He maintained in *Man Is Not Alone* (1951) that a person could not hope to arrive at relation to God via reason, but rather needed to cultivate the sense of awe and mystery—severely neglected in modern societies—in order to be open to climactic religious experience. In our technological age man could not conceive of this world as anything but material for his own fulfillment. He considered himself the sovereign of his destiny. Only a moment of despair can impel us to break through the "cage within a maze, high as our mind, wide as our power of will," which keeps us from God.[13] Joseph Soloveitchik contrasted the self (or aspect of the self) who pursues mastery and control of the world (Adam I) with the self in search of covenant, love, and commitment (Adam II). Both are gifts of the Creator, and, as such, intrinsic to the human person. Neither is dispensable, let alone evil. Science is meant to help us know and repair God's world. Jews have an obligation to study it. But the balance between the two selves has been lost in the modern West, Soloveitchik argued. The modern "man of faith" is particularly "lonely" because modern culture values only the pursuits of Adam I and devalues those of Adam II. "The situation has deteriorated considerably in this century, which has witnessed the greatest triumphs of majestic man in his drive for conquest.... His pride is almost boundless, his imagination arrogant, and he aspires to complete and absolute control over everything."[14]

Theological critique of reason's claim to self-sufficiency and the Promethean attempt by human beings to do without God is of course as old as religion. But the challenge to modernity put forth by Heschel and Soloveitchik and anticipated by Rosenzweig is striking nonetheless. It stands utterly at odds with the dominant tendency in modern Jewish thought, which has been adjustment of Jewish belief to the strictures of rational (especially Kantian) philosophy and adjustment of Jewish behavior to the demands of modern Western cultures and societies. Modernity has been the standard by which Judaism has been measured, reason (especially Kantian reason) the bar by which truth-claims were judged, autonomy the ideal to which Jewish selves have aspired. Rosenzweig, Heschel, and Soloveitchik all saw the need to challenge that view of self in order to bring Jews back to God—and health. The self whom they rejected is, in their view, overly rational, smugly self-confident, and utterly self-possessed; that self mistakenly believes that he or she is in control of personal destiny, ever-knowing, ever-capable, and unimpaired in its exercise of free agency. Such a person is not subject to the disabilities and distortions of mind and of body in which moderns have been well instructed by Freud, Marx, Weber, and a host of more recent philosophers and social theorists, in which we all receive further instruction from life. Nor is this self seriously threatened or damaged by the state, society, and culture in which he or she lives—with the two exceptions of assimilation and anti-Semitism.

That is why it is so refreshing to encounter, in Rosenzweig and elsewhere, the self who, like us, moves in and out of doctors' offices and hospitals, suffers from anxiety and depression, is vulnerable, and feels pain. Heschel and Soloveitchik, too, seem convinced that the self who knows that he or she is sick is one who can be healed. It should be added, lest we misread them, that Rosenzweig never asked his readers to abandon reason or responsibility. Nor did Heschel or Soloveitchik.

All three aimed only to deny a certain sort of reason dominance over how modern men and women seek truth and live their lives. In pursuit of that aim they opened a discussion about the sickness of the modern self that provides essential background for our current concern with healing.

Why has there been a lack of sustained critique of modernity in modern Jewish thought as a whole? Why is Rosenzweig's talk of "sick and healthy" so rare? The reason, I suspect, is twofold.

For one thing, Jewish thinkers have struggled to strengthen Jewish commitments in the face of social and cultural forces that have constantly threatened to distance Jews from Judaism, and have often succeeded in doing so. Rather than attack a pervasive reality that they seem powerless to change, Jewish thinkers have left the critique of the regnant culture to others and have focused instead on the work that no one but they can undertake: providing reasons and direction for Jewish commitment. The division of self most often analyzed or advocated in modern Jewish thought is the one separating the Jewish from the Gentile parts of the modern Jewish self. The only weaknesses widely acknowledged in the self are those imposed on Jews by minority status in a Gentile society.

Modernity, moreover, has in many ways been very good for the Jews. Enlightenment and Emancipation have presented Jews with unprecedented opportunities and enabled them to participate in political, economic, and cultural life to an extent Jews had never before experienced. These opportunities arguably extend not only to the Jewish (and Gentile) body but also to the spirit. Enlightenment and Emancipation have opened new vistas for the spiritual imagination, including faith. Jews have therefore been loathe to highlight modernity's failings, much less to pronounce these deficiencies incurable; it would have seemed false to their experience—and seemingly ungrateful—to attack the source of precious freedoms and opportunities. In the words made famous by the other Jewish Marx, Groucho, an attack on modernity by Jews would have meant critiquing the first Gentile club to which Jews had ever been admitted as full members. Jews have in fact overwhelmingly rejected the ultra-Orthodox rejection of modernity. They have instead embraced modernity with both arms opened wide—to the point of regarding the Holocaust and even modern anti-

Semitism as aberrations for which modern society, culture, and political institutions as such cannot be held responsible. They do not see the Shoah or lesser modern ills as by-products or consequences of the modern order, intrinsic to that order. Modern Jewish thinkers have by and large shared this view.

The remedy for anti-Semitic hatred and persecution, it is widely believed, is more Enlightenment rather than less, more dominance by reason rather than less, wider access to the goods that science—and particularly medicine—have made available. Rather like the philosopher Jürgen Habermas, Jewish thinkers have believed that the cure for the ills of modernity is more modernity.[15] They have not called for a change in the rules of the modern order as regards minority religious and ethnic affiliation, or for a fundamental change in the nature of the ideal modern self, even when critiquing aspects of this society and this self that discourage or preclude Jewish commitment.

If American Jewish thinkers have engaged in more explicit critique of modern society and culture in recent decades—a change without which, I suspect, widespread concern with health and healing would not have emerged—the reason was in part the fact that Jews have, since World War II, become more fully a part of America. Acceptance of Jews by America increased the risk of assimilation. The concern of rabbis and Jewish religious thinkers therefore shifted in the 1950s from adjustment to survival and authenticity. What is more, Jews for the first time felt at home enough in America to criticize it strongly. Anti-Semites could not deprive Jews of full participation; that participation brought with it a sense of responsibility, ownership, right, and duty to point out failings and correct them.

No less important, and perhaps more so, Jewish and Gentile thinkers began in the late 1960s to struggle to make sense of the fact that human beings (and, some have argued, God too) had perpetrated and/or acquiesced in the Holocaust. Jewish thinkers such as Heschel, Soloveitchik, Emil Fackenheim, and Eugene Borowitz shared in the postwar disenchantment with technology and with the claim of scientific rationality to a monopoly on our minds and souls. Reason seemed to have failed humanity in major respects, even as its successes in other areas such as medicine continued to be celebrated, and even as individuals and nations alike sought to marshal reason to save the planet from poverty, disease, and nuclear holocaust. In contrast to Mordecai Kaplan's prewar insistence that reason and science be the standard by which all truth-claims be judged (Kaplan was born in 1881, and his conceptual universe was shaped when faith in progress through reason seemed justified), Heschel, in the shadow of the Holocaust, argued the inadequacy of reason when it comes to faith and piety.[16]

One simply cannot imagine a book such as Michael Wyschogrod's brave, original, and controversial *The Body of Faith*—which maintains that Jewish election is corporeal, inscribed upon the very flesh of Jewish bodies—being written before the Holocaust, let alone being taken seriously by its American Jewish readers. "Man is a being who prefers light over darkness," the book begins. "Human intelligence is powerless before the power of God." The Bible sheds more light on ultimate matters than reason ever could. "The reason of Israel," based upon the Bible, "is therefore a dark reason, a reason that remains entangled in the dark soil in which the roots of reason must remain implanted if it is not to drift off into the atmosphere."[17] I am not claiming that Wyschogrod's book (which, like Rosenzweig's work, bears marked connection to the philosopher Yehuda Halevi) is typical of postwar Jewish thought. It is not. But the book bears marked affinities to work by other thinkers in the postwar period (e.g., Heschel and Soloveitchik) as well as to the renewed interest in Kabbalah and spirituality that has likewise become a major thrust in contemporary Judaism. It, too, was virtually absent from the work of major Jewish thinkers in the West several decades earlier.

For all these reasons, Rosenzweig's essay on sickness and health strikes a chord, after several decades of post-Holocaust and postmodern reflection on the failings of modernity, which could not have resounded in previous eras of American Jewish life. It is evident that Jews are now willing to entertain possibilities that formerly would have been scorned, perhaps because they have been forced to admit insufficiencies in humanity and in themselves that would formerly have been denied. The postmodern turn away from "grand narratives" (such as the modern story of Emancipation and Enlightenment) in favor of "local narratives" about flawed individuals or groups is but one more sign of the distrust in claims to absolute Truth. Even many scientists and physicians no longer claim certainty, "the facts," but rather seek to navigate in the uncertainty that they know to be a fact of life, a feature of the medicine that is more and more spoken of as "art" rather than as "science." Many of us, in the current cultural moment, no longer expect to find Truth through either science or faith. Such people rather seek solace, instruction, "healing wisdom."

One other major transformation has accompanied and nurtured the concern with health and healing in recent decades, and it finds no anticipation in Rosenzweig whatever. I refer to feminism. It is surely no coincidence that renewed attention to the need for healing has coincided with the entry of women into public Jewish discourse (including the writing of Jewish thought) and to leadership roles in the synagogue.[18] For one thing, as historians Shulamit Magnus and Marion Kaplan have argued, Jewish women never embraced the rationalist promise of secular modernity as much as the men who went out every day to work in the rational world and so had to dress their minds for the part.[19] Whether there is as well a more "essentialist" reason for women's greater attention to body and the embodied character of thought, biological or cultural (i.e., childbearing and/or childrearing), I will leave it to others to decide. But it seems clear that if Jewish men and women, responding to the powerful cultural forces that have made books and conferences about the body legion in the academy in recent years, are now more likely than they would have been a few decades ago to think of Jewish selves as bodies as well as souls, one reason is that members of our culture cannot avoid thinking of ourselves as gendered—and therefore as embodied.

All of these developments have left their mark on contemporary American selves, Jewish and Gentile. We now know—far better than we would like to know, in many cases—the degree to which we *are* our bodies. Illness and pain force us to recognize that we are less than entirely rational agents, plagued not only by doubt or the diseases of philosophy but by death and the manifold diseases of body and psyche. We not only live with pain, loss, and inadequacy—that is not new, of course—but we "thematize" them, as the postmoderns would say. We articulate these matters more thoroughly than in recent decades, make them into major subjects of cultural conversation (including conferences!) and major aspects of self-conception. The emerging self-conception, aided and abetted by the triumphs of medicine, the resultant longer life spans, and our greater exposure to illness and its treatment, features the body prominently as both a friend who accompanies us well into ripe old age and as an adversary who afflicts us even in youth. The change was bound to affect the belief and practice of Judaism in fundamental ways that are only now beginning to be understood.

Excursus: The Self at Yom Kippur

Heschel, like Rosenzweig, was ahead of the crowd in this respect. At the climactic moment of *Man Is Not Alone*, right before a magnificent description of personal religious experience that in my estimation constitutes one of the greatest passages in modern Jewish thought, Heschel explains one last time that we cannot think our way to God. Modern human beings inevitably have trouble "telling to our minds" what we have experienced thanks to our capacity for wonder. Other factors, too, compel us to resist the acknowledgment of God's presence, which tends to come, if it comes, at moments of shattering personal crisis.

> The world in which we live is a vast cage within a maze, high as our mind, wide as our power of will, long as our life span.... But even those who have knocked their heads against the rails of the cage and discovered that life is involved in conflicts which they cannot solve, that the drive of possessiveness, which fills streets, homes and hearts with its clamor and shrill, is constantly muffled by the irony of time; that our constructiveness is staved in by self-destructiveness—even they prefer to live on the sumptuous, dainty diet within the cage rather than look for an exit to the maze in order to search for freedom in the darkness of the undisclosed. Others, however, who cannot stand it, despair.

My point in citing Heschel at length is not to endorse the psychology of religious experience that he so beautifully articulates in this passage, and surely not to embrace the apparent claim that only despair opens the way to knowledge of God. I am not sure that Heschel meant to make this claim in any case; indeed, as I have argued elsewhere, he was surely aware that the three-fold progress from wonder to God to *mitzvot* described in this book is not the only path Jews walk.[20] Rather, I want to emphasize one final time, as we move from discussion of the nature of the self to focus on anxiety in the face of death, how unusual it is for a Jewish thinker in the modern West to speak in terms of self-destructiveness and despair—and to point out once again how commonplace such views of the self have been in other periods in the history of Judaism. Heschel's language directly recalls that of hasidic forebears,[21] who in turn call to mind previous texts and traditions.

Consider for a moment the Yom Kippur liturgy that Jews still recite each year. That liturgy, like the passages from Heschel and Rosenzweig that we have examined, presumes and depicts a very different and more complex Jewish self than the one usually encountered in modern Jewish thought. It also forces the Jew to face directly the fact of his or her mortality. I think it is worth dwelling on the Yom Kippur liturgy for a moment, the better to understand how the current interest in healing, far from innovating, has in fact returned Jews to themes that before the modern period stood at the very foreground of thought, as of life. Jewish religious culture has long made possible and normative a sort of self discouraged or precluded in modern secular societies and philosophers.

Perhaps we can approach the matter through the following question. Why were the rabbis of old not afraid of injuring fragile selves with the verbal battering rams of accusation and indictment so pronounced in the Yom Kippur liturgy? The congregation's individual and collective sins are repeated many times over in the course of the day. Confessions of guilt seem innumerable. Fists pound the chest in ritual self-flagellation. Worse still, Jews time after time encounter, and give voice to, the frightening image of a divine hand ready to write in—and seal—the book of life and death. Why subject them to this torment year after year? Is it only that the rabbis were well acquainted with human sinfulness and inadequacy? They certainly did know the human material with which they worked. The alphabetical catalogues of human faults supplied for the Yom Kippur liturgy are both exhaustive and inventive. Generations of rabbinic liturgists recognized that human beings "sin" much of the time, in the sense of the Hebrew root *hata*: miss the mark, fall short. Human beings are far from perfect in the rabbis' eyes. All claims to mastery are clearly suspect. "Who is the [true] hero? He who masters himself." The rabbis knew how hard that is to do. They had a healthy respect for *yetzer ha-ra*, the drive that aims at other things than the good. Did they feel they needed to disabuse Jews of overconfidence, break through repression, wear down resistance, and force Jews back to what really matters from the willful distractions with which we surround ourselves? Is that why the critique of self in the liturgy is so relentless?

Perhaps. We know, too, that the rabbis aimed to build up the human beings their liturgy broke down. They trusted in the power of words to heal and not only to harm. They believed that the words they placed in the liturgy would be effective, in some cases at least. They also believed fully in the human ability to "return": repent or change one's ways. There is no notion in the Yom Kippur liturgy of original (i.e., inevitable, inherent) sin. The unending litany of sin is paired with the constant call for *teshuvah* and the promise of divine forgiveness to those who "return." The rabbis insisted that Jews were capable of returning.

However—the point I wish to stress here—the rabbis also seem to have believed that the Jews who used their liturgy could be brought to repentance rather than destruction because those Jews were strong enough to hear—and bear—whatever the rabbis instructed them to know about themselves. Jews were strong not only because they were, as the psychologists put it today, "well defended" (why else the repeated reminders of mortality and sin?), but also because they were loved, and therefore in love with life. They trusted God to seal them in the book of life for another year. Their experiences of Torah and community, on Yom Kippur as throughout the year, would get them through the Day of Atonement, as they got Jews through every other day of life.

I am suggesting, in other words, that the rabbis' strategy of self-repair presumed two precious goods largely absent in contemporary Jewish life: devotion to an authoritative scripture and participation in an integral community composed of human beings who share that devotion. Jews reciting the Yom Kippur liturgy, as the rabbis imagined them, do not sit alone in their rooms but stand and sit surrounded by people whom they know and can lean on. The music and the words of the prayers become old friends after years of repetition. They reprove Jews as only old friends can do, chastising them in a way that reaches the soul without driving it to despair. Sometimes it seems, in fact, that Jews are not serious enough about the reproofs pronounced on Yom Kippur. The most terrible things are said about the self in singsong melodies that seem calculated to soften the blows. There is palpable enjoyment in congregational chanting of ancient and beloved words, even if those words carry brutally harsh threat and critique. However, this, too, is part of the rabbis' strategy for moving Jews to repentance. Jews look into the void during Yom Kippur services, as it were, but are brought back to life by the experience of the goods those services have to offer.[22] God may be distant at times, or fearfully close. But life is all around as Jews pray, inviting the congregation back for another wonderful year inside the blessings of tradition and community. That is why the liturgy's litany of transgression is neither too harsh nor in vain.

The conviction that Torah and community are the necessary vehicles to choosing life seems to me one of the most profound, life-giving, and healing Jewish teachings. Modern Jewish thinkers perhaps cannot be faulted for missing the balanced view of self that it presumes. If they have stressed Jewish capabilities at the expense of other truths about Jewish human beings and the world, if they have devoted relatively little attention to sin and frailty and death, the reason is perhaps that they wished to emphasize how much Jewish men and women, assisted by Torah and joined in community, can accomplish in the world despite the manifold obstacles to such achievement. They have articulated the original Jewish chutzpa that is now popularly called *tikkun olam*, "repair of the world": the contention—arrogant on the face of it—that the world is not good enough as it is, and that we—you and I, mere human beings—are required and empowered to make it better. Rosenzweig would have added, in the spirit of the rabbis, and against the grain of much modern Jewish thought, that you and I, mortal and sometimes ill, powerful and sometimes compassionate, self-destructive, self-deceived, neurotic, insecure, mortal you and I—we are capable of these things. It is, I believe, an affirmation that the movement for health and healing in Judaism at its best learns from the classic texts and rituals of the Jewish tradition, none more potent than those encountered and celebrated on Yom Kippur.

The power of the day, as Rosenzweig noted in *The Star of Redemption*, derives in no small measure from its intimate association with death. Jews pray ardently, over and over again, to be written and sealed in the book of life. They ask to be spared unnatural death, to be remembered when no longer walking the earth, to merit life hereafter.[23] Anxiety in the face of death, and the provision of a strategy to cope with that anxiety, are nowhere better articulated than in the book of the Torah chanted at both the morning and the afternoon services on Yom Kippur: Leviticus. If you can overcome resistance to the book's apparent obsession with purity and pollution, the hierarchy of priest and tabernacle, the blood and gore of animal sacrifice; if you can learn to appreciate the sheer detail of priestly accouterment and practice, you discover a book with much to teach contemporary selves. I believe I am not alone in coming to value Leviticus only in middle age, and to value it precisely for its sense of human frailty and temptation. This book of the Torah meets its reader not on the peaks of Sinai, as it were, but where we live every day: among the minutiae and detail that, the book insists, we can sanctify. Leviticus conveys the assurance that ordinary existence can be wonderfully rich and good despite the very real terror that haunts us in the recognition that one day death will take all we love from us, including life itself.

The book does not let us forget for a moment that we will die. Its chosen symbolic ritual idiom, sacrifice, places us imaginatively in front of the altar, our hands on the body of a throbbing animal about to die. We hear its scream, see its blood, and smell its death. Each of us cannot but think: there but for the grace of God go I, today.[24]

Leviticus reminds us of death repeatedly: not to make us morbid, in my view, or to have the prospect of the grave dominate our lives, but for exactly the opposite reason. It wants to help us contain death inside a life of order, richness, and meaning—and to contain not only our individual deaths but the threat posed by all of the world's pointless suffering and terrible chaos to the sacred order that the Torah seeks to build. Learn how to live, the text advises, in the awful presence of so many deaths—and in the awesome presence of God. Do not focus on death to the point of obsession, but do not repress knowledge of it either. Death will come to you one day, but life can be beautiful and joyous. You can live it well. Ritual—including the liturgy of Yom

Kippur, which originates in chapter 16 of Leviticus—is meant to help us face up to what is hardest and to stare it down.

It is for a similar reason, I think, that the injunction to love our neighbors as ourselves—likewise found in Leviticus—is surrounded by warnings against forbidden sexual relations (another topic virtually absent from modern Jewish thought). Leviticus recognizes that sex is the master passion, indispensable to human relationships, not to mention to creation. Sex is the source of pleasure and an aspect of life, but it also destroys many marriages, friendships, and communities. We don't have to agree with the details of the book's permissions and prohibitions where sex is concerned to appreciate the havoc wreaked in our lives by sexual transgression—probably now more than ever before. Harassment and other violations are much in the news. Adultery is not much in the news because it is so common. Leviticus once again does not seek to repress sexuality but to contain it within a sacred order of love and community.[25]

Love and death are not entirely absent from the discourse of modern Jewish thought (though sexuality is almost never mentioned). Rosenzweig said some important things about love in *The Star of Redemption*, as did several other thinkers in their works. There are even a few memorable passages in the "corpus" of modern Jewish thought about death. Heschel, for example, ended *Man Is Not Alone* with an eloquent meditation on death as the return to God of the life that has been loaned to us. Death, he averred, marks the end of doing, not of being.[26] Rosenzweig's little book on sickness and health ends with the notion—"difficult to realize," he wrote—that:

> All verification lies ahead, the ultimate verification of life, that to live means to die. He who withdraws from life may think that he has avoided death; however, he has merely foregone life, and death, instead of being avoided, closes in from all sides and creeps into one's very heart.... If he is to be restored to life he must recognize the sovereignty of death. [At the end it] will speak: "Do you finally recognize me? I am your brother."

It is extremely telling, however, that Nahum Glatzer, in his introduction to Rosenzweig's "little book," tried to explain this passage away, reminding us that Rosenzweig ended his great work with the teaching: "Into Life." Glatzer suggested that the passage on death may be one reason Rosenzweig found the book unsatisfactory and decided not to publish it.[27] It is as if the subject of death is off limits for a respectable modern Jewish thinker—and certainly cannot be discussed in the terms chosen in this passage by Rosenzweig.

That is unfortunate, I believe. We value Rosenzweig and other great thinkers precisely because they push against and past the limits of what they can in good conscience assert. They do so because they cannot in good conscience deny their readers important truths that they feel compelled to witness but that they can only verify in life. I wish more of modern Jewish thought had dared to join classical Jewish texts such as Leviticus or the Yom Kippur liturgy in moving "beyond the bounds of reason alone." Neil Gillman, in his book *The Death of Death: Resurrection and Immortality in Jewish Thought* (Jewish Lights), has pointed out the lack of attention to death and the afterlife in much of modern Jewish thought.[28] The same could have been said, until recently, of Jewish concern with a host of other bodily matters: sexuality, mental illness, healing. That has not stopped Jews who are unsure of their beliefs where these matters are concerned from taking action: joining burial societies, for example; praying for healing; and comforting mourners with traditional messages of eternal life, and meaning every word.

In these and other cases, I believe, the practice of modern Jewish thinkers, as of ordinary Jews, has been way out in front of the theory designed to make sense of that practice or to authorize it. Many Jewish thinkers, like many Jews less learned in the history of their tradition, have negotiated modernity not so much by the formulation of new beliefs as through the activities that they have continued or innovated. Commitments bespeaking a sense of commandedness have survived the loss of belief in divine Commander or the issuance of commandments at Sinai. Prayer occurs regularly even in the absence of belief in a God who hears or answers prayer. Belief in many such cases lags behind practice and struggles to catch up.[29] Were this not the case, contemporary observance of Yom Kippur among non-Orthodox Jews would long since have lost much of its appeal—and there would likely have been no healing movement in American Judaism.

Legacies of Life and Death

That priority of "life" over "theory" is one reason I now turn to a work of fiction. *Aggadah*, story, narrative, has from the very beginning of Jewish tradition served to articulate matters that defy statement in rigorous philosophical form. Fiction teaches truths accessible in no other way; it has long helped Jews, adopting Heschel's words, to take up the lessons learned from experience and "tell [them] to our minds." When the Jewish philosopher Emil Fackenheim found himself, in the wake of the Holocaust, unable to make logical sense of *God's Presence in History*, he turned to midrash. The distant example of rabbinic stories, and the proximate example of Elie Wiesel's fiction, served him where philosophy had failed. Midrash, he explained, made possible "Jewish affirmations" that "philosophical reflections" alone could not offer. For midrash, unlike philosophy, "refuses to destroy" the root experiences of Judaism (believing in God's commanding and saving presence) "even as it stands outside and reflects upon them." Midrashic thought, he argues, "cannot resolve the contradictions in the root experiences of Judaism but only express them." Yet it does state both sides of those contradictions, positive and negative. It continues to affirm what much of experience denies, and never despairs of the ultimate solution that it cannot in good faith provide. "Midrashic thought, therefore, is both fragmentary and whole." It finds adequate form only in story, parable, and metaphor.[30]

The need for narrative has become a major theme among philosophers in recent decades as well. Martha Nussbaum argues eloquently in her book *Poetic Justice* that the literary imagination is "an essential ingredient of an ethical stance that asks us to concern ourselves with the good of other people whose lives are distant from our own." She rejects charges that literature is of no value for the purpose of fixing law or ethics—that it should be left off to one side of political, economic, or legal thought because it is unscientific, irrational in its commitment to the emotions, and lacking in impartiality and universality. On the contrary, the novel in particular "constructs a paradigm of a style of ethical reason that is context specific without being relativistic, in which we get potentially universalizable concrete prescriptions by bringing a general idea of human flourishing to bear on a concrete situation, which we are invited to enter through the imagination."[31] I would add that the tools of the modern novelist—insight into the complexities of character; plot surprises adequate to the twists and turns of actual lives; language attuned to the multiple registers into and out of which contemporary selves move with irregular regularity—are particularly suited to capturing the nature of selves as we know them, now subject to postmodern dislocations as well as eternal anxieties and troubles, lives spent on the boundary of belief and community rather than inside Levitical sacred order. The novel I discuss here, Saul Bellow's *Humboldt's Gift* (1975),[32] illustrated well these literary resources. In Bellow's energetic prose, all the issues with which we have been dealing in essay form come boldly and vividly to life.

They do so, I should add, precisely for the reasons that prevent Bellow's work from falling readily into the category of modern Jewish thought. His novels offer no systematic reflection on the condition and prospects of Judaism or the Jews, and they are not written from a standpoint of avowed commitment to their survival and enhancement. But in *Humboldt's Gift*, as in other works by Bellow, not only the author but also the leading protagonists are Jews, even learned Jews. The novel's concerns and themes touch on venerable matters of Jewish and of other religious thought. It captures a widespread Jewish sensibility and outlook on the matters of concern to us—precisely because it is attuned to and immersed in matters of popular as well as elite culture, drawing energy, plot, and characters from life as actually lived by contemporary American Jews. And, last but not least, *Humboldt's Gift* abounds in Jewish quotations and Jewish teachings. Bellow has his lead character sound the prophetic call to wakefulness (46), stresses the need for metaphysics to be joined to ethics (357), issues forceful condemnation of those who have eyes but see not (46), and criticizes the "single self, independently conscious, proud of its detachment and its absolute immunity, its stability and its power to remain unaffected by anything whatsoever—by the sufferings of others or by society or by politics or by external chaos. In a way it doesn't give a damn"(203).

That sentence and others could have been written (in less felicitous prose) by Rosenzweig. Bellow is always careful to couch his reflections in universal rather than distinctively Jewish terms—a modern Jewish proclivity if ever there was one! His meditations on what Walt

Whitman called the question of questions, the death question (66), are not expressed via Kabbalah (though Joseph Caro is cited) but via Rudolf Steiner's "anthroposophy," his radical educational philosophy. This is strategy on Bellow's part, I believe, as it is strategy that—lest we dismiss these reflections as the ravings of an author who takes himself too seriously—Bellow conveys via the consciousness of two characters who are not entirely trustworthy.

The first is Von Humboldt Fleischer, a great poet who was also a drunken, wife-abusing lunatic. "Humboldt said that history was a nightmare during which he was trying to get a good night's rest"(4). He saw his task as conducting raids behind enemy lines—American lines, materialist, big, drunk on power and achievement, adolescent, "uncorrected by the main history of human suffering"—to bring back things of beauty (5). "Humboldt wanted to drape the world in radiance, but he didn't have enough material" (107). His story is narrated by the second character of questionable character: Charlie Citrine, Pulitzer prize–winning biographer and playwright, erstwhile student of literature and perpetual dabbler in great ideas, unreformed chaser of young women, compulsive philosophizer, "an idiotic old lecher ... leaving two children to follow an obvious gold digger to corrupt Europe," as he himself puts it at one point (293), but a man who is also deeply loving and wonderfully reflective. Charlie tells us early on that he "had a funny feeling sometimes, as if I had been stamped and posted and they were waiting for me to be delivered at an important address. I may contain unusual information. But that's just ordinary silliness." Silly or not, he spends the rest of the book looking for the message, and finds it with the help of his deceased friend Humboldt.

He is motivated, in the first instance, by guilt. Visiting New York one day at the height of his fame, Charlie spies his old friend, now looking like a derelict, across the street—and Charlie looks the other way.

> I knew that Humboldt would soon die ... he had death all over him. He didn't see me. He was gray stout sick dusty.... Concealed by a parked car, I watched. I didn't approach him. I felt it was impossible.... I was, as they say, "in great shape" myself.... My belly was flat. I wore boxer shorts of combed

Sea Island cotton at eight bucks a pair.... So how could I talk to
Humboldt? It was too much. (7–8)

The result is that Humboldt talks to Charlie for years after his death.
He visits his friend's thoughts both with reproach and with life lessons.
The latter constitute the gift we all offer our friends. We offer lessons
in words and ideas as well as in doings and undoings. (We have all that
is needed, Rosenzweig wrote—the moment; the rest is provided by
God and the world.)

Prompted by Humboldt's death, Charlie resolves to take up the
death question once and for all, and to do so—in the spirit of
Leviticus—amid all the circumstances of everyday life.

Under the circumstances (and it should by now be clearer what
I mean by circumstances: [girlfriend] Renata, [ex-wife] Denise,
children, courts, lawyers, Wall Street, sleep, death, metaphysics,
karma, the presence of the universe in us, our being present in
the universe itself ...) (107)

He realizes quickly that it is not the world that is, as Max Weber famously put it, "disenchanted." We are. Or rather, our heads are.
Charlie, as if following instructions from Rosenzweig, tries to use his
head well to think past the disenchantment and past death, the fear of
which he believes is sapping him and all of Western culture of vital energy. His ruminations lead to the realization that "our present state of
waking sleep is the result of a desire to evade an impending revelation"
(293). That revelation is all around us, given our felt connection to
other beings in the universe. This is where Kabbalah in the person of
Joseph Karo's Maggid (a nightly angelic visitor who brings Karo instruction of law and metaphysics) enters the novel, his welcome prepared for the reader by anthroposophy. And then comes the ultimate
realization—

that life was a hell of a lot more bounteous than I had ever realized. It rushed over us with more than our senses and our
judgment could take in. Our life ... is after all only a tin dipper-
ful of this superabundance. (331–32)

Consider this climactic passage:

> Suppose, then, that after the greatest, most passionate vividness
> and tender glory, oblivion is all we have to expect, the big
> blank of death. What options present themselves? (357)

Nothing great, Charlie concludes, precisely the conclusion at the core
of modern culture.

> Suppose, however, that oblivion is *not* the case. What, then,
> have I been doing for about six decades? I think that I never be-
> lieved that oblivion *was* the case....

Charlie wants to say to his brother, the day before Julius has bypass
surgery, but cannot get the words out:

> that this brilliant, this dazing shattering delicious painful thing
> (I was referring to life) when it concluded, concluded only what
> we knew. It did not conclude the unknown, and I suspected
> that something further would ensue. But I couldn't prove a
> thing to this hard headed brother of mine. (391)

He could not, as it were, tell it to Julius's mind, or his own. So Charlie
saves the declaration for us—and showers him instead with what
Julius *could* receive from his brother. He shows him love.

In the end, Charlie does penance for his years of sleep and distor-
tion, and in particular for his sin against Humboldt. He spends months
in a broken-down hotel babysitting the child of his girlfriend Renata,
who has gone off and married a mortician after growing tired of waiting for Charlie to commit. Most important of all, Charlie comes to this
statement of how things are:

> The soul of a civilized and rational person is said to be free but
> is actually very closely confined. Although he formally believes
> that he ranges with perfect freedom everywhere and is thus
> quite a thing, he feels, in fact, utterly negligible. But to assume,
> however queerly, the immortality of the soul, to be free from

the weight of death that everybody carries upon the heart presents … a terrific opportunity. The first result is a surplus, an
overflow to be good with. (441–42)

It turns out that, aside from the life that prompted this realization,
Humboldt has also left Charlie another valuable gift: a wild idea for a
screenplay that makes Charlie a lot of money, which he promptly gives
away.

Conclusion

"Overflow to be good with" is a lovely formulation for what
Rosenzweig was after in his book on sickness and health. It also captures one major aim of the Torah and of the Oral Torah added by the
rabbis, when they command Jews to choose life and point out the way
that enables us to do so. The courage needed to overreach ourselves
rarely comes from words, they knew, even the Torah's words. It comes
instead from facts in our experience that the Torah helps to place
there: the children to whom we have transmitted life and wish to
transmit good; the love of our spouse and friends; a just and caring
community; astonishing encounters with the kindness of strangers; the
presence of God. All convey the assurance that life is good. Death is
not good—but it might be okay. One can usually live with it.

I think we step into healing prayer in much this way. Our steps are
not prepared by theological or philosophical affirmation of what it
means for God to heal or for us to ask for healing. We don't have
knowledge in anything like the scientific sense of whether God heals by
any agency other than human activity and care, or how this and other
purported divine interventions in the world can be reconciled with
human freedom, let alone why God would alleviate some suffering,
write some into the book of life and good health without inscribing all
of God's children there, all the time. Premodern as well as modern
Jewish thinkers have had a lot of trouble with these matters. We pray, if
we pray, because we need to and we can; because our tradition author-
izes and encourages us to do so; because we have a proximate source of
blessing, our immediate and distant ancestors, who taught us to pray;
because they and others we know have proven to be sources of strength

who witnessed before our eyes to the power of such strength, demonstrating that life can be a blessing (I paraphrase Debbie Friedman's well-known and widely beloved prayer for healing here).

Jews at the start of the twenty-first century have perhaps reached a point—as citizens of America and card-carrying participants in modernity—at which they are at home enough in both their country and their culture, confident enough in both memberships, to acknowledge that they need healing of body and spirit—and to ask for it from God and one another, out loud. This seems a good thing for modern Jews to do, and for modern Jewish thought to contemplate. It is a development to which I for one can gladly say, Amen.

Rabbi William Cutter, PhD, is Steinberg Professor of Human Relations and Professor of Hebrew Literature and Education at the Los Angeles Campus of the Hebrew Union College–Jewish Institute of Religion. He is the author of numerous articles on Hebrew literature, educational theory, and (most recently), aesthetic issues regarding health and healing. He is director of the Kalsman Institute on Judaism and Health.

Literature and the Tragic Vision

William Cutter

Literature has a dual function with regard to healing. On the one hand, stories are most often about rupture and repair, as they chronicle the problems humans face and often yield hopeful affirmations in the midst of those problems. On the other hand, the very task of literature is to encompass the vastness of human experience; in other words, to present a comprehensive if not fully coherent view of the world. For some people literature's mode trumps the selective and summative efforts of rationalist philosophies. That is why Arnold Eisen's essay combines a description of the healing movement with the examination of a great novel.

Eisen opens his chapter with reference to a little-known book by Franz Rosenzweig entitled *Understanding the Sick and the Healthy*. The chancellor of the Jewish Theological Seminary, an institution that has fostered so many leaders of the healing movement, now takes his turn at trying to understand it. He begins in artful irony, since Rosenzweig's little book was not actually about sickness or about health in the way we normally conceive those subjects. I myself was first drawn to this "book" because it seemed that it might have something to do with my pastoral work, and because I thought it might foreshadow Rosenzweig's own legendary illness. I was, at the time, both disappointed and surprisingly intrigued by what the great German thinker meant. And that leads us to consider another irony, since Rosenzweig's essay actually *did* foreshadow something that Professor Eisen talks about in his: the relative failure of Jewish thought until the beginning of the twentieth century to address the individual on an individual's terms, terms for which sickness, along with all manifestations of mortality, is more a part of an individual human being's consciousness than of communal mandates and needs.

The failure to address the individual when he or she is suffering is part of what has stimulated our current discourse about health and sickness, in the more conventional definitions and in the way in which we use the terms in our daily speech. That is, the philosophical worlds of logic and of empiricism, the worlds of historical description and classical *Wissenschaft* (science), have not seemed adequate to consider the affective status of people or the spiritual condition of individual Jewish people. Although often associated with a kind of nihilism, the writings of Friedrich Nietzsche, the German thinker and aesthete, intrigued many of the thinkers of the early twentieth century. His work certainly appealed to many of my generation who were stifled by traditional modes of Jewish scholarship and thinking. While hardly in the genealogy of Nietzsche, the emergence on the Jewish stage of Martin Buber, Joseph Soloveitchik, Franz Rosenzweig, and (later) Abraham Joshua Heschel was a kind of response to the classic limitations (some would say failure) of traditional philosophical and historical ways of examining the world.

Joining in that response, in my opinion, have been numerous contemporary instances of popular religious expression and folk practice. The early writers of belles lettres (art literature), in both Yiddish and Hebrew, seem to me to be part of this very struggle for some kind of freedom. Rosenzweig's critique of philosophy for its having addressed the wrong questions is an invitation to consider further aspects of Jewish experience, aspects that Saul Bellow's character Charlie Citrine might have seen as part of "superabundance."

I would add to Arnold Eisen's report of Rosenzweig's critique a genre of literature that Rosenzweig did not know much about but whose flowering occurred at more or less the same time as Rosenzweig was thinking and continued long after his sad death. Under some of the same impulses as those that propelled Rosenzweig, late nineteenth- and early twentieth-century Eastern European Jewish intellectuals began to develop one of the great original universes of Jewish discourse: modern Hebrew (and Yiddish before that) belle lettres, which described and addressed those who felt that the Jewish individual had to gain a kind of liberation and dignity that trumped the communal agenda. This was no "bowling alone" kind of argument, or a simple retreat into privacy, but rather an assertion that until Jewish individuals became socially and spiritually healthier, the Jewish polity would remain sick.

Strange as it may sound, then, Judaism's quintessential modern nationalist movement, Zionism, was propelled by many writers who privileged the individual's status and aspirations over community. I am speaking of writers like Micah Yosef Berdyczewski, Josef Hayim Brenner, Devora Baron, and the poet Shaul Tschernichowski. Each of these writers used plenty of illness metaphors to describe the Jewish people. In the lineage of literature, there are those historians who have argued that another great healer of individuals, Rabbi Nachman of Breslov, anticipated a century earlier this literary movement with his ideology of stories.

Professor Eisen suggests, and I agree, that impulses that inspired this attention to the self can be directly associated with the movement to embrace health and healing as part of Jewish life, which this book celebrates, and which is a response to a similar absence. The optimism of the Enlightenment, which seems to have come from outside of religious circles, joined with the system of Jewish practice as a joint enemy of those who wished to emphasize attention to the affective side of human spirit and to the individual struggle against the authority of community and its approach to experience. The existentialist's proposition (as in Rosenzweig or Kierkegaard)—that death and finitude are really what drive the human spirit—had now evolved into a movement that would pay attention to individual needs, to the suffering of people as the "subject," and to the way in which we take care of those who are suffering. Although the healing movement has surely embraced the communal side of the public Jewish agenda, and while it accepts the rationalist expressions of science and clinical cure, the goal of the healing movement surely has expanded to find a greater space for the private self. In the early literary movement I have just cited, the most rebellious writers seemed to feel (against Ahad haAm) that community health is a consequence of liberated (healthy) individuals. That emphasis has had remarkable implications for the emergence of Jewish modernity.

At the end of his essay, Professor Eisen turns his attention to a novel, and he seems to do so because, in his own words, "belief ... lags behind practice and struggles to catch up." Story has from the beginning of the Jewish tradition articulated matters that defy statement in rigorous philosophical form.

This point needs some elaboration. How does story do this? Do we mean story as emphasizing a moral, as is often the case in aggadah? Or is something else at stake? I want to elaborate on this point from the perspective of someone who has not participated as vigorously as would be polite in the organized articulation of system—either systems of hope and affirmation, or systems of halachic behavior, which seemed designed to create a sense of order in the chaotic sociology of our lives. In lieu of one system or another, literature became my way of articulating Jewish life in creative terms, what Cynthia Ozick has called "the last trustworthy vessel of the inner life" (*The Din in the Head*), a way of recognizing the subjectification of things and the valorization of the private self. I noted early on in my own pastoral career that the *Code of Jewish Law (Shulchan Aruch)* speaks primarily of the obligations of the visitor to the ill and says too little of the suffering of the patient who is being visited, or of the specific experiences that are part of that suffering—the back story, as it were.

Not only is the self valorized in literature, but literature also seems to respond critically (in a negative sense) to the systems that others have built, and to embrace the apparent randomness that the Creator presents us with. With regard to that randomness, Philip Roth has somewhat wryly argued that what he likes about novels is the serial aspect of the form, its "and, and, and.... "

My own preference as an example of the importance of prose literature might not originally have been Bellow's *Humboldt's Gift*, but perhaps a novel with more apparent redemptive qualities or plot results. But, upon reflection, I realized that the redemptive themes of modern literature are always equivocal and nuanced. As Bellow himself wrote early in his career, "If you hold down one thing you hold down the adjoining" (*Adventures of Augie March*). Professor Eisen offers us a bold reading of an important novel too rarely understood in its consolation dimension, and that is part of what makes his essay so interesting for us. I would argue, however, that the issue of literature and redemption—and its responses to philosophy's "illness" (to use Rosenzweig's term)—requires a theoretical examination of how literature works. I would like to borrow from Eisen's helpful exposition of the connection between healing and the American condition that has rendered Jews free to express their anxieties about human frailty and to be assertive enough to seek solutions for that frailty on the individual's terms. Bellow's most famous opus is *Adventures of Augie March*, and from the opening line of the novel, it seems to speak to Eisen's ideas: "I am an American, Chicago born.... " Today's Augie, following Professor Eisen's logic, might begin: "I am a Jewish American—and I belong wherever I have been born."

There are many theories and suggestions as to how story has come to replace systematic philosophy as part of the modern expression. And I would cite here Yosef Hayim Yerushalmi's assertion that literature may even replace formal history as a means of tracking memory. As for literature, some critics have followed Lionel Trilling's social ideas that literature is unmatched for assimilating a modern world in which individuals can exchange social positions and thus be worthy of novelistic place. Ian Watt argued in a similar vein that modern literature was actually a chronicle of that mobility. We have already met Ozick's vessel of inner life and Roth's fascination with the serial-ness of things. We could turn to the work of such thinkers as John Gardner, Wayne Booth, or even Robert Coles, who argued that prose literature leads readers through ethical choices. We could extend the choice a bit further into the abstract and find a home in the more elusive notions of J. Hillis Miller that the act of reading literature is a kind of exercise in making choices, where the choices characters make in stories are allegories of the choices we make as readers.

For my own solace about the importance of literature in the Jewish canon, I have turned to the master Jewish storyteller of early modernity, Rabbi Nachman of Breslov, whose tragic vision of the human condition could only be encompassed by faith and by the telling of stories that reflected all of the paradoxes and sufferings that challenged faith but led to it at the same time. One of the authors in this volume, Professor Arthur Green, has treated the great hasidic master most convincingly. Nachman's own stories were described by him, and by his followers, as messianic experience. The act of telling the story (in the proper way, of course) was an exercise in redemption, and redemption is always incomplete in life and in stories. As Bellow says, in his great first novel (again, right off the bat), "there isn't any way to disguise the nature of the knocks by acoustical work on the door or gloving the knuckles." Stories were the only way Nachman could see to include it all and—further—to move from an idea to narrative experience of the idea, and to extrapolate from the narrative experience a further idea in an endless round of concrete and abstract. It's what I think Professor Eisen might be suggesting as a solution to Rosenzweig's claim. Rosenzweig had a different solution, of course, than Eisen or Bellow. Nachman went even further in his insistence that tragedy emerges from the fundamental nature of God's world.

Arnold Eisen's case for the relationship of story to modern pain, of the struggle to locate ourselves differently in the face of stubborn Jewish insistence on proper behavior and commitment, reflects on the nobility of its author. I would add only that the authority to which Conservative Judaism's leader ultimately attaches himself is challenged by the rejection of authority in which modern writers have excelled. Striking, isn't it, that the word for a modern writer is "author"—the anti-type who has come to inform so much modern Jewish experience, since one part of the Jewish Enlightenment began to create in negation of that other part, the artist challenging the systematizer. Only in a story would the chief character find redemption in the demonstration of simple love, without endless centuries of commentary and explanation, and without an ethical system to explain why that love ought to come about.

Narrative prose remains a highly inclusive means of capturing human experience in subjective ways that Professor Eisen seems to understand. With the individual at its center, story challenges tradition, just as it illuminates suffering. That is how I view the healing movement, and I happily and admiringly share that vision with Arnold Eisen.

The concrete and the abstract are always struggling, as are issues of form and content. Only a few masters are willing to take on that struggle. Many of those masters are found in this volume, and my partner in this discourse is unique among them.

2

Health and Healing among the Mystics

Rabbi Arthur Green, PhD, is the Irving Brudnick Professor of Philosophy and Religion and rector of the Rabbinical School at Hebrew College in Newton, Massachusetts He is also professor emeritus of Jewish Thought at Brandeis University. Green is a widely published author in the areas of Jewish mystical thought and contemporary theology.

Mystical Sources of the Healing Movement

Arthur Green

I am surprised to be addressing this subject. A student and teacher for many years of the Jewish mystical tradition—a body of lore to which, and to the teachers of which, many have turned for healing over the centuries—I have always kept myself distant from this aspect of Kabbalah. I think it important, for the sake of full disclosure and honesty, that I explain why that is the case.

The crucial event of my psychological life, that which determined more of my future biography than any other single occurrence, was the death of my mother when I was eleven years old. She died of a terrible cancer, one the doctors in 1952 were unable to heal and one that even today, if allowed to advance as it did then, would be beyond medical help. The fact that my sister and I have now made our fiftieth *yahrtzeit* pilgrimage back to New Jersey allows me to speak about it, but of course it does not complete the healing.

A child already attracted to religion before this shocking event, one for which I was quite totally unprepared, I spent the next seven years seeking the solace of God's presence, the assurance that this death was not without meaning and somehow not final, and the embrace of various surrogate parents. My life as an adult began only as I broke free from the near suffocation of this embrace. I had to accept the arbitrariness of natural processes that often determine life and death as well as our inability to control them either by medicine or by appeal to divine mercy. This meant a denial of the faith in particular providence that had sustained me through those years and a willingness to confront the possibility that life and death are indeed without meaning, other than what we construct out of our own aspirations and longings.

I came to Kabbalah several years later, having crossed a desert peopled by Friedrich Nietzsche, Franz Kafka, and Albert Camus. Nietzsche taught me of the death of God. Kafka taught me that the Nietzschian exultation at the death of God lasts but a moment, leaving you quite alone in an absurd and horrifying universe. From Camus I learned that meaning happens in that universe only as you fashion it yourself. That desert is the place that Rabbi Nachman of Breslov, one of my greatest teachers, calls the "void" or the empty space, from which God is necessarily absent, so that we can become ourselves. Although I have tried to follow Nachman's invitation to live on the far side of that void—the world of faith beyond emptiness, the faith that stands in defiance to meaninglessness and chaos—the void is always there for me, as I believe it was for him.

There is no naïveté in my faith, no room for pretending that "God's in His heaven and all's right with the world." My theological enterprise has been about articulating what I call a "Judaism for adults," which means those who stand with me in having abandoned—or, perhaps more accurately, having been abandoned by—the naïve religion of childhood fantasy and yet seek meaning in the symbols and textual traditions of Judaism. I have marshaled the rich resources of Jewish mystical teachings in this effort, to which all of my theological writing, and much of my scholarly and educational work, is devoted.

My early attraction to the language of Kabbalah and Hasidism had to do both with the profundity of religious ideas, some of which I first encountered in the writings of Gershom Scholem, and the richness of metaphor and poetic imagination with which these teachings are sometimes graced. Later I came to appreciate the unitive mystical consciousness that underlay these and the ways they used all of Judaism as a path toward deeper rungs of human experience. All of these I have tried to reinterpret in our own language to render them accessible to seekers.

While engaged in this process, one that has now stretched over more than forty years, I was of course aware that other uses were being made of the kabbalistic tradition as well. Jerusalem taxicabs and market stalls adorned with pictures of a Moroccan or Baghdadi Jewish saint told me that popular Kabbalah was alive and well among certain sections of the Jewish community. Over the years various tales would come to my ears of someone who was cured from illness or saved from disaster by the blessing of the Lubavitcher or another hasidic rebbe. These, of course, echoed a great deal of what was present in the sources I studied, but I remained uninterested in the alleged curative powers of either kabbalistic amulets or the blessings of hasidic masters. I considered this popular use of Kabbalah a betrayal of the deeper mystical tradition, that which saw all worship as an act of pure giving, not seeking even such reasonable earthly rewards as health and longevity.

Following in the tradition of Martin Buber, I tended to skip over such promises when seeking materials for translation or teaching. For years I listened to the late Shlomo Carlebach make a very different selection from the hasidic teachings than I did, one that sought out and glorified naïve faith, while I was trying to pick up and paste together shards of meaning—"broken tablets," as I called them—on the far shores of its destruction. While I might enjoy the account of child-like faith in the tales of one hasidic master or another, any move in that direction on my own part felt dishonest, as though I were abandoning the hard-fought truth that I had come to know.

Decades of involvement with mystic teaching do have their affect, however. I am engaged with a realm of human understanding that by definition goes beyond ordinary rules of reason or scientific explanation. I am not much attracted to those experiments that try to lend greater "scientific" credibility by measuring the alpha waves of meditators or analyzing the brain chemistry of apocalyptic visionaries. My approach is rather more phenomenological: I seek to take the mystic's testimony seriously, to analyze it in its own terms, perhaps to compare it with language heard elsewhere, and to be especially wary of reductionist or dismissive explanations. This involvement with the realm of inner mystery has forced me to admit how much there is that I—dare I say we—do not understand. I certainly cannot judge whether the visions or recounted experiences of mystical teachers throughout the world are "true" or not on the basis of my meager ability to explain them. I have come rather to accept them as strivings to express the ineffable, as attempts to describe an inner reality that makes powerful claims, both on the original visionaries who describe them and on later generations of faithful readers, sometimes including myself, who are inspired by them.

I have come to accept that there are forces or energies present in the world that we have not yet found ways to measure or describe. In ways we do not understand at all, there are people who have the psychic ability to "tune in" to the frequencies of these energies and come to see or know things that are otherwise beyond explanation. The field of psychic research is as yet very young and overwhelmed by both charlatanism and the excessive skepticism that comes in its wake. But I believe we still have much more to learn in this area than we know at present, and humility behooves our ignorance. This does not mean, of course, that we are to become patsies for the many spurious and suspicious claims in this area that appear every day.

The same has slowly come to be the case with regard to accounts of healing, whether based on the blessings of a tzaddik or simply the power of prayer. As I have become aware of the defensive role that a certain cynicism about such claims plays in my own psychic life, I have been forced to become more open to the reality of experiences recounted by others. This was best brought home to me in a conversation with a group of rabbis that I have had the privilege of teaching over the past several years. I went to them for help in preparing for my appearance at the "Mining the Tradition" conference. I wondered whether I could speak without somehow pretending to be a mystical healer, or without, at least by implication, lending support to something that might border on quackery.

"Suppose," I said, taking a worst-case scenario, "there are cancer patients in the audience, there looking for hope of a cure. What shall I say to them? If I give them a sense that Kabbalah and its teachers do have healing powers, I'll be sending them off to buy holy water from one or another quick-buck phonies. If I tell them I think it's all nonsense, I'll be unfairly destroying their hopes, something I surely have no desire to do!"

Had I looked around for a minute at these ten or twelve rabbis, most of whom I know quite well, I would have counted two cancer survivors among them, one other whose spouse had just survived a heart attack, and yet another who had lost her husband to illness at a terribly young age. And all of them wanted to tell me of the power of prayer in their lives and in confronting illness or loss, while none of them sought to make a naïve claim that it was prayer alone, rather than medical intervention, that stopped the cancer's growth or saved the life.

Our conversation brought forth all kinds of important thoughts, some previously stored in my own memory, that belong to such talk. The Talmud's declaration that "Outcry is good for a person, whether before or after the decree has been issued" makes it quite clear that what is "good" about outcry or prayer is not its ability to change the decree. A distinction that was crucial to our conversation is that between "healing" and "cure," one surely familiar to many readers. The fact that we cannot offer a cure should in no way stop us from seeking to offer healing. This applies even to the use of materials from the mystical sources that indeed did claim to have curative powers; we may find them valuable resources for healing even without being literal believers in their curative effects.

This healing begins with a gift of empathy, companionship, and being present. It shares an awareness of the pain, suffering, or fear that is the lot of both the patient and those fearing or experiencing the loss of a loved one. Teachings that speak of a deep, mystical faith, where the gulf between the divine and human is transcended, are an important part of the healing resources our tradition has to offer. We should indeed mine deeply that aspect of Jewish teaching, using it in this context as a tool of healing, without any pretense to curative powers.

A most striking comment offered by one of the rabbis was a rereading of the *amidah* phrase *refa'enu hashem venerape* to mean "Soften us up, O Lord, so that we may be able to receive healing." Open our hearts so that we can receive the gift of those who seek to heal. Help us to break down our own resistance to Your healing love! This stimulated in me a memory of an old reading of my own of another passage in the *amidah*: *hamerachem ki lo tamu chasadecha*—"You are compassionate, Lord, even when Your love is not simple." Help us to accept Your compassionate presence, Lord, even when compassion means just that—You are present with us in our suffering—and not that You will "avert the decree."

Not long before that conversation, I had written in a book:

> I do not know much about the power of prayer to affect others: to heal the sick, to bring home the lost, to protect those we love from harm. I remain somewhat neutral to the claims now being made again, on this far edge of the age of skepticism, for the efficacy of prayer in the external world. But I know that prayer heals the one who prays, restoring a wholeness or a balance that can be lost when we are beset by concern or worry. And since the One who lies within us, to whom we give the words of prayer, lies as well in the heart of the one for whom we pray, we would indeed be setting false and unnecessary limits to say that the energy of our love, expressed in that prayer, *cannot* reach the other.

After that conversation, I would probably add the line: Listen to the testimony of those who have been healed no less carefully than You listen to the outcry of those who have not.

But the conversation with my rabbi friends led me somewhere else as well, and that brings us closer to my subject. Our healing, as important as it is to us and those who love us, is ultimately a small matter. The world will go on without us. Generations in families will come and go, some longer and some shorter. The real healing that is needed is not only of the sick and the bereaved, but of the whole human situation. This leads me back to some of the great ideas of Kabbalah that I mentioned earlier.

The Kabbalists understand that the world is a broken place. Somehow, in the flow of energy from its boundless source into the finite beings that populate the world as we see it, there was a break, a flaw, or a moment of painful separation. There are various versions in kabbalistic lore as to how this loss of wholeness came about, and much of the myth-making creativity of the Kabbalists is devoted to this question. The human heart longs to return to its source, to unite with the wholeness of God, but it cannot, at least not for more than brief interludes. The human being longs to feel fully at home in the universe, to celebrate life as we once did in Eden, but this, too, is not given us; the gates to paradise are closed. Paradoxically, our very longing for

God, or oneness, or an undivided heart shows us how very far away we are. Nobody in Jewish literature, and indeed few among the world's religious teachers, has described this aspect of the human situation with the poignancy of Rabbi Nachman of Breslov:

> There is a mountain, and on that mountain there stands a rock. A spring gushes forth from that rock.
>
> Now everything in the world has a heart, and the world as a whole has a heart. The heart of the world is a complete form, with face, hands, and feet. But even the toe-nail on that heart of the world is most heartlike than any other heart.
>
> The mountain and the spring stand at one end of the world, and the heart is at the other. The heart stands facing the spring, longing and yearning to draw near to it. It is filled with a wild yearning, and constantly cries out in its desire to approach the spring. The spring, too, longs for the heart.
>
> The heart suffers from two weaknesses: the sun pursues it terribly, burning it because it wants to approach the spring. The second weakness is that of the longing and outcry itself, the great desire to reach the spring. The heart ever stands facing the spring, crying out in longing to draw near.
>
> When the heart needs to rest a bit or catch its breath, a great bird comes over it and spreads forth its wings to shield the heart from the sun. But even at its times of rest, the heart looks toward the spring in longing.
>
> Now if the heart is filled with so great a desire to draw near to the spring, why does it not simply do so? Because as soon as it starts to move toward the mountain, the mountaintop where the spring stands would disappear from view. And the life of the heart flows from seeing the spring; if it were to allow the spring to vanish from its sight, it would die....
>
> If that heart were to die, God forbid, the entire world would be destroyed. The heart is the life of all things; how could the world exist without a heart? For this reason the heart can never

approach the spring, but ever stands opposite it and looks at it in longing.[1]

To be human is to be distant from God, so very distant, as one end of the world is from the other. Our deepest desire, our greatest need, is to stare into the divine face, to drink at the deep well of God's presence. Yet we cannot do so; we cannot come any closer than we are. Every prayer we utter, every time we say the vital word "You" in prayer, proclaiming God our beloved, we are also confirming our distance and separation from the One that we hope would embrace us all.

This is what needs healing, and it is to this work of healing that religion, in the profoundest sense, must address itself. This is its true message of salvation, the promise to bring us forth from the *mitzrayim* (Egypt) of *galut hada'at*, the narrow perception of ordinary consciousness, and to give us a taste of that deeper reality, the one on the far side of the void, where the oneness of being is total and where the "Thou" of our prayers gives way to the single silent sound of the divine *anochi*, "I am."

This general healing of human alienation cannot, of course, gloss over the unique situation of any single human being. Each of us needs to seek out and come into the arms of this wholeness in ways that are appropriate to who we are, to our needs, to our particular pains in life's journey. But each of us also needs to learn how to step beyond our individual situation and to see the ongoing process of healing, called *tikkun* by the Kabbalists, in its fullest ramification.

Indeed it is the process of individuation—the process that makes each of us into the unique self that we are—that separates us from our deeper root in being as a whole, which we later seek to recover. Individuation itself should be seen as a holy process: the emergence of a healthy, balanced ego is as much a revelation of God's image as is the conquest of that ego and its dedication to a higher purpose. The whole cycle of human life is thus nothing but the intake and outflow of divine, cosmic breath. Our healing lies in our becoming aware of that all-pervasive underlying truth.

Judaism is not primarily a religion based on the need to atone for an original sin. The rabbis mostly believed that the struggle with evil and temptation begins over again with each person. But the tale of Eden does belong to our scripture, and the faint memory of a lost paradise haunts our tradition. Indeed one way of reading the entire Torah is to see it as a response to our expulsion from Eden. The sin for which we were expelled, according to the Kabbalists (and later also discovered by Kafka), is that of having separated the two trees, having broken off the Tree of Knowledge from its own root in the Tree of Life. The quest to satisfy curiosity leads us to make that separation. Knowledge that is about mere curiosity, "just the facts," unaccompanied by a commitment to *live* the truth learned, to transform our lives into vessels that serve such truth, leads us down the path that will take us to "evil," knowledge in the service of self promotion, aggression, "my" truth arrayed against "yours." Torah as the new Tree of Life is given to us as the antidote to this alienation, a way of learning, a path of moral as well as intellectual development that leads us toward a new Eden, toward our Promised Land.

One piece of what needs healing in our lives, to say it differently, is our intellectual lives. Those of us who have spent large parts of our lifetime in academic communities know how true this is. As the Western university abandoned its claim to being a bastion of wisdom, becoming instead a temple of scientific detachment, "objectivity," and, finally, "professionalism," generations of young wisdom-seekers throughout the latter twentieth century have abandoned it for the ashram, zendo, madrasa, yeshiva, and monastery, places that had not yet given up the claim. Judaism, especially as reflected in the mystical tradition, is home to an ancient and venerable tradition of wisdom. It is access to this wisdom that we seek when studying Torah.

The Torah that we find in this quest is meant to lead us to a life of service. The commandments of Torah, the forms of religion, are there to provide shared outward structures within which the true *avodah*—a rich word embracing "work," "service," and "devotion"—is to take place. This work is nothing less than a transformation of the self into a mirror of divinity. To say it in a way more widely acceptable to the Western mind: a realization of the potential in each human being to truly become the image of God. This process of self-transformation requires *investigating* the deeper truth, *realizing* that truth in the way we live, both individually and in community, and *communicating* the value of that work to those around us. This three-part task is the true purpose of religion.

The Jewish esoteric tradition offers a particular set of tools through which this work can be done. Although Kabbalah is often presented as an abstract metaphysic or theosophy, it is best understood as the hasidic masters did, as a form of religious *avodah*, a way to do our inner "work." All reality, according to the Kabbalists, is constructed according to a tenfold pattern, a divine structure that unfolds from within the most hidden recesses of divinity. We humans can understand that reality primarily through our own inner experience, since the cosmic pattern is repeated in the soul-life of every person.

While there is not room here to explicate this system in full,[2] a very general outline can be offered. Within your deepest self (connected to the single Self of Being, or God), there are infinite resources of energy. You are initially unaware of these deeper levels of being; they belong to the self of the unconscious mind. Slowly they begin to filter into consciousness. In doing so, however, they necessarily become constricted, as the conscious self is so much smaller, narrower in focus, than the infinite realm of potential within. As the mind becomes aware of these inner energies, however, they begin to coalesce around two poles.

One is a center of love-energy; we feel loved and blessed by the Source of our energy and seek to pass that blessing on, whether to partner and offspring through the physical love-act or in sharing love with those around us. The other center feels the energy as a surge of strength, a way to build up the self, to achieve power. Human life involves a great struggle between these two, a tension between the impulse to give, to be generous in spirit, to let flow, and the impulse to hold back, to stand firm, to build for yourself a bastion of strength, even if that means withholding giving. As we mature we need to resolve that tension, to find a way of proper balance.

As we do so, however, a second great tension appears, that between the demands of perfectionism and the grace of self-acceptance. One side of us wants to accomplish it all; it is the Type A personality within us, striving for great accomplishments, improving our lives, maybe even improving the world and bringing the messiah. The other pole in this struggle is that of humility, a virtue not much known in our aggressive culture. Accepting yourself for who you are, loving yourself (and knowing that you are loved by God) even if you can't transform the world, cook like a Cordon Bleu chef, or write the great American novel. When we resolve these two tensions—love versus power and demand versus acceptance—we are ready to be proper givers and receivers of the divine energy that continues to course within us. We learn the dynamic of giving/receiving from our sexual roles as male and female, although the experienced lover always learns to play the other role as well as his or her primary biological one. Thus we are all male and female, givers and receivers of love.

That is the essential kabbalistic system, read here as a textbook of religious psychology. The grid of the ten *sefirot* (primal numbers) and especially of the seven "lower" of these, known as the *middot* (personal qualities), is a set of tools for doing our inner work, for achieving balance, for making sure that one or another of these inner drives has not run amok, as they so often do. This achievement of proper balance is the healing work that each of us needs to do. While we must take great care never to blame the victim and imply that "your illness has come about *because* your spirit was out of balance," those who do this work know how much better illness can be managed and wholeness achieved by a person who is set on the course of proper balance among these forces.

Of course the great changes spoken of here in our intellectual life—Torah—and our struggle for moral growth—*Avodah*—have to lead us to the third pillar of what the ancient rabbis said would make the world stand firm: *Gemilut Hasadim*, or acts of lovingkindness. Ultimately it is only in the realm of deeds that our spiritual lives and struggles are tested. How we act with regard to others and where we stand on the great social issues of our time will be the only true reflections of our inner process.

I end this essay with a few words about broader issues, about the social context within which our discussion of healing takes place.

The illness with which we are afflicted, and from which we need to heal, is societal and collective, not just individual and private. All of us are shaped daily by our social context and the powerful forces that surround us. The very matters we have been discussing—how to love and accept ourselves, how to free ourselves from excessive pressures to achieve, how to be strong and yet generous, open to others' needs without becoming victimized by them—all of these are affected by such societal forces as advertising, peer pressure, and the expectations of those around us. Our own struggle to maintain and communicate decent values must be seen against this backdrop.

We live in a society struggling collectively, and often not very wisely, with such issues as benefits for the unemployed and impoverished, medical care for the elderly, the provision of a "safety net" for all those most in need. Supporting the creation of a caring and generous society—in the midst of the great collective wealth we as a nation enjoy—is an essential part of our work as healers and as Jews. One of the favorite Yiddish expressions I recall from childhood is *me'tor nit araynlegy a gezunten kup in a krenken bettl*: "You mustn't lay a healthy head down in a sick bed." This advice applies to our situation as well. The comfortable circumstances in which we discuss Judaism and healing should inspire us to ever greater concern over the growing gap between rich and poor, between privileged and forgotten, in those societies where we live and for which we bear responsibility. Healing is not just for ourselves, but reaches, as the prophets would say, to the ends of the earth, to the humblest and lowliest places.

Eitan P. Fishbane, PhD, is assistant professor of Jewish religious thought at the Jewish Theological Seminary, and was formerly on the faculty of the Hebrew Union College. He specializes in Kabbalah and Hasidism, and their place within the broader spectrum of Jewish thought. He received his PhD from Brandeis University in 2003, and has already distinguished himself through numerous articles and essays. He is preparing two books on the Kabbalah and on the construction of the self in Jewish mystical literature. His work has already helped place the study of Jewish mysticism within the canons of Jewish learning.

Wisdom, Balance, Healing: Reflections on Mind and Body in an Early Hasidic Text

Eitan P. Fishbane

We live in a marketplace of spirituality and wellness. Charismatic holy men, fueled by the engines of commercial outreach, sell the promise of health and cures for physical illness. The right price, the right incantation, the right belief will secure that most coveted of all human desires: the ability to evade the grasp of ailment and weakness. Hold on to this holy object, recite the following divine names, stand in the presence of the energy-bestowing master, and you shall be healed. The appeal of such promises often translates into a cult of the holy man, the belief that the sainted figure has more power to save the individual from disease than does the science of modern medicine.

As Arthur Green notes in his essay, it is this disturbing trend among contemporary manipulators of kabbalistic teaching (though such beliefs are by no means new to Jewish piety and folk belief) that leaves others of us so wary about utilizing the mystical tradition in the formulation of a contemporary spirituality of health and healing. Such New Age phenomena are a fascinating intrigue to us as historians and anthropologists of religion—and there can be no doubt that very similar beliefs and practices were pervasive in the golden periods of kabbalistic and hasidic mysticism. But the degree to which we shall give voice to our own view of the matter as twenty-first-century American Jews is another issue entirely.

And yet the matter may be framed in a different way: can we posit a relationship of interdependence between the ongoing healing of our physical selves and the cultivation of a state of mindful attention, a therapeutic posture of cognition? What is the impact of meditative centeredness on the tumult of our bodies? Is there any correlation between the turbulence of our psychological lives and that of our physiology?[3] This last question has been answered in the affirmative by a significant number of medical experts and healing practitioners. Indeed, such connections are perhaps most manifest in the current medical treatment of stress and anxiety conditions—an impact that has been researched and documented most famously by Dr. Herbert Benson and his team of investigators at the Mind Body Medical Institute of Harvard Medical School.[4]

One of the most striking features of Benson's research as it pertains to our reflection concerns the potent use of cognitive-behavioral therapy and the meditative techniques of mantra repetition, visualization, focal-point centeredness, and attentive, controlled breathing. Benson effected a major transformation in thinking and practice on this issue by consciously adapting the meditative techniques of various mystical traditions for medical and therapeutic healing. The basic conclusion that emerges from all of this research is that the happenings of the mind are not divorced from the workings of the body—that consciousness can have a powerful impact on the state of our physiological health.

All of this is of course well known to medical professionals and interested patients alike; it has become common practice to integrate cognitive therapies with pharmacological prescription and other medical interventions in the treatment of an array of ailments and disorders. But to what extent are such perspectives on healing visible in the spiritual traditions of Judaism? Are there insights to be gleaned from the sources of Kabbalah and Hasidism that may add further texture to the contemporary integration of spirituality and healing? To what degree did the masters of this literature believe the mind (when properly directed) to be capable of major impact on the health of the body, and of what value might these beliefs be for our own contemporary articulation of the matter?[5]

In seeking answers to these questions, we shall give close scrutiny to one representative text from the hasidic mystical corpus of late-eighteenth-century eastern Europe. It is drawn from the *Degel Mahaneh Efrayim*—a collection of homilies attributed to Rabbi Moshe Hayyim Efrayim of Sudilkov (though these in all likelihood constitute the written record, composed by disciples, of the Rebbe's oral sermons), the grandson of the putative founder of Hasidism, Rabbi Israel Ba'al Shem Tov. The passage embeds a fascinating reflection on integrated mind-body healing in the context of a multifaceted exegesis. My method in what follows shall be one of *metacommentary* (the exegesis of exegesis)—an annotation and interpretive reflection that will proceed alongside the words of the original text.

We shall strive to understand how our contemporary struggle with the relationship between mind and body in the healing process may be illuminated by classic sources from within the Jewish spiritual tradition. We shall seek to answer several interrelated questions: What are the spiritual messages conveyed by the Rebbe of Sudilkov, and how do they shed light on his conception of healing and personal transformation? How does the text function as an exegetical process of thinking and creativity, or, how is scripture interpreted within the hasidic homily? What messages and teachings in this text are applicable to our contemporary concerns in the realms of Jewish spirituality and healing?

In one of his interpretive ruminations on the deeper meaning of the Genesis creation narrative, the master offers his insight into an individual's ability to utilize the power of the mind, the focus of consciousness, to effect palpable change and healing in the physiology of the body. As we shall see, the homilist (preacher) arrives at his ultimate point quite gradually, first setting the stage with characteristic midrashic and sermonic skill. Utilizing a classic exegetical play on the opening words of Genesis, the preacher leads his audience toward a remarkable theological claim: the divine name *Elohim* symbolically alludes to the world of nature, a correlation that allows the interpreter to view mundane reality as permeated with a divine presence and energy of life:

עוֹד יֵשׁ לוֹמַר

בְּרֵאשִׁית בָּרָא אֱלֹהִים.

Concerning the words *bereishit bara Elohim* (literally "In the beginning God created…"), the following may also be said:

יֵשׁ לְפָרֵשׁ

דְּהִנֵּה אֱלֹהִים גִּימַטְרִיָּא הַטֶּבַע

וְרֵאשִׁית הַיְנוּ חָכְמָה

כְּמוֹ שֶׁתִּרְגֵּם יְרוּשַׁלְמִי עַל בְּרֵאשִׁית בְּחוֹכְמָתָא.

The word *Elohim* is numerically equivalent (*gematria*) to the word "nature" (*hateva*), and *reishit* is to be understood as "Wisdom" (*chochmah*), just as the Targum Yerushalmi translates *bereishit* as "through wisdom" (*bechochmeta*).

דְּהִנֵּה אֱלֹהִים גִּימַטְרִיָּא הַטֶּבַע This striking correlation, based on the numeric equivalence of the words *Elohim* and *hateva* (each of whose letters total eighty-six in numeric value), is rooted in earlier Jewish mystical literature.[6] The implications of this creative midrashic move are quite extraordinary in that some degree of identity is posited between the deity and the natural world. To what extent is a thorough-going pantheism and monism implied or hinted at here (i.e., that all of reality is in fact part of the unified and integrated deity, that God is nothing other than the great One of all Being), and to what extent can it still be read as *panentheistic* (the belief that the divine presence *fills* all of reality, but is not One with it)? It does appear that this correlation is meant to startle the reader into the awareness that Divinity is to be found in the natural realm of mundane reality, and is not necessarily to be read as an unequivocal equation of deity and Nature. Nevertheless, the blurred lines of textual rendering do intrigue the theological imagination.

וְרֵאשִׁית הַיְנוּ חָכְמָה Already in the midrashic sources of late antiquity,[7] the word *chochmah* (wisdom) was playfully substituted for the word *reishit* (as in *bereishit*—in the beginning) in Genesis 1:1, yielding an alternate reading of the first verse of the Hebrew Bible: "through *chochmah*, God created the heavens and the earth." This apparently surprising move was the result of a correlation between the standard creation narrative in Genesis 1 and the reflection on origins placed in the mouth of Lady Wisdom in Proverbs 8:1. As part of an extended soliloquy delivered by this personified female "Wisdom," we hear that God created her (*chochmah*) at the beginning of His way (*reishit darko*), before all the other creations mentioned in Genesis 1. Wisdom—in a primordial form—antedated all other created reality.

The rabbis of (the relatively early text) *Genesis Rabbah* were quick to assert that this primordial wisdom was nothing other than Torah itself—the blueprint of existence that was utilized by the Great Architect of the universe. The fact that Lady Wisdom states that she was created at *reishit darko* (the beginning of God's way) further stimulated the interpretive imaginations of the early midrashists and led them to a brilliant deconstruction of that first verse in the book of Genesis. Wisdom herself (or in this version, Torah herself) is to be called by the name "*reishit*," insofar as she was the first entity to be created. That stretch made, the midrashists then moved to read Genesis 1:1 in the following manner: "Through Torah [*chochmah/reishit*] God created the heavens and the earth."[8]

וְזֶה יֵשׁ לוֹמַר
שֶׁמְּרַמֵּז הַפָּסוּק בְּרֵאשִׁית
הַיְנוּ בְּחָכְמָה בָּרָא אֱלֹהִים
הַשִׁי"ת בָּרָא הַטֶּבַע בָּעוֹלָם.

And this goes to say that the verse beginning with the word *bereishit* alludes to the following meaning: "through wisdom _____ created *Elohim*." That is to say: God, blessed be He, created the natural order in the world (since *Elohim* equals *hateva*).

בְּחָכְמָה בָּרָא אֱלֹהִים Standing in the background, and crucial to a full understanding of this fresh twist, is the manner in which medieval kabbalists had themselves adapted the midrashic exegesis discussed above. Particularly in the Zohar, the great classic of kabbalistic literature composed in late-thirteenth-century Castile (and also in the Hebrew literature contemporaneous with the Zohar), the equating of *bereishit* with *bechochmah* yielded a startling transformation of the meaning of Genesis 1:1. Within the mindscape of kabbalistic symbolism, the verse came to mean: "Through *Chochmah* (the second of the divine emanations, called *sefirot*, and the primal point of revealed cosmic Being in which infinite nothingness is channeled into the first sparkle of perception), *Ein Sof* (the Infinite ground of divine Being that unfolds and becomes manifest through the ten *sefirot*) emanated *Elohim* (a classic name for the third *sefirah* of inner divine emanation, called *Binah*, or Understanding)."

Thus, the name *Elohim* ceases to be read as the persona of divine actor and creator (the clear meaning of the word in the biblical and rabbinic discourses) and is instead interpreted as the dimension of God that is third in the succession of emanation (the first, *Keter*, is not discussed in this context, in that it stands on an ambiguous threshold between *Ein Sof* and the *sefirot*)—the *object* of the sentence when read through a kabbalistic lens. In this passage, the hasidic Rebbe takes the exegesis to a bold, even radical, new level. For in his teaching, the word *Elohim* is not even read as a *sefirah* (as in kabbalistic interpretation of this verse), but rather as earthly Nature! To be sure, a continuum (and even partial identity) is implicit between the deity and the natural world in this exegesis, but such a caveat does not diminish the highly startling deconstruction of the divine active persona in the verse. Through wisdom, God created *Elohim* (understood here as the natural world)!

וְזֶהוּ חָכְמָה נִפְלָאָה
כִּי הַטֶּבַע הֵם הַד' יְסוֹדוֹת
אֵשׁ רוּחַ מַיִם עָפָר
וְכֹל עִיקָר בְּרִיאוּת הַגּוּף תָּלוּי
כְּשֶׁהַיְּסוֹדוֹת הֵם בְּמֶזֶג הַשָּׁוֶה.

This is a wondrous wisdom, for Nature is composed of the four foundational elements—fire, air, water, and dust—and the essence of the health of the body depends on these foundational elements being in equal balance.

וְכַאֲשֶׁר יְסוֹד אֶחָד מִתְגַּבֵּר עַל חֲבֵירוֹ ח"ו
מִזֶּה נִמְשָׁךְ לְאָדָם אֵיזֶה מִיחוּשׁ וְחוּלְשַׁת הַגּוּף ח"ו
רַק לְחַזֵּק וּלְגַבֵּר הַטֶּבַע
שֶׁלֹּא יִהְיֶה שׁוּם רִפְיוֹן בְּאֶחָד מֵחֲבֵירוֹ
רַק כּוּלָם יִהְיוּ בְּמִשְׁקָל הַשָּׁוֶה.

And when one element dominates the other (heaven forbid!), this causes a person to feel pain and a weakening of the body (heaven forbid!), as is known to the sages of natural science. For all forms of healing are only attempts to strengthen and to fortify the natural constitution. There must not be debility in any one of the elements—all of them must be in equal balance.

שֶׁלֹּא יִהְיֶה שׁוּם רִפְיוֹן בְּאֶחָד מֵחֲבֵירוֹ ... רַק כּוּלָם יִהְיוּ בְּמִשְׁקָל הַשָּׁוֶה.

In these lines we finally arrive at the heart of the matter—at least as regards a conception of health and healing in the *Degel Mahaneh Efrayim*. Physiological wholeness and strength is related directly to the degree of equilibrium that reigns in the human body, for that body parallels the composition of nature more generally, and therefore requires the disparate elements of its makeup to exist in harmony. If one element overwhelms the others, if the equilibrium of the body is disrupted, a weakening of physical strength will follow—pain and disease in its wake. The implicit theory behind these remarks is that physical health is rooted in an integrated understanding of the body—that seemingly separate aspects and regions of physiognomic composition are in fact inextricably bound to one another.

Just as the baseline of health rests on this integrated conception of physiology, so, too, the practice of healing must follow such a holistic approach. If the healer seeks to treat a physical ailment without attention to the interconnected nature of the human body, if a symptom is addressed in isolation without any awareness of how one part of the body relates organically to a whole integrated self, then true healing will not be achieved. All of the elements of physical composition must be taken into account by the responsible healer, and health will only be restored through attention to the interconnected balance of an individual's physiology.

This outlook on wholeness and healing comports well with contemporary conceptions of total body medicine and healthcare. Many physicians and alternative medicine healers have expressed the importance of an integrated awareness of the patient's whole body, of the manner in which particular symptoms must be treated in relationship to the other interwoven aspects of the body.[9] Such a view emphasizes that one element of a person's physiology cannot be healed in isolation—each symptom is always a part of a larger interconnected web of life. So, too, the balanced equilibrium of seemingly disconnected parts of the body is the critical foundation for the conception of health articulated in the *Degel*. When the body is brought back into harmonious alignment (the role played by the mind in this process will emerge shortly), pain and physical weakness are conquered.

וְהַתּוֹרָה הִיא נִצְחִית
וּמָה שֶׁיֵּשׁ בָּעוֹלָם
יֵשׁ בָּאָדָם עַל דֶּרֶךְ עָשָׂ"ן
ע'וֹלָם שָׁ'נָה נֶ'פֶשׁ.

The Torah is (the force of) eternity, and that which exists in the world also exists in the human being [i.e., human being as microcosm]. This is demonstrated through the correlation [originating in *Sefer Yezirah*] of "world, year, and soul" (*olam, shanah,* and *nefesh*).

וּלְכָךְ בְּוַדַּאי אָדָם שֶׁהוּא בַּר־שֵׂכֶל
וְיֵשׁ לוֹ חָכְמָה
יָכוֹל לִבְרוֹא לְעַצְמוֹ טֶבַע חֲדָשָׁה
וּלְשַׁנּוֹת טִבְעוֹ שֶׁהִיא לוֹ מִכְּבָר.

And therefore, a human being who is a person of intellect (*sechel*) and who possesses wisdom can surely create a new state of nature for himself, and can alter the natural constitution that he had before.

דֶּרֶךְ מָשָׁל
אִם נוֹלַד בְּטֶבַע שֶׁהָיָה כַּעֲסָן אוֹ חַמְדָּן
כְּשֶׁהוּא בַּר־שֵׂכֶל
יָכוֹל לַהֲפֹךְ טִבְעוֹ וְלִכְבּוֹשׁ כַּעֲסוֹ
וְיִהְיוּ דְּבָרָיו בְּנַחַת
וְכֵן לֹא יַחְמוֹד וְיִרְדּוֹף אַחַר מוֹתָרוֹת
רַק יִסְתַּפֵּק בַּמֶּה שֶׁיֵּשׁ לוֹ
וְהַכֹּל תָּלוּי בְּחָכְמָה
כְּמוֹ שֶׁכָּתוּב
שֵׂכֶל אָדָם הֶאֱרִיךְ אַפּוֹ (משלי י״ט י״א)
וְעוֹד
כַּעַס בְּחֵיק כְּסִילִים יָנוּחַ (קהלת ז׳ ט׳).

This is exemplified through the following parable: If a person
is created such that his nature is to be angry or covetous—if
he is a person of *sechel* then he will be able to invert and
alter his natural state, and he will be able to conquer his
anger and his words will be calm. Likewise he will not covet
and chase after greater things, but he will be satisfied with
what he has. All of this depends upon wisdom. As it is written (Proverbs 19:11): "the *sechel* of a man defers his anger,"
and also (Ecclesiastes 7:9): "for anger rests in the bosom of
fools."

כִּי הַצּוּרָה צָרִיךְ שֶׁתִּדְמֶה לְיוֹצְרָה
כְּמוֹ שֶׁיּוֹצֵר הַכֹּל בָּרָא הַטֶּבַע בָּעוֹלָם עַל־יְדֵי חָכְמָה
כֵּן הָאָדָם יָכוֹל לִבְרוֹא לוֹ עַל־יְדֵי חָכְמָה טֶבַע חֲדָשָׁה.

For the form must resemble the One who formed it. Just as the
Creator of All created the natural order of the world through
wisdom, so, too the human being can create a new state of nature for himself through wisdom.

הָאָדָם יָכוֹל לִבְרוֹא לוֹ עַל־יְדֵי חָכְמָה טֶבַע חֲדָשָׁה   In these last few segments we see a highly striking move: precisely because primordial Torah was the divine instrument for the creation of the natural world *and* the human body, a person who knows the ways of Torah in wisdom is able to tap into that repository of divine energy and power that lies latent in the instrument of Torah. In this way, an idealized state of mind—one in which the sage has mastered and connected himself to the creative forces and mysteries of Torah—can bring about the healing of the physical body. To be in command of this potent wisdom is to bring the mind to bear overwhelmingly upon the body; what occurs in the mind has direct and serious ramifications for the physiological state of the person.

Despite the fact that this point is articulated within a radically different belief system and set of assumptions than those of modern medicine and alternative healing, the reader may easily observe the correlations that can be extrapolated from this hasidic conception. As I noted earlier, the research of various medical experts (the most notable of which is Herbert Benson's *The Relaxation Response*) has demonstrated the degree to which a meditative mind and cognitive-behavioral therapies can have concrete effects on the physiological indicators of stress, anxiety, heart disease, and other ailments.

Of course, it would be hyperbole to imply that such a contemporary view is exactly foreshadowed in the *Degel*'s teaching. The hasidic master argues that physical and psychological healing are effected by the mind's ability to tap in to a metaphysical, divine force of energy. Torah, the instrument of divine creation, can be harnessed by the wise adept to transform and alter his own natural constitution—through his cultivated *sechel*, bound to the wisdom of Torah, he is able to *create* a new state of nature for himself, just as the deity created a new state of Nature through Torah at the dawn of primordial time. For if the energies of Torah do indeed lie at the root of all natural reality, then it stands to reason that the skilled mystic might be able to utilize those energies for the sake of effecting a healing.

Perhaps most resonant to a contemporary sensibility, the *Degel* asserts that a person of such wisdom will be able to conquer and transform one of the greatest ailments of the *moral* life—a weakness that eats away at a person's emotional health: he will be able to invert his

anger and jealousy into calm and compassion. Mental attachment to
the wisdom of Torah, to the eternal force of divine creativity, allows
the individual to still the scalding waters of anger, to attain control
over the bestial and wild instincts of our most unrefined selves. Here
the power of the mind reigns over untamed emotion, as it wields the
ability to generate healing in the physical body.

We conclude with the Sudilkover Rebbe's formulation of this very
power, of the need to maintain balance in mind and body as an integrated and interdependent organism of life:

וּמִזֶּה נָבִין אֵיךְ בְּגַשְׁמִיּוּת יְכוֹלִין לְהָשִׁיב נֶפֶשׁ
עַל־יְדֵי הַתּוֹרָה
כִּי בִיטוּל וְחוּלְשַׁת הַנֶּפֶשׁ
בָּא מֵחֲמַת רִפְיוֹן אֶחָד מִיסוֹדוֹת הַנִּקְרָאִים טֶבַע
וּכְשֶׁמְּתַקְּנִים הַיְסוֹדוֹת
לִהְיוֹת כּוּלָם מִתְנַהֲגִים בְּמִשְׁקָל הַשָּׁוֶה
בָּזֶה נִתְיַישֵׁב הַנֶּפֶשׁ עַל עָמְדוֹ הָרִאשׁוֹן.

We can understand how it is possible, in the physical realm, to
restore a soul through Torah. For the nullification and the
weakening of the soul comes about because of the weakening
(or debilitation) of one of the foundational elements that are
(collectively) called Nature. But when the foundational elements are repaired such that all of them function in equal balance, then the soul is restored to its former position.

וּכְבָר אָמַרְנוּ
בְּרֵאשִׁית הַיְנוּ בְּחָכְמָה
בָּרָא אֱלֹקִים הַיְנוּ הַטֶּבַע נִבְרָא בְּחָכְמָה
וְחָכְמָה הַיְנוּ הַתּוֹרָה
כְּמוֹ שֶׁכָּתוּב
כֻּלָּם בְּחָכְמָה עָשִׂיתָ (תהלים ק"ד כ"ד).

And we already said that it was through reishit (bereishit),
which is to say "through wisdom" (bechochmah) that _____

created *Elohim*. That is to say: the natural order (*hateva*, which is numerically equivalent to the word *Elohim*) was created through wisdom. And wisdom (*hochmah*) is the Torah. As it is written (Psalms 104:24): "You made them all with wisdom."

וּלְכָךְ תִּיקוּן וְחִיזּוּק הַטֶּבַע
הוּא גַּם־כֵּן עַל־יְדֵי הַתּוֹרָה
שֶׁיֵּשׁ בַּתּוֹרָה עִנְיְנֵי רְפוּאוֹת גַּם־כֵּן כנ"ל
וְהָבֵן.

And thus the repair and the strengthening of Nature also occur through the Torah, for the Torah contains matters of healing. Understand this.

For the hasidic master, the forces of divine healing may be harnessed through the Torah—the living water of that tradition is the nourishment that restores the thirsty soul and heals the suffering body. In Torah, in God, he finds his spiritual and physical center—the Source of complete healing, *refu'ah sheleimah*, the Great Equilibrium of life. And we, too, arriving as we do with premises so different about the very nature of scientific truth and the healing process—we, too, stand before the mystery of those living waters, seeking to discover our own perfect balance between the spiritually centered mind and the body restored from the weariness of its pain and its burden. With eyes lifted to the mountains, we still seek the support of that hidden river, the Source of all spirit and strength.

3

HOPE AND THE HEBREW BIBLE

Tamara Eskenazi, PhD, is professor of Bible at Hebrew Union College–Jewish Institute of Religion in Los Angeles. She is a reknowned popular lecturer and publishes her scholarly work in numerous journals and periodicals. She is currently working on a women's commentary to the Torah and has conducted some of her most important research on the Books of Ezra and Nehemiah.

READING THE BIBLE AS A HEALING TEXT

Tamara Eskenazi

Introduction

The Bible is a book of hope and a book of healing. It is, of course, many other things as well. It functions in many modes: as the book that establishes, defines and sustains religious faith; as a work that shapes a community by reconstructing or constructing a shared history and identity; and as a source of spiritual and practical guidance to everyday life, to mention but a few of the roles that the Bible has served throughout the millennia. But one of its most pervasive agendas from the very beginning was to provide hope and healing.

As most scholars concur, the driving impetus for the formation of the Bible came about after the destruction of the Jerusalem Temple in 587 BCE and the exile that followed. The Bible began, then, as a response to crisis. Its early compilers aimed at restoring hope and providing a healing to a people whose world had come undone. It thus represents one particular expression of the human need to retrieve meaning even when all seems lost. Empirically speaking, the Bible successfully accomplished the goal of providing healing and hope to people long after the initial crisis and to those far beyond the small Judean community that first put it together. The books that made their way into what we call the Hebrew Bible, or the *Tanach*, are those that accomplished this task and were therefore preserved, generation after generation.

Given that the Bible has been such a perennial source of healing wisdom, the task of mining it for healing wisdom would appear to be easy. So much of the Bible readily speaks to the full range of human experience, from despair to fulfillment, that twenty-first-century readers, like those before them, can find solace and strength in countless passages. The Psalms allow us to pour our heart out to God who sometimes seems absent but soon responds. The prophets assure us that justice will prevail and that we will again be restored in body and soul. Chapter after chapter in the Book of Isaiah urges us to rejoice, to be comforted: "Comfort, oh comfort My people ..." (Isaiah 40:1). Hope is on the way.

What I wish to do in this essay, however, is engage texts that less readily appear as texts of hope and healing and then to illustrate some ways in which they can also become sources for us today. I will review some of the circumstances to which the Bible is an answer and then review the answers themselves in a manner that allows us to appropriate them in a new way.

Certain developments in the twenty-first century help us recover some of the anxiety that our ancestors felt in the past. It is not so long ago that fear of the SARS virus infected the globe and caused panic across borders. More recently we have been monitoring with great concern the global spread of the H5N1 virus, colloquially known as avian flu. The ravages of AIDS continue worldwide even though we have tools that help control the disease. Such experiences that shake our confidence in our medical, scientific, or social capacity to protect ourselves can give us a taste of how vulnerable the ancestors felt before the discovery and invention of true cures.

In the ancient world, disease could spread rapidly and unchecked and literally obliterate thousands of people, a large portion of the human population. It could well have been your own child, coming home with some infection picked up along the road, who could destroy the entire village. Historical and archaeological sources confirm the devastation caused by disease. Most scholars agree that between the Bronze Age and the Iron Age, most of the population in the Middle East was wiped out by disease. It is even more likely, despite the amount of time and glorification given to war in the Bible, that disease killed far more people during biblical times than did war. The Epic of

Gilgamesh, one of the oldest texts from antiquity, expresses this phenomenon. When the gods wish to find ways to destroy humankind, one of them explains that there is no need to use war; one can simply let disease and famine do their job.[1]

Within such a context, when human frailty is self-evident, the Bible makes healing a central concern. The healing it seeks encompasses the physical, spiritual, economic, and social aspects of life. Two distinct systems undergird and dominate the overarching perspectives of the Bible on the questions of healing in response to the disease and disasters that were experienced in the past. One is represented in the book of Deuteronomy, and the other, the priestly perspective, is in Leviticus.

The Deuteronomic Perspective

The perspective of Deuteronomy shapes many parts of the Hebrew Bible, including prophetic books such as Jeremiah. At a time of crisis the prophet Jeremiah asks, "Is there a healer?" Jeremiah himself answers the query with a negative: There is no healer. There is no balm. Therefore, calamities will follow. Therefore, God weeps. Like many others in the *Tanach*, Jeremiah holds that there is an inevitable connection between sin and human suffering. This ideology comes especially from Deuteronomy and forms the backbone of large portions of our Bible. This ideology, commonly labeled "Retribution," has a particularly vivid expression in the blessings and curses at the end of the Book of Deuteronomy.

These chapters represent Moses's final words to the Israelites who are about to enter the Promised Land. They disclose a theology that is often hard to swallow. In chapters 27 and 28 Moses instructs the Israelites to proclaim the curses that will befall them should they fail to follow the teachings of Deuteronomy. The list includes famine, disease, and all other manner of devastation. According to these chapters, the curses that follow are the inevitable result of Israel's sin, especially their breaking the covenant and disobeying God. Such threats and their supporting ideology are, at first glance, anathema to us. Readers cringe when reading the lists. Over the years, I have come to know many a rabbi who bemoaned these chapters and asked, "WHAT am I going to say about THIS text on Shabbat?"

But before we toss out Deuteronomy, let's be clear about the Deuteronomic claims. Deuteronomy maintains that the various disasters, the "curses," are not simply natural phenomena to be endured passively. They are contingent upon the behavior of the society. The underlying presumption is that the moral society, constructed along the lines the *Tanach* commands, uses its human and natural resources responsibly. The respectful use of land and the compassionate care for the disenfranchised create and sustain a healthy society. And that is what secures the entire world. When a society fails to construct an equitable life-support system, the entire ecosystem suffers and disaster follows.

Epidemics, according to Deuteronomy, are not accidents. They signal, on some level, human disregard for the physical, religious, and moral aspects of life. It is tempting to read these threats from Deuteronomy as another case of simplistic theological cause and effect. Even worse, it has been possible to use the curses as another chilling excuse for blaming the victim, claiming that those who suffer must have done something to deserve their fate. This misguided theology and ideology represents the outlook of Job's friends in the Book of Job. Responding to the death of Job's children, one so-called comforter states: "If your sons sinned against Him, He dispatched them for their transgression" (Job 8:4; JPS). God, however, unambiguously chastises these friends for their position (see Job 42:7).

To attribute this simplistic perspective to Deuteronomy is to misread. Deuteronomy is not proclaiming a simple, individual cause-and-effect theology. For Deuteronomy, the world remains an interlocking system, governed by a just and compassionate God who cares deeply for those in the world, and who is trying to shake those of us who are part of the covenant to care and to take care as well. Moses is addressing those about to "arrive" ("When you enter the land," *ki tavo*, Deuteronomy 26:1). By listing the diseases and disasters that would follow disobedience, Deuteronomy is essentially saying to those who have arrived, or who are on the verge of arriving: "When you come to the land, you have the privilege and the power to make a difference. You have arrived. Your life as an individual is woven into the larger fabric, for which you are also responsible." It claims that suffering individuals in our midst are evidence not of their own transgressions, but of the corporate, communal failure to build a healthy society of economic and social responsibility rooted in a covenant. Deuteronomy therefore urges those among us who have arrived to monitor ourselves and our communities, to care and to act. Optimistically, it assumes that we are capable of doing just that.

Many of us remain troubled by the picture of wholesale punishment for the crimes of the few. We cringe at the prospect that the innocent perish along with the guilty. Yet, when we look around us, we must admit that today, as in our past, we are living in a world where countless people suffer because of the crimes of the few. The few, in many ways exemplified by those of us privileged to live in North America and Western Europe, are the cause of so much that is economically rejected by the rest of the world. We help perpetuate disease not by wanton transmission and infection (as was once the case), but because we have not devoted nearly enough of ourselves or of our vast resources to creating solutions. We have not taken responsibility.

Inadvertently and without our consent we in fact exemplify the phenomenon that Deuteronomy describes. Our ancestors explained this perspective through theological language in which God plays a direct role, and sought to remedy it by invoking the fear and love that the relation with God can generate. By recognizing these diseases and disasters as communal problems, the ancients learned to lift from the individual the guilt that is so often attached to suffering. They made it clear that the source is not with the lone sufferer, but those who have the means and options to make a difference yet fail to do so.

The Leviticus Perspective

Leviticus has a different focus than Deuteronomy, representing another mode of communication altogether. Whereas Deuteronomy thinks of what we might call "body politic," Leviticus is concerned with the politics of the body. In reading Leviticus I am particularly indebted to the work of the anthropologist Mary Douglas. Her book *Leviticus as Literature*[2] provides the lens through which I approach the text in this essay. I share the view of my former student Rabbi Jocee Hudson, who sums up Douglas's interpretation well; and I paraphrase here:

> Douglas explains that the Israelite purity system surfaces within the context of an emerging Israelite theodicy. What happens when a people that is supposed to believe in God can't (as Douglas points out) get rid of their belief in demons? How can they explain why seemingly healthy people fall ill if demons didn't cause the illness? How can they explain the death of a new mother or a newborn baby if some malevolent creature doesn't cause the terrible act? The biblical purity system and its bizarre complexity not only separated people from that which they feared. It granted our people a qualified coping mechanism that allowed them to feel protected from the terrifying forces in the universe.[3]

The purity system (according to Douglas) provided the bridge. It should be noted, however, that Leviticus does not explain the theories that link the physical and the spiritual. It aims to help us know how to get past obstacles that jeopardize the balance in the universe, how to move on; it does not seek to rationalize, but to guide actions that can restore balance to the world as the Levitical worldview understood it.

For Leviticus, the physical body itself is a locus of theological meaning, enacted ritually. Leviticus works like an artist who paints virtual spaces and describes what happens in them, while instructing adherents on how to move in and through that space. The priestly writer "is teaching the people of Israel to honour in their lives the order of creating, and by doing so to share in its work. The living body is his paradigm."[4] In the space of the body the author of Leviticus finds analogies with the Tabernacle and the history of God's revelation to Israel."[5] Maimonides—much later—concluded that the Tabernacle/ Mishkan as described in the Book of Exodus (chapters 25–31 and 35–40) is analogous to Mount Sinai itself in that it is composed of three circles of holiness, in gradation of holiness moving from periphery (open to the public), to the more exclusive realm of trained personnel, to the holiest space of all, restricted in terms of time and personnel: the outer court, the Sanctuary, the Holy of Holies.

Douglas goes further. She demonstrates that Leviticus envisions three microcosms each mirroring the same symbolic structures of holiness: Sinai, the Tabernacle/Mishkan, and the embodied person. One route to holiness moves vertically with a mountain peak as the Holy of Holies. The other, the Mishkan, moves horizontally with the Holy of Holies as the culmination. And the body, following the same structure, moves from the outside to the inner recesses. Each of these virtual spaces is a recreation of an encounter with the divine, which is why there are so many prohibitions. What cannot go onto the altar cannot go into the person. The body, like the altar, is the place where the encounter with the divine occurs.

What we might call "health care" is addressed in Leviticus more advertently than any other biblical component. Chapters 13 and 15, in most explicit terms, focus on illness. The biblical scholar Hector Avelos refers to the Bible as a whole as the complete biblical health care package, one address for all.[6] However, the statement is not quite right because it implies that the Bible, or Leviticus, provides a cure. Leviticus, however, is not about the cure of a disease. Rather, it is about the healing of the person—and through the person, also the healing of the world.

The difference between "cure" and "healing" is significant and is correlated with two different terms for sickness: disease and illness. According to Arthur Kleinman: "*Disease* refers to malfunctioning of biological and/or psychological processes, while the term *illness* refers to the psychosocial experience and meaning of perceived disease."[7] Kleinman observes further that "modern health professional health care tends to treat disease, but not illness; whereas in general, indigenous systems of healing tend to treat illness, not disease."[8] As a result, curing pertains to disease and healing to illness. Leviticus focuses on how to heal the person in the community.

For many modern Jews, the Torah portions *Tazria* and *Metzora*, especially chapters 13–15, represent an obstacle to be overcome. They appear to be a tremendous affront to many of our sensabilities because these texts isolate and exclude from the community persons with certain physical conditions, such as a woman who bleeds after childbirth or a person inflicted with *tzaraat*, the skin disease once translated erroneously as "leprosy." I propose that we revisit these sections in

Leviticus to discover whether, in fact, they can be a friend, not a foe, and a veritable source of healing wisdom.

Perhaps the best way to begin is to bear in mind that in Leviticus, priests supervise stages of infection to determine whether a person is cured. They do not themselves engage in the curing. Their first task is to protect the community from conditions that might be contagious, and this is accomplished by isolating the infected individual. Leviticus, thus, is concerned with the integrity of the body and of the community, with wholeness. It is fair to argue that this echoes the very beginning of the Bible, Genesis chapter 1, with its focus on the marking of boundaries, the separations of sea from land, earth from sky, and so on. Leviticus simply brings this cosmos of separation to a human level. The goal is for wholeness, on an individual level as well as a communal one. Bodily fluids, accidental seminal emissions, and irregular bleedings, for example, all mark punctures in that wholeness. Dialogue between persons or between persons and the divine require that the integrity of the body must be restored. What Leviticus depicts, time and again, is this process of restoring such wholeness so that a dialogue can resume. After offering many details about the conditions that require separation and isolation, Leviticus in these chapters also concentrates on reconnecting the persons who have been isolated and on bringing them back into the center. The more marginalized the ill persons have been, the greater the effort to bring them back into the fold.

The most extensive procedure is for *tzaraat*, the skin disease sometimes mistranslated or misdiagnosed (as noted above) as leprosy. This highly contagious disease often marks the person for life. Leviticus 13 focuses on diagnosing the disease and isolating the inflicted person during stages of the disease's development. The isolation, at first, is complete. These precautions, although disturbing, are comprehensible in terms of the danger that infection poses for the community as a whole.

What is striking about Leviticus, however, is the extensive ritual that signals the safe restoration of the afflicted person into the community. The event entails an odd and ultimately astounding ritual in the final stages of this particular healing ritual. In Leviticus chapter 14, we read about the person who had been afflicted with *tzaraat*. The person is to sacrifice an animal, and then, "The priest shall take some of the blood of the guilt offering, and the priest shall put it on the ridge of the right ear of him who is being cleansed, and on the thumb of his right hand, and on the big toe of his right foot" (Leviticus 14:14). There follows a ritual in which the priest handles oil and then, "Some of the oil left in his palm shall be put by the priest on the ridge of the right ear of the one being cleansed, on the thumb of his right hand, and on the big toe of his right foot" (14:17). After a few more steps comes the conclusion that pronounces the previously isolated person as ritually pure: "Then he shall be clean" (14:20). The word "clean/cleanse" used in this Jewish Publication Society version translates the Hebrew term *taher*, which pertains to ritual purity, that is, freedom from ritual contamination that forces isolation from contact with the holy.

This process of restoring the *metzora* (person afflicted with *tzaraat*) to the community has to be compared with the ritual for ordaining the priests, first described in Exodus 29 and then enacted accordingly in Leviticus 8. Here is how the commands in Exodus describe the ordination of priests:

> Slaughter the ram, and take some of its blood and put it on the ridge of Aaron's right ear and on the ridges of his sons' right ears, and on the thumbs of their right hands, and on the big toes of their right feet; and dash the rest of the blood against every side of the altar round about. Take some of the blood that is on the altar and some of the anointing oil and sprinkle upon Aaron and his vestments, and also upon his sons and his sons' vestments. Thus shall he and his vestments be holy, as well as his sons and his sons' vestments. (Exodus 29:20–21)

Here is how Leviticus 8 describes the actual consecration or ordination of priests: "Moses then brought forward the sons of Aaron, and put some of the blood on the ridges of their right ears, and on the thumbs of their right hands, and on the big toes of their right feet" (Leviticus 8:24). After a few more steps, we read: "Thus he consecrated Aaron and his vestments, and also his sons and their vestments" (8:30).

All three texts demand the odd ritual of placing consecrated blood and/or oil on the right ear, right thumb, and right toe. What is crucial for understanding Leviticus is the fact that these three texts are the only ones in the Bible in which the odd ritual of right ear, thumb, and toe appear. This means that the ordination of the priest and purification of the formerly infected individual share some fundamental and unique features. Such parallels express a profound statement about the rehabilitation of the person who had been excluded. Leviticus 14 illustrates the tremendous investment in the social and religious reconnection and rehabilitation of persons formerly stigmatized and excluded by virtue of the disease. The most marginalized, isolated person is reintegrated with an elaborate ritual, comparable only to that of the ordination of the High Priest. What is absent in these chapters of Leviticus, and in Leviticus as a whole, is as crucial as what is in it. At no point does Leviticus suggest that a person's illness or disease results from that person's sin.

One reason I have been focusing on Deuteronomy with its curses and Leviticus with its preoccupation with isolation of an infected person is that these texts in particular have been used throughout history either to punish persons or to reject the Bible. Patients suffered cruelty in isolation and ostracism, followed by social and religious stigma. (For some details, see William McNeill, *Plagues and Peoples*.)[9]

As Professor Bill Whedbee notes in an article on plagues and pestilence in ancient Israel, we could write a horrifying history of applications of these texts in Leviticus and Deuteronomy in Western culture. It is the persistence of horrifying applications of both Deuteronomy and Leviticus, either implicitly or explicitly, that makes me eager to emphasize the part that I myself have usually ignored. Far from seeking to perpetuate the dreadful discrimination in the ancient world against people afflicted with skin diseases, Leviticus aims at finding a way to restore and rehabilitate persons in the most public way. An awareness of the prejudice in the ancient world may explain precisely why the integration of these persons stricken with or disfigured by isolating diseases receives in Leviticus the highest attention and most ennobling validation. The *metzora*, the person afflicted with *tzaraat*, is the only person radically isolated. The *metzora* is also the only person restored with a ritual that evokes sanctification of priests. I trust that we can easily see the many contemporary applications and analogues, mostly noted by their absence, because we do not, as a rule, have a ritual to mark the reentry of a person to the community after an isolating illness (although the *Gomel* benediction could serve that function).

The parallel with the High Priest, whose holiness is recognized once he has been consecrated (see Exodus 29 and Leviticus 8 above), raises the question about the meaning of holiness or sanctification. The dictionary definitions of "holy" begin with the words such as "Set apart for the service of God." The standard authority for biblical definitions, Brown, Driver, and Brown,[10] has several explanations for *kodesh*, and they all begin with words such as "separateness," "withdrawal" and "apartness" before mentioning dedication to God. In all these definitions sanctity is marked first and foremost by separation, and this understanding of holiness is repeated in virtually all discussions of holiness in the Bible. This focus on separation is understandable, but it is insufficient as a description of the biblical notion of holiness. Now, it is time to move forward, beyond these definitions and understandings.

The fullest exposition of what it means to be holy in terms of the Bible is in Leviticus 19. Here, the articulation of personal boundaries is coupled with powerful affirmations of necessary, unshakeable connections, to the parents we must honor, to the stranger, to the poor whose gleanings we must secure, to the neighbors and strangers whom we must love, and to the deaf, the blind, and the otherwise "weak" whom we are obliged to protect. These connections, demanded in the name of God, delineate what it means for us to be holy. To be holy in the Bible, then, is to connect to the highest power by means of connecting to others in responsibility and in love.

Thus far I have focused on troubling texts, texts that some have called "texts of terror."[11] The Bible typically moves from crisis to hope and thus we must look at "texts of hope" as well. Here I wish to linger briefly on a much-neglected biblical source for our work on healing. I am referring here to the canonical shape of the Bible, to the very shape of the whole, which functions as a path of healing and a resource for personal and communal renewal.

The five Megillot, or scrolls, that we read as a community on designated holy days—Song of Songs, Job, Ruth, Lamentations, Ecclesiastes, and Esther—are remarkable as a response to the different times in our lives. When we read them together in a sequence, they mark a trajectory of life and illustrate processes for thriving and coping. These books have the advantage in that the theological claims in most of them are more muted and can speak readily to persons with ambivalent or negative connections to the overriding theologies of the Bible. This makes the Megillot more accessible and more "user-friendly" for people who are not already at the heart of the biblical traditions.

The Megillot follow the Book of Job, the book and the character that have raised the most acute cry of the heart about the fragility of the human condition and the consequences of hopelessness. The Megillot chart a path of healing as one moves through the seasons of life. Song of Songs leads us back into the processes of human regeneration, rekindling the appetite for life. It sustains a person through the intimacy of love, a "love as strong as death" (Song of Songs 8:6). This book envisions love that can stand in the face of death and empower us to rediscover and be born in new ways into the next stage of our life.

Song of Songs inspires our potential to be vibrant, radiant persons, reveling in life's abundance. It recreates the Garden of Eden and its evocations of what it means to be human and whole. In Song of Songs, this possibility is not depicted as a nostalgia for some primordial time back in history but as a possibility to be lived in the here-and-now of ordinary women and men. Song of Songs is also an extraordinary resource for articulating the Jewish spirituality of wholeness. It celebrates and embodies spirituality, a love that celebrates the body as a holy place, a *Mishkan*. It restores us to the role of gardener in that garden where everything flourishes with great profusion. It recreates the time of fresh discovery, the emerging of a self in dialogue with an other who invites us to blossom. The other, whether human partner or Divine Entity, is the essential element.

The woman describes her lover saying to her "Rise up, my beautiful one, my friend, and go forth" (2:10). (This line from Song of Songs is often mistranslated as "come away," a translation that changes the meaning entirely.) The passage invites the woman to go forth. She understands her beloved to say, "Our relationship (human-

human or human-God) is for you to blossom and move forth and become your whole self in relation to me." The image is not singular, and
has many possible interpretations and readings. But among these is a
vision of wholeness. There, Song of Songs also offers a vision of integration. "Set me as a seal upon your heart and a seal upon your arm" (8:6).
The arm and heart are integrated here. The heart, that innermost part of
us, animates everything we do from within; and the arm, the part of us
that acts in the world. In this universe, in Song of Songs, fragments are
made whole, the inner and the outer selves encountering the other, and
become whole by virtue of the dialogue between "me" and "you."

The rabbinic sages of antiquity read Song of Songs, theologically,
as a spiritual journey describing the relationship between God and
Israel, as well as a dialogue between the individual and God. If read
through such rabbinic lenses, Song of Songs portrays God as not so
much a shepherd but as a lover, and love here encompasses body and
soul. The book traces this love affair in a rhythmic dialogue of mutual
nurturing and of the connectedness between differentiated persons. It
sets a vision before us of how we can be related to each other, to God,
and to the earth. It prepares us to hold on to that vision when things
begin to go awry, as things inevitably do.

The book that follows, Ruth, prepares us for a different journey.
It is a journey that begins in futility and moves to fertility. This journey
ends as a manifesto of the human capacity to generate *chesed* (kindness). It illustrates the kinds of steps that can be taken by an ordinary
man or woman to enable goodness to become as contagious as bird flu
or SARS. When Naomi returns home she essentially says, "I'm empty.
I do not have anything. I went away full and came back empty. I have
no one. There is nothing for me." (See, for example, her self-description
in Ruth 1:20.) Saying so, she completely ignores the one who stands
next to her, namely Ruth, the woman who left everything in order to
join herself to the widow, the stranger, which is what Naomi was.
Ruth, after all, had been living in her own land. But she made herself
into the stranger in order to join, protect, and sustain another. Naomi
fails to see Ruth or her other resources because she wallows in loss and
a sense of futility. Only when Ruth comes home with some food and
an image of hope (2:20–22) does Naomi rally strength and begin to act
creatively.

The story of Ruth is a story about relationship. How do you put bread on the table when you are poor, when you are a stranger, when you are a widow, when you have no one? The book of Ruth suggests how, and it begins with one person igniting the awareness of life's possibilities in the other. In chapter 3, Naomi begins to see a possible future. She tells Ruth she needs a man. For Naomi, the only way to make it in the world is to have a husband. Ruth has a different understanding of her situation, but this is not where I want to focus my argument. I would like to take a closer look at Boaz.

When Ruth and Boaz first meet, Ruth is essentially destitute, forced to gather the gleanings of Boaz's fields. Boaz, however, senses something more in her and discovers her story. When Ruth asks Boaz why he is paying attention to her, Boaz replies:

> I have been told of all that you did for your mother-in-law after the death of your husband, how you left your father and your mother and the land of your birth, and you came to a people that you had not known before. May Adonai reward your deeds. May you have a full recompense from Adonai, the God of Israel under whose wings you have sought refuge. (Ruth 2:11–12)

This is a very nice sentiment, a very traditional understanding of the relationship between the individual and God. Boaz is offering charity, food, water, and a blessing. But once the harvest is over, the good deed is done, and there is no sign that Boaz intends to do anything more. He will return to his normal routine and the two destitute women will have to rely on what Ruth had gleaned beforehand.

It is Naomi who steps in and counsels Ruth to attach herself to Boaz. And it is on the threshing floor where Ruth and Boaz make their connection. Under the cloak of darkness, Ruth echoes Boaz's earlier statements, but with a difference. She says to him, "Spread your wings over me, for you are a redeemer" (3:9). In essence, she is saying: "Don't wait for God to reward me and give me shelter [as you did in chapter 2]. You are my redeemer. Spread your wings over me." Boaz rises to the occasion, and he doesn't only redeem her by taking responsibility. He marries her. What begins as admiration from afar becomes a matrimonial bond that leads to the birth of Israel's most famous king, King David.

Surprisingly, God does very little in this story. For the most part, God is little more than hearsay in the Book of Ruth. The people, Boaz, Naomi, and Ruth, bring God into the story through their blessings of each other in their work and actions. And God is, of course, at the very core of these actions. But God becomes a partner only after the human beings in the story have done their work. In the end, the Book of Ruth celebrates the extraordinary achievement of ordinary people who create and recreate relations and possibilities, building the world into one that is suitable for children.

Next comes the Book of Lamentations, which commemorates and mourns the destruction of the Temple in 587 BCE. When read in sequence, as reference to life's seasons, this becomes a book that speaks to the time when all that had been achieved (in the Song of Songs and in Ruth) comes crashing down. The Hebrew name of the book, *Eicha*, goes to the heart of the book's message. The word *eicha* opens three of the five poems in the book (1:1, 2:1, 4:1). It means "How!" and expresses the overwhelming grief and dismay of the poet. "How has Adonai, in wrath, shamed Daughter Zion, cast down from heaven to earth the majesty of Israel?!" (Lamentations 2:1; my translation).

Rehearsing the sorrow of our people over the destruction of the Temple in the sixth century BCE, the Book of Lamentations also speaks to the crises in our personal lives. It speaks to the times when the ecstasy of love described in Song of Songs has vanished and the security of family, friends, and community that have been arduously built in the Book of Ruth give way to sorrow and irreparable loss. It is a book for the season when one confronts personal tragedies, such as the suffering of loved ones, the onslaught of illness, or the encounter with death. It speaks to a time when our trust has been betrayed, our business has collapsed, our home and our city have been laid to waste by war or some natural disaster. And we ask, both of ourselves and of our God, "How? How could all of this have happened to us? How can I live through this moment? How can I respond?" Until "How?" becomes an expletive.

Yet these poems, part plea, part protest, and part rehearsal of everything that has gone wrong, also offer a catharsis that enables the process of healing to begin. Four of the five poems are alphabetical acrostics; each begins with aleph, the first letter, and concludes with the last letter of the Hebrew alphabet, having gone through the other letters in sequence to describe the experience and the pain. This process of pouring out grief also begins the healing process. It gives a voice to those who suffer and words for their pain. The form of this rehearsal of sorrow, the acrostic, serves to diminish the impact by structuring the pain and helping contain it.

Speaking about loss from A to Z, as it were, Lamentations gives shape and perhaps also closure to the chaos that invades a person's life when disaster strikes. With the acrostic, the book helps in restructuring the world. Using the most basic building blocks of language, at a time when physical and emotional resources have been stripped from us, it provides us with a ladder back to hope. Language that brings order out of chaos through the most basic materials that we humans possess, the letters, helps reassemble our broken world.

Following Lamentations, Ecclesiastes, or *Koheleth*, picks up the next stage of life's seasons and the next step toward healing after loss. Here the writer surveys the journey from ecstasy to despair and asks, "What remains? What endures? What matters?" The conclusion has famously been (mis)translated as "vanity" or "futility." Thus we read in the JPS edition Koheleth's repeated theme as "Utter futility—said Koheleth—Utter futility! All is futile!" (1:2). The New Revised Standard Version has "Vanity of vanities, says the Teacher, vanity of vanities! All is vanity."[12]

These translations misrepresent the word that *Koheleth* uses by translating it as either futile or vain. The Hebrew word, *hebel*, more accurately means "vapor" or "mist." It refers to the ephemeral nature of seeming substance, to that which is fleeting. It is the breath you see emanating from you on a cold day. It is the steam from a teapot. It is what appears briefly, and, just as quickly, vanishes. The writer of this book emphasizes that the most precious aspects of human life are fragile and pass quickly. They are not like a diamond that can be stored for some future use without losing its value. This can be construed as futile if such concretization is the only thing that matters. But *Koheleth*'s message aims at sensitizing the reader to the preciousness of those aspects of life itself that are precious because they vanish all too quickly.

Ecclesiastes/*Koheleth*'s advice is clear: be sure to celebrate and relish what you have, including the most simple things, for these are the gifts that we get to enjoy. The transitory nature of the most precious aspects of life does not make these aspects either futile or absurd. It calls for the fullest appreciation of each aspect of life, each season of life. Thus the famous lines from Ecclesiastes/*Koheleth* describe human fate and journey: "To everything there is a season and a time for everything ... a time to give birth and a time to die, ... a time to kill and a time to heal, ... a time to wail and a time to dance" (*Koheleth* 3:1–4; my translation). None of these seasons endures forever and none can be stored as we would a diamond.

Therefore, *Koheleth* offers clear advice in the face of the changing nature of life's seasons. It tells us, "Go, eat your bread in gladness and drink your wine in joy ... Let your clothes always be white and your head not lack ointment" (9:7–8). It is not recommending the use of, say, corn oil. Rather, it is referring to expensive perfumes. Its message: always dress your Shabbat best. Treat every day and every event as the special moment that it is. Always, as it were, put on your Chanel No. 5, and don't just store it for some future date. Life is a great feast that, inevitably, is going to end soon enough. Appreciate it now and celebrate it now. "Enjoy happiness with the person you love all the fleeting days of your life.... Whatever is in your power to do, do it with all your might" (9:9–10).[13]

The last book in the collection of the Megillot is the Book of Esther. To read Esther as a book that teaches about a healing and wholeness is to recognize the book as a time for crossing the threshold back into history, leaping into the carnival of life. This is what Esther herself does when she takes a frightening risk and comes to the king uninvited. Esther is a story of fasting and feasting, and of learning to laugh, first and foremost at ourselves. Before we know it, the year passes and Song of Songs returns for another cycle of going forth through another cycle of life.[14]

The *Tanach*, the Jewish Bible, contains these stories and poems that help us recognize the different seasons in our lives. The Megillot honor each season in its time. They help us gain wisdom by teaching us to move with, rather than struggle against, the inevitable ebb and flow of life. In reading the Megillot we learn to recognize the seasons not only in our own lives, but also in the lives around us, our friends, lovers, communities, and the strangers in our midst. We discover that because there are seasons, there is also, as Koheleth says, a time for everything under the heaven.

What final lesson can we take from this journey through the Megillot? The recognition that love is as strong as death (Song of Songs 8:6), that practicing *chesed* wisely can lead from futility to fertility (Ruth), that nonetheless the time comes when we experience deep, even devastating loss (Lamentations), but that loss and love must and can be integrated into a larger picture of life as both fleeting and precious (Ecclesiastes). Finally, as the seasons are about to begin again, we get to cross the threshold with Esther into the world of laughter and liberation.[15]

Adriane Leveen, MSW, PhD, has taught at Hebrew Union College–Jewish Institute of Religion in Los Angeles, and at Stanford University as a senior lecturer in the Hebrew Bible in the Department of Religious Studies. She will soon be teaching at HUC-JIR in New York. Dr. Leveen has published in *Prooftexts,* and the *Journal for the Study of the Old Testament* and is a contributor to a forthcoming volume, *Women's Torah Commentary*, sponsored by Women of Reform Judaism. Dr. Leveen's book *Memory and Tradition in the Book of Numbers* will be published by Cambridge University Press.

"CALL ME BITTERNESS": INDIVIDUAL RESPONSES TO DESPAIR

Adriane Leveen

In her eloquent reflections on biblical understandings of healing and hope, Tamara Eskenazi reminds us that the Bible emerged as a response to both national and individual crisis. "Time and time again it was necessary to gather the fragments of what had been shattered and bring them together."[16] The Bible depicts the people Israel as collectively experiencing deep anxiety and dread, violence, exile, and displacement. Yet the Bible also depicts Israel's recovery and restoration in the Promised Land. Eskenazi's insight into the Torah's ability to shape meaning out of despair, hope out of hopelessness, convincingly explains its extraordinary power to endure. But, as she goes on to remind us, the Torah endures due to its compassionate attention not only to national trauma, but also to moments far more personal than collective. In its pages we encounter individuals who experience what we recognize and know ourselves—relief after a much-anticipated birth, loyalty in friendship, enduring love, and also, in equal measure, infertility, deep disappointment, abandonment, and bitter loss.

Eskenazi argues that whether as a collective or as an individual, we respond to crisis by seeking out, and even demanding, an interpretation of events that involves a struggle for meaning. Only then are we able to find comfort and dare to begin again. To combat despair Israel must recognize itself as embedded in a larger story that points in a direction that leads beyond the bleakness of the present to a new chapter in the life of the nation. The biblical writers, especially the prophets, took upon themselves nothing less than the delineation of the process—crisis with its concomitant fury and disappointment, loss and sorrow, hope and restoration. Thus the Bible "combats despair and inscribes processes of healing in a number of ways."[17]

In this essay, I want to take up Eskenazi's compelling insight into the Torah as a work of healing and analyze its depiction of despair and recovery at the level of the individual rather than the nation. To do so I will examine the stories of four individuals—Tamar, Hannah, and Naomi and Ruth. As each story opens, the female character is in the midst of a crisis—whether it be the loss of a husband, the loss of sons, or the fear of infertility. In each story crisis takes a different form, but in all three, a woman hovers on the brink of capitulating to a life of grief and bitterness. Yet she turns away from despair. All three stories end on a note of renewal and celebration as each woman does nothing less than rewrite what appears at the outset to be a very grim future.

When I set out to write this essay I did not intend my examples to include only women, nor did I expect to focus so heavily on issues of family ties and fertility, as profound and fundamental as they are. Yet when looking at each of these three stories through the particular lens of despair and recovery, I discovered how each actually delineates the process of crisis and resolution as a subtle psychological event. I was struck anew by the rich and astute literary depiction of the characters' determination and personal power. Thus the task at hand created the opportunity to revisit these familiar stories with a fresh appreciation of their astonishing power. To discover that power, we must carefully observe how the Hebrew text delineates the process, conveying the writer's insight into how individuals combat despair through such resources of language as poetic form, repetition, play on words, and/or the deployment of key terms.

And she sat down at "the opening of eyes" (Genesis 38:14)[18]

Tamar's story is delayed. First we are told of Judah's move away from his brothers, his marriage, and the birth of his three sons in rapid succession.

Note that the theme of conception and birth is introduced from the very beginning of Genesis 38. The chapter concludes with another conception and birth, as Tamar succeeds in conceiving and giving birth to twins. The presence of such an obvious frame suggests a precisely constructed story whose events are carefully intertwined. The continuation of the line of Judah, and Tamar's role in that continuity, is the story's main concern.

Yet Tamar is only introduced in verse 6—"taken" by Judah as a wife for his son. Inexplicably that son dies. Refusing to perform the obligated act of intercourse on behalf of his brother's line, the second son dies as well.[19] We know nothing of Tamar's response to this double disaster but we do learn of Judah's response. He is struck with fear that his only surviving son will share the fate of his two brothers. "For he thought, 'lest he, too, die like his brothers' " (Genesis 38:11). At this point in the story, the reader reasonably assumes that Judah and Tamar are traumatized by events, united in a shared grief over the unexpected loss of a son and a husband. Yet Judah chooses to withdraw from the grief and from his daughter-in-law, figuratively locking away the problem by literally sending Tamar back to her father's house with a promise to give her the third son at a later time. Judah chooses the route of avoidance to cope with his grief. Thus Tamar's tragedy is worsened by Judah's action, however understandable. Tamar has no choice at this point but to comply.

Time passes without fulfillment of Judah's promise. Tamar remains in her father's house. The writer does not inform us of her thoughts, but we can imagine her increasing sorrow as she realizes that Judah will not act to change her isolated, childless state. Someone tells Tamar of Judah's whereabouts. That in itself is a fascinating detail. Is this anonymous someone a mere plot device or does it suggest that at least one member of Tamar's community is aware of her plight and desirous to help her? At the very least the resolution of Tamar's plight would not occur without this anonymous intervention.

In verse 14 the woman who was passively taken as a wife, sent away, and ignored suddenly and dramatically acts. Tamar is now the subject of a string of verbs:

> And she took off her widow's garb and covered herself with a
> veil and wrapped herself and sat by the entrance to Enaim

[literally, "the opening of eyes"] ... *for she saw* [emphasis mine] that Shelah had grown up and she had not been given to him as wife. (Genesis 38:14)

Only the last verb in the series is passive while the key word, *saw*, is in the grammatical perfect, suggesting completed action. She has finally reached the inevitable conclusion that Judah broke his promise. Thus her actions emerge directly from reflection.

Yet, ironically, Judah does not yet see anything but an appealing prostitute whom he desires: "And *Judah saw her* [emphasis mine] and he took her for a whore" (Genesis 38:15). The verb in verse 16 for Judah's turning aside to speak to her— וַיֵּט —is identical to that in verse 1 describing Judah's initial movements. The repetition of verbs invites the reader to look back at the course of events that led Judah to this point. Judah's initial turning away from his brothers and his subsequent acts culminate in this crucial encounter with Tamar, an encounter that eventually opens his eyes. Tamar unhesitatingly seizes the opportunity that she has in fact created by placing herself directly in his path. By choosing to leave her confinement Tamar rectifies her isolated and abandoned state. She is quite purposeful in negotiation with Judah, requiring as a guarantee precisely those objects that most readily identify an individual of that time—a signet ring and a cord.[20] Note the end of verse 18 and verse 19: "... she conceived by him. And she rose and went her way...." In other words, throughout the entire encounter with Judah, Tamar is the agent of her own fate, brought home by the fact that she now voluntarily goes on her way. What a different journey it is than the earlier exile forced upon her by Judah!

In verse 24 Judah is informed that Tamar is pregnant. With ruthless indifference and astonishing brevity, he orders her taken out and burned. On the way, she sends him the objects that identify him as the father. Tamar's survival at this point depends on the thinnest of threads— the sending of messages. Note that the groundwork was laid for "sending" as a key word in the passage by its use in their negotiations in verses 17 and 20 when Judah gave Tamar his markers of identification in anticipation of sending her payment. The terms of exchange—sending (used five times) and giving (used eight times)—are the crucial means through which reconciliation and restoration are accomplished after Judah failed to give Tamar his third son. Of course Tamar is physically saved in the end because of Judah's willingness to recognize and acknowledge the injustice he did to her.

How then does Tamar respond to a crisis and combat the despair of losing a husband, of being sent away, and of the loss of a future? This story suggests that she combats despair by daringly acting on her own behalf. Instead of remaining a passive victim of Judah's fear and indifference, she finds her way by rejecting the confinement he imposes on her. She will not resign herself to such a fate. She rectifies the wrong and in so doing ensures the continuity of Judah's line. To revert to Eskenazi's line of argument for a moment, Tamar acts in a present moment to secure a different future for herself than that imposed upon her. Yet she could not succeed entirely on her own. She needed someone from the community first to inform her of Judah's whereabouts and then to send Judah word of his part in her pregnancy. Finally Tamar needed Judah to acknowledge his responsibility. The story moves from actual and threatened death to life, ending with the birth of twins.

And her face was no longer downcast (I Samuel 1:18)

The writer emphatically defines Tamar as the chief actor in her own destiny but acknowledges that Judah is crucial to the ultimate "happy ending" of that story. Human interdependence is also present in the story of Hannah but to a lesser degree. Eli the priest will play a role in Hannah's recovery from despair. More than Eli's contribution, however, I will argue that it is Hannah's articulation of the justice of her complaint that restores her hope.

We are introduced to Hannah's untenable environment as her husband minimizes her pain at being barren while Penina repeatedly mocks her state. The writer goes out of his way to suggest that as painful as barrenness might be for Hannah, it is the human responses of those around her that exacerbate the situation. A cycle of humiliation at the hands of Penina endures over time. In other words, Hannah is trapped in a psychologically damaging situation. The key image that captures that torment can be found in verse 7: "and thus it was done year after year—when she would go up to the house of the Lord, the other would torment her and she would weep and would not eat" (I Samuel 1:7). These details of physical distress are quite unusual for the typically laconic biblical narrative. Her crying, lack of eating, the heaviness of her heart, and her sadness are in fact biblically astute descriptions of real depression and anguish. Yet just as in Tamar's case, Hannah combats despair by taking her fate into her own hands. She does so through prayer and, I want to argue, through a self-definition that emerges out of a strong sense of the legitimacy of her desires.

As Hannah prays, weeping the whole time, she makes a vow: "Lord of Hosts, if you really will look on your servant's woe and remember me, and forget not your servant and give your servant male seed, I will give him to the Lord all the days of his life … " (I Samuel 1:11). In this speech Hannah uses the emphatic form: אִם רָאֹה תִרְאֶה "if you *really* will look," suggesting her need to have her distress accepted without minimizing it or mocking it. Her impulse to negotiate with God turns her powerlessness into a state of activity, even though she's negotiating over the future of a child she does not yet have. She is moving into a state of agency through negotiation.

Eli misreads her internal process, mistaking her for a drunk. Their dialogue captures Hannah's ability not only to correct his mistake but to do so in such a way that she also gains his admiring respect. How she does this provides the key to her success in combating despair.

> "No my lord! A bleak-spirited woman am I. Neither wine nor hard drink have I drunk, but I poured out my heart to the Lord. Think not your servant a worthless girl, for out of my great trouble and torment I have spoken till now." And Eli answered and said, "Go in peace, and may the God of Israel grant your petition which you asked.… " (I Samuel 1: 15–17)

Hannah refuses to be checked by the priest. When he rebukes her, she clarifies and explains with simple directness her exact emotional state. She begins by telling him he has in fact carelessly categorized her (as worthless), therefore utterly failing to recognize and define her correctly. True discernment is a complex skill that he apparently lacks. She is someone who can pour out her heart to God. Implicit in her comments is the definition and valorization of direct prayer as speaking from a fullness of trouble. Note how Eli concedes the point and sends her on her way in peace. "And the woman went on her way, and she ate, and her face was no longer downcast" (I Samuel 1:18). Why does the brief exchange with Eli comfort Hannah? What has he done? I would argue that he has acknowledged the rightness of her self-definition, learning to respect an emotional truth he can't help but recognize. Not only that, he allows himself to be corrected. Finally, note that a key part of Hannah's recovery is her ability to articulate her experience. This saves her. But it is also the simple human understanding and acceptance of her self-definition that allows her to rise from her place, return home, and conceive the prophet Samuel.[21]

Why should you go with me?
(Ruth 1:15)

My last example will be the briefest since Tamara Eskenazi has already highlighted aspects of the tale of Naomi and Ruth. I turn to this story because it is the clearest example within the biblical corpus of the response to grief and despair as one of simple companionship. Naomi is bitterness itself: "Do not call me Naomi, she replied, call me Mara [i.e., bitterness]" (Ruth 1:20). No argument can move Naomi away from this totalizing self-definition. It is only Ruth's determined physical action of remaining by her side that softens Naomi enough over time to relinquish this deeply felt and tightly held bitterness.

I will limit my comments mainly to chapter 1 of the Book of Ruth. There is ample evidence in this chapter of the writer's understanding of connection to others as the key to recovery after crisis. With breakneck speed verse 3 of the first chapter informs the reader of Naomi's first crisis—the loss of her husband. She is left (the Hebrew verb is in passive voice). Two verses later, both of her sons die, and again the same verb in the passive announces that she is left, but now, not only without a husband but also without her sons. Thus her state is one of solitude and, we could surmise, utter devastation. Through its quick establishment of crisis the story suggests that Naomi's predicament is one of its main concerns.

Yet Naomi is not utterly alone. Her two daughters-in-law remain and begin the return journey with her. Urging them to return to their mothers' home, Naomi wishes that they will find security, מְנוּחָה. A biblical lexicon translates the Hebrew in a variety of ways: security, resting place, equilibrium (on a scale), assurance, peace, and relief from sorrow.[22] Having none of that herself, Naomi believes she is incapable of providing or securing such things for her daughters-in-law. She cannot understand why they would accompany her, asking: "Why should you go with me?" (Ruth 1:11). Naomi sees herself as a solitary figure, bereft of husband, of sons, of a future, and even of God: "The hand of YHWH has struck out against me" (1:13). Orpah leaves but Ruth remains.

The verb describing Ruth's reaction captures the main dynamic: Ruth clings to Naomi. This same verb describes the clinging of the first man to the first woman in the Garden of Eden in Genesis 2:24. In so doing Ruth attempts to break through Naomi's strong desire to succumb to her solitary despair, to cut herself off from comfort and relationship. Ruth's famous speech is an expression of attachment. Not only its content but also the reciprocal and interconnected parallel form embodies the point: "wherever you go, I will go ... wherever you lodge, I will lodge" (Ruth 1:16). Ruth demands a share in Naomi's fate.

The Hebrew for "accompanying" (or more literally, walking) appears frequently enough to function as a key word of the passage. A key word appears so often in a brief amount of text as to draw the reader's attention to its use. In the present case, "accompanying" appears nine times in verses 1, 7, 8, 11, 12, 16, 18, 19, and 21 in chapter 1 alone. This verb negotiates the emotional issue best—will Naomi accept company on her journey into despair? At least initially Naomi refuses to acknowledge the gift Ruth offers her: "I went away full and YHWH has brought me back empty" (1:21). But the writer ensures that we understand the gift Ruth has given by emphasizing Ruth's return with Naomi immediately after Naomi's failure to do so: "And Naomi returned, and Ruth the Moabite, her daughter-in-law with her..." (1:22, translation mine). Placing Ruth's presence in the middle of the verse makes the point.

As discussed by Eskenazi, Naomi does eventually recover, awakening to the possibility of securing a future for Ruth through Boaz. Naomi announces her intent in 3:1 to seek a resting place for Ruth, a possibility she was convinced she was incapable of securing for her daughter-in-law. By realizing Boaz could play a role, Naomi considers an alternative she could not contemplate in the early stages of her grief. The possibility of considering things from a different angle or new perspective is a sign that recovery is under way.

So how does Naomi combat despair? How does she move from grief and utter bitterness to hope and plans for the future? The story suggests that it is Ruth's insistence on accompanying Naomi in her grief, to share the fate awaiting Naomi, that in turn allows Naomi to move eventually from bitterness to hope. Rather than persuasion or lengthy exhortation, Ruth offers Naomi silent companionship, loyalty, and attentiveness. These best fit what Naomi, overwhelmed by grief, needed at the time. Eventually Naomi can envision a far different future than the emptiness she assumed to be her fate in the early stages of her grief. She can place herself alongside Ruth in that " ongoing future." As Eskenazi writes, between them, Ruth, Naomi, and Boaz have created a community "and a world into which you want to bring a child."

Tamar, Hannah, and Naomi and Ruth, each in their own way, have something to teach us. When crisis hits, we can succumb to despair. It is understandable. It is certainly necessary to grieve and allow ourselves to experience the gamut of emotions that arise from loss and abandonment. Yet healing happens when you can move from powerlessness to activity, crossing a threshold, perhaps on your own, to acquire some form of restitution. Or healing happens when you can directly articulate your emotional turmoil without excuses, and experience gratitude in the recognition that someone else suddenly understands. Or if need be, healing happens silently as you comes to understand and recognize a patient companion who makes few demands but waits until the grieved person can eventually reciprocate. So it is that the "faltering are girded with strength" (I Samuel 2:4, translation JPS). So it is that each of these characters comes to rewrite her own story, securing a far different end than that threatened at the outset.

4

From Disability to Enablement

Rabbi Elliot Dorff, PhD, was ordained by the Jewish Theological Seminary of America in 1970 and earned his PhD in philosophy from Columbia University in 1971 with a dissertation in moral theory. He currently is rector and distinguished professor of philosophy at the University of Judaism. Rabbi Dorff is vice-chair of the Conservative Movement's Committee on Jewish Law and Standards and served on the editorial committee of *Etz Hayim*, the new Torah commentary for the Conservative Movement. He is author of twelve books and over 150 articles on Jewish law and thought and on issues of health and healing.

JUDAISM AND THE DISABLED: THE NEED FOR A COPERNICAN REVOLUTION

Elliot Dorff

Our civilization needs a revolution in the way it manages people with so-called disabilities. As Jews we may begin within our own religious and cultural community, aiming to modify our behavior and possibly influence general culture as well. Part of my purpose in this essay is to see what Judaism might contribute to the desired changes.

Before changing the way we manage this dimension of our communal life, we must look at the tradition itself and try to understand it more fully.

I think it is fair to say that traditional Judaism's approach to disability is remarkably enlightened and compassionate, especially when compared to the treatment disabled people received in other cultures. We should note that almost all of the biblical heroes were disabled in some way. Sarah, Rebekah, Rachel, and Hannah were all barren for some time in their lives.[1] Isaac and Jacob suffered from blindness in their old age,[2] Jacob was lame for much of his life,[3] and even the greatest biblical hero, Moses, suffered from a speech impediment.[4] Similarly, a number of talmudic rabbis were disabled; for example, Nahum of Gimzo, Dosa ben Harkinas, Rav Joseph, and Rav Sheshet were all blind.[5] The more "manly" biblical models—Esau, Gideon, Samson, and even David—are all portrayed as flawed in character.

In contrast, the heroes of Greek and Roman culture were all physically perfect—even extraordinary. American secular culture applauds those who overcome disabilities, along with those who triumph over any obstacles. Some popular movies, like *Philadelphia*, and some country songs, like Mark Wills's "Don't Laugh at Me," warn us not to ignore or denigrate the homeless or ill, but very few, if any, commercials depict disabled people or even old people, because Americans honor youth and ability. That is why Franklin Delano Roosevelt insisted on hiding his wheelchair in the last years of his presidency. Thus the fact that so many of the biblical and rabbinic heroes were disabled in various ways speaks volumes about how our tradition from its very beginnings thought of this group of people: in contrast to the Greek, Roman, and American cultures. In Jewish sources the disabled were to be construed like everyone else, and they were often leaders.

This stems from some deep Jewish convictions. For the Jewish tradition, humans are all created in the image of God,[6] and, as such, we have divine worth independent of what we do. That does not mean that we may do whatever we want, because what we do must occur within the framework of 613 commandments. Moreover, the fact that each person is created in the image of God does not mean that we have to like everyone or what everyone does. It does mean, though, that even when we judge a person harshly for his or her actions, we must still recognize the divine worth inherent in that person. The extreme illustration of that, from my perspective, is that the Torah demands: "If a man is guilty of a capital offense and is put to death, and you impale him on a stake, you must not let his corpse remain on the stake overnight, but must bury him the same day. For an impaled body is an affront to God"[7]—literally, "a curse of God." That is, the image of God inherent in even such a person must be honored. How much the more so must we honor the image of God in those who have not committed heinous crimes but happen to be disabled in some way.

The Jewish tradition is remarkable not only in how it *thought* about the disabled, but also in the *actions* it demanded with and for them. In Greek and Roman cultures, "imperfect" infants were put out to die, and disabled adults were left to fend for themselves and often mocked to boot. In Jewish culture, in contrast, killing an infant for any reason constitutes murder,[8] and the Torah specifically prohibits cursing the deaf or putting a stumbling block before the blind.[9]

As Jews, we dare not forget these fundamental features of our tradition's thought and practice. Given how other cultures treated the disabled, we should take pride in the fundamental humanity embedded in Judaism, whether or not individual agents have always been true to that tradition.

It is also important that we acknowledge that Jewish sources *did* put the disabled at some disadvantage. This especially affected the Temple and the biblical concept of the holy. Specifically, while disabled men born into the priestly class were not denied their part of the priestly portions, they were not allowed to serve in the Temple and were instead put to menial work such as cleaning the kindling wood from worms, for which a special area was set aside: "No one at all who has a defect shall be qualified [to offer a sacrifice], no man who is blind, or lame, or has a limb too short or too long; no man who has a broken leg or a broken arm; or he who is hunchback, or a dwarf, or who has a growth in his eye, or who has a boil-scar, or scurvy, or crushed testes."[10]

Maimonides explains the exclusion on the grounds that "most people do not estimate a person by his true form, but by his limbs and his clothing, and the Temple was to be held in great reverence by all."[11] Somehow, for the Torah and Maimonides, a person could be disabled and still function as the people's political leader, but that person could not serve in the sacred precincts of the Temple. One verse in Deuteronomy even says that a man who has crushed testes or a severed penis "may not enter the congregation of the Lord"; it is not clear whether that only refers to a man who voluntarily maimed himself in service of some Canaanite god or whether it refers to any man in that condition, and we also do not know the meaning or implications of "may not enter the congregation of the Lord,"[12] but it clearly constitutes an exclusion of such men from normal status.

As we turn from ancient rites to Jewish law now in practice, I shall summarize the various categories of disability and how the Rabbis treated them. In all fairness, by and large the Rabbis limited any legal restrictions on the disabled to the specific tasks the disability prevented them from doing, seeing such people otherwise as full-fledged Jews. That is, the Rabbis did not dismiss the disabled categorically from Jewish responsibilities and roles; they instead sought to empower them as much as possible. Still, rabbinic law does impose some limitations on them in both ritual and civil law.

The disabilities the Rabbis discuss are the following: someone who is insane or sufficiently mentally retarded to lack the mental ability to be held legally responsible (*shoteh*); blind (*suma*); epileptic (*nichpeh*); sexually neuter (*tumtum*) or hermaphrodite (*androgenus*); or sterile (*saris* for a male; *aylonit* for a female). In addition, they speak about a *cheresh*, a term the Mishnah defines as someone who is both deaf and mute, although the Gemara defines *cheresh* as someone who is deaf but not mute, *ileim* being used to describe a mute.[13] That ambiguity will affect later rulings about that category.

Here, then, are some of the rulings regarding the disabled in Jewish ritual law:

1. Blind people should say the blessing before the Shema that praises God for creating light because even though they cannot see the light of day, they benefit from it because others see them and keep them from accidents.[14]

2. Similarly, even though the third paragraph of the Shema (Numbers 15:39) commands us to wear fringes so that we may *see* them and thereby remember God's commandments, blind people are obligated to wear fringes because others can see them.[15]

3. Along the same lines, even though the Shema begins with "*Hear O Israel*," a deaf person, who by definition cannot hear either the command or his or her own voice saying the prayer, can nevertheless fulfill the commandment of reciting the Shema because others can hear him or her saying the prayer.[16]

4. Since the Torah must be read and not recited by heart, blind people may not serve as the Torah reader, but they may be called up to recite the blessings over the Torah and they may read the Haftarah from a Braille text or even recite it by heart.[17] A deaf person may read from the Torah as well as recite the blessings over it.[18]

5. A blind person may lead the congregation in prayer because blindness does not free a Jew from the duty to pray and, unlike when reading the Torah, a person may pray by heart.[19]

6. A *cheresh* (probably here a deaf-mute) cannot fulfill the obligation of the community to hear the Purim megillah read because such a person cannot speak audibly.[20]

7. Despite some arguments to the contrary, a blind person is obligated to recite the Haggadah of Passover, as two great, blind talmudic scholars, Rav Sheshet and Rav Joseph, did.[21]

8. A blind person may not serve as a kosher slaughterer, for a slaughterer must see clearly to cut firmly and quickly to minimize the animal's pain. A deaf-mute or even a *shoteh*, however, may serve in this capacity *if* supervised by a person who knows how to do this and who attests that the slaughter fulfilled the requirements of Jewish law.[22]

9. Finally, a *cheresh*, *shoteh*, and a minor are not obligated to hear the shofar blown on Rosh Hashanah and therefore are not eligible to fulfill the commandment for others if they blow the shofar. The later codes specify that this applies only to a deaf person, but a hearing person, even if mute, is obliged to hear the shofar blown and therefore can fulfill the commandment for others.[23] This is a good example of a general tendency embedded in all of these Jewish ritual laws and in Jewish civil law as well—namely, that the rabbis restricted a disabled person's duties and eligibility only to those areas affected by the disability.

Now let us look at a few Jewish civil laws related to the disabled. In general, deaf-mutes were categorized together with insane people and minors because the rabbis had no way of knowing whether deaf-mutes understood what was happening or not; as a result, deaf-mutes, like minors and the insane, were not given much legal status. The blind and the crippled, on the other hand, were presumed to have full legal competence, except in areas that required someone to see or to walk. In other words, Jewish law worried most about legal competence (what American lawyers call "mens rea"), and that was much more likely to be compromised by mental, rather than physical, disabilities.

Here, then, are some examples, of Jewish civil laws relating to the disabled:

1. An insane person and a minor who does not realize the value of an object cannot acquire title for themselves or for others; only an agent of sound mind (such as a parent) can acquire title for them. A deaf-mute and a minor who *can* understand an object's value, however, can acquire title for themselves, although not for others.[24]

2. Because inheritance to and from blood relatives requires no legal transfer of property but rather occurs automatically at death, both an insane person and a deaf-mute can make bequests and receive them. In both cases, though, a trustee or guardian must be appointed to look after their affairs.[25]

3. An insane person cannot buy or sell property, but a deaf-mute and even a minor can buy or sell movable property (but not real estate) in order to sustain themselves.[26] Special care had to be taken, though, to assure that the witnesses to the sale correctly understood the gestures made by the deaf-mute to indicate an intention to buy or sell.[27] Someone who is mute but not deaf, however, can effect an acquisition or sale even of real estate.[28] Someone who sometimes is of sound mind and sometimes not, such as an epileptic, has full ability to buy or sell both movable property and real estate while of sound mind, but the witnesses must take steps to ensure that that is indeed the case during the transaction.[29]

4. Even though there are restrictions on the ability of deaf-mutes, insane people, and minors to acquire property, someone who takes away anything such people found has committed theft.[30]

5. Insane people are not held liable at law, and if the situation requires it, a guardian is appointed to protect the interests of both the insane person and those who might suffer as a result of his or her legal immunity.

6. An insane person may never serve as a witness, and even a sane person who is confused about a given matter may not serve as a witness about that matter. Those who are sometimes sane and sometimes insane must be tested to ascertain their eligibility as a witness.[31] The deaf and mute were also excluded from most testimony because the rabbis, interpreting Leviticus 5:1, determined

that one must be able not only to hear, but also to speak in order to testify.[32] The deaf and mute could, however, testify to free a woman from becoming chained to her first husband and thus unable to remarry (an *agunah*).[33] The Torah's verse requiring that witnesses see what happened also excluded the blind from testifying, even if they recognize the voices of the parties.[34] Moreover, since these disabilities barred a person from serving as a witness, they also excluded them from being eligible to serve as a judge.[35]

7. An insane person cannot marry because such a person cannot legally consent, but a deaf-mute can.[36] Sterile people can marry as long as both parties are aware of that fact at the time of marriage, but otherwise the marriage is void. Someone who exhibits no sexual characteristics (a *tumtum*) can marry either a woman or a man, although the marriage has doubtful status. A hermaphrodite (*adrogenus*) may marry a woman but not a man because the rabbis considered such a person male.[37]

8. Finally, and perhaps most indicatively, just as a person who disgraces an able-bodied person must compensate the victim with money as well as seek forgiveness, so, too, anyone who demeans a disabled person must pay such damages. Only an insane person is not paid for this, according to the Talmud, because being insane, in the rabbis' judgment, already constituted a disgrace second to none.[38]

That last provision may disturb our modern sensibilities, but what is remarkable is that Jews were forbidden to embarrass all other categories of disabled people and had to pay damages if they did.

My Copernican Revolution

Of course this is not a perfect picture; there are parts of the story and the law that we might wish were different. Those who would like to see changes in Jewish attitudes toward the disabled or the laws governing them base their arguments on the immense changes that have taken place in recent times in technology and medicine, enabling even paraplegics to get around, the deaf to communicate through sign language, and the blind to read texts translated into Braille. Psychotherapy and drug therapies have made good progress in relieving a variety of psychological disorders. Obviously such disabilities often still compromise a person's competence to do some things, but, many maintain, the advances in what the disabled can do should move us to change Jewish law in a number of particulars. I agree with such moves, and I think that they are completely in line with the rabbis' careful analysis of identifying exactly what people suffering from a particular disability can and cannot do.

In this essay, though, I want to try a completely different approach. I call it a "Copernican revolution" because like Copernicus, I want to invert our perceptions. (Copernicus, we recall, got us to think of the earth as going around the sun rather than the other way around.) I suggest that we think of a world in which *the norm* is what we now call "disabled," and we able-bodied and sane people are the abnormal ones. What would, or should, Jewish perspectives and law look like then?

Before I develop this idea, I would like to point out two things that might make it seem more reasonable. First, the idea struck me because of what a disabled person told me long ago—namely, that from the point of view of the disabled, all the rest of us are *temporarily abled*! We all know, of course, that they are right: even Olympic athletes will, in the course of life, most likely lose at least some of their vision and hearing, and even the most nimble and those who exercise regularly will not escape the slowing down and the aches and pains that age inevitably brings. We nervously joke about it, but even our mental processes may dull; you do not have to have full-blown Alzheimer's to become increasingly forgetful—and yes, often more crotchety—as time goes on. My wife, Marlynn, told me that the first time she heard about disabilities was at a conference of the Bureau of Jewish Education in Los Angeles in 1971, when a young woman who was wheelchair-bound told the assembled teachers: "Don't care about the disabled out of sympathy. Care for them for your own selfish reasons, for you, too, will be like me some day." My intention is not to depress you; it is only to point out that it is not so far-fetched to think of everyone as disabled, especially as the American and Jewish populations age.

Second, a person is not just abled or disabled; there are *degrees* of disability. I, for example, have worn glasses since I was seventeen, and it was also during that year that I had my first asthma attack. Ever since then, I have lived with these disabilities. The asthma, in particular, prevents me from engaging in fast sports. In my younger days, when the test of a male's masculinity was all too often connected with his athletic abilities, and when asthma medications were much less helpful than they are now, that particular malady took quite a toll on my psychological well-being and my social standing. I mention these things not to seek your sympathy, but just to indicate that each of us is disabled in some ways—physical, mental, interpersonal, or all of the above—and even if we learn to cope with these problems, they do change our image of ourselves and what we can do. So all of us who think of ourselves as able-bodied should not have too much difficulty picturing ourselves as at least partially disabled.

In such a world, then, in which the norm is being disabled and the unusual thing is to have full control of our physical and mental faculties and full ability to interact socially with people without any psychological problems whatsoever, how would we want Judaism to treat disabilities? Instead of thinking about humane treatment for the disabled as being motivated by our own compassion or God's commandment, we would see it as simply caring for ourselves—much as we see any of the services that we Americans expect the government or others to provide for us.

With that as the norm, wheelchair access, for example, would not be a new and sensitive thing; it would be what we normally assume. "Walk" and "Don't Walk" lights at intersections would naturally have ticking sounds so that the blind would not have to depend on the sighted or what traffic they hear to know when to cross. As many college classrooms are now equipped with Internet access, so, too, they would have facilities for Braille transcriptions of materials being discussed in class, and they would be routinely staffed by people who sign for the deaf. The same would be true for business meetings, court proceedings, and the like. Even private homes would be easily accessible for people in wheelchairs and would be arranged to ensure that the blind would have an easy time finding their way without tripping.

As the objects of society—the nouns—would change, so, too, would daily activities—the verbs, so to speak. That is, daily activities and special events, including trips, would be planned assuming that most people are disabled in some way. So, for example, there might still be sports for the able-bodied, together with teams and league competition, and there might even be professional sports teams for the able-bodied, but such activities would be seen simply as a subset of the larger social efforts to provide athletic expressions for all of society's members. Thus, just as there are now professional men's and women's basketball teams for the able-bodied, so, too, there would be professional teams for the blind, deaf, and wheelchair-bound, perhaps differentiated by sex as well.

Courses in schools and colleges would be taught in a multimedia way so that people of all kinds of abilities and disabilities could participate. It would be obvious that school districts would need to schedule and pay for classes for autistic children and those with other developmental disabilities, with teachers specially trained for helping such children. Business meetings, court proceedings, and visits to the doctor, the accountant, the barber, and everyone else who provides a service or sells a product would all be easily handled by all people, regardless of their forms and levels of ability or disability. Even those inviting others to their homes would automatically think about not only the activities that they plan, but even how to give directions to get to their home for people of varying abilities and disabilities.

What kind of society would this be? Clearly our whole way of looking at the world and what we expect of people would change. That would bring with it a number of objective, subjective, and interpersonal innovations.

First, objectively, massive economic and social changes would be entailed in the kind of Copernican revolution I am proposing. As I indicated through only a few examples, both the objects and activities of our lives would have a very different character. Much of that would cost considerable sums of money, and that is a real concern, but the economic outlays to make this happen would be nothing like the 14 percent of gross national product that we currently spend on cosmetics.

The real difference would be one of attitude. Instead of thinking of ourselves with all kinds of abilities and coping with whatever disabilities we have, and instead of modeling ourselves after people with no apparent disabilities, we would instead think of human beings as coming in all kinds of shapes and sizes, abilities and disabilities.

The Costs and Benefits of Such a Copernican Revolution

While I very much encourage us to entertain my proposal, I must warn that it entails significant costs. First, in the most literal sense of the word "cost," my plan, as I indicated above, would require major financial expenditures. To do anything like what I am proposing would require major outlays of money. We have already tasted that in the costs of complying with the Americans with Disabilities Act (ADA), but my proposal would require much more. If anything, American society today seems to be moving in the opposite direction, as we have seen the U.S. Supreme Court chip away at the ADA's protections and its costs over the last several years. The current administration, and American society generally, may not be ready to spend more money on these issues, and that raises real questions about the viability of what I am suggesting.

Even apart from current spending priorities, it must be acknowledged that one important reason why society is structured as it is does not stem from fear of the disabled or prejudice against them, but from the fact that the vast majority of us, for the vast majority of our lives, are, in fact, remarkably abled. We may require glasses, asthma medications, and the like; but God has given most of us bodies that enable us to do many things for many years, and God's agents in the form of doctors and other mental and physical health care personnel are extending our abilities and their longevity yet further. Thus there is a certain plausibility in treating the abled as the norm and the disabled as the exception, not only in conception, but also in creating social policy.

Furthermore I fear that my proposal may understate the pain involved in being disabled. After it is all said and done, it *is* harder to cope with life if you are blind and most people are sighted, deaf when most people are hearing, unable to walk when most people can, or unable to learn or interact with people as most people do. This increased difficulty encompasses not only the physical trials of getting around in the world of the abled, but also the emotional challenges of feeling a sense of self-worth and the social obstacles of creating friendships. I certainly do not want to minimize those problems in the least; on the contrary, my proposal aims at mitigating them by resetting the default option in society, as it were—that is, by making us think of everyone as disabled in some way. Even less do I want to stand in the way of efforts to develop cures for disabilities or better tools to cope with them; on the contrary, I want to encourage such efforts as much as possible. So my proposal of making the disabled the norm should *not* be construed as minimizing the pain involved in disabilities or as discouraging efforts to alleviate that pain.

What I am proposing would require us to do some considerable emotional work in readjusting our American way of thinking and feeling about ourselves. Currently, with the exception of doctors and other mental and physical health care personnel, most of us live in a state of denial for most of our lives about the disabilities that we ourselves will most probably incur at some later date. We do that, in part, by choosing to engage with only able-bodied people in at least the vast majority of our daily activities. We avoid visiting the sick at hospitals, not only because it is a bother and poses a real risk for infection, but also because hospitals remind us of our own vulnerability and even our own mortality, and we do not like to think about those things or feel insecure.

In the society I am proposing, though, very much like the society of our great-grandparents, people will encounter others of all ages of ability and disability on a daily basis; the disabled will not be sequestered into specific institutions for them, but will instead live at home and will regularly study and work with the more able-bodied. That may make some of us today, who are used to being protected from daily reminders of our vulnerability, uncomfortable. Such feelings may pass, however, as we again get used to such a society. In many ways, this is similar to the process by which Jews of my generation gradually accepted women—and, for that matter, men—participating in many areas of life where they had never been before. But like the opening of roles in society to people of both genders, so, too, the opening of society's spaces and activities to people of all levels and forms of ability and disability will take at least some getting used to.

So much for the costs of my proposal. What are its benefits? First of all, making the disabled the norm would make all of us *feel* better about ourselves, for such a society would be much more accepting of high degrees of disability in the various areas of life. That would not stop a bad baseball player from striving to be a better one, or a person ignorant of science from becoming more adept at it, for we would still try to develop our physical and mental abilities, as we do today.

At the same time, this social arrangement would help control our egos, for it would remind us that our human claim to worth is *not* a function of our abilities. In the Torah, God warns us against claiming that "My own power and the might of my own hand have won this wealth for me. Remember that it is the Lord your God who gives you the power to get wealth"[39]—and, for that matter, to do anything else. We certainly can and should feel proud of our achievements, but seeing the world from the vantage point of the disabled should restore and reconfirm in us a needed sense of humility.

My proposal would also make society as a whole a kinder, gentler, more inclusive place to be. People would not be judged primarily by how much they can do or how beautiful they look; since the norm would be a lack of many abilities, people would be judged primarily by what they do to help others in coping with life. That is, *character* would more likely be the criterion of worth in such a society—and that, I dare say, is a very nice result.

And what about the trappings of Jewish law? The intriguing part of this proposal is that it might prompt us to look with a completely new lens at a number of the details of Jewish law regarding the disabled. As I indicated earlier, in most cases Jewish law makes every effort to include the disabled as much as their disabilities will permit, and we should be proud of the extent to which ancient Jewish law did just that. Some provisions of Jewish law, though, would become hard to justify if we were to look at the world from the vantage point of most of us being disabled. For example, if most of us were blind, we certainly would not require the Torah to be read from a scroll that is only accessible to the sighted; we might *allow* reading from such a scroll, but we would presume that most people would read from a Braille text. Similarly, if most of us were deaf or blind, we certainly would not exclude deaf or blind people from giving testimony to what they did perceive through their functioning senses. Now that we know that mute people are not necessarily or even usually insane, we would treat them at law like everyone else. And we probably would maintain, contrary to the Talmud but very much in line with its reasoning regarding those asleep, that those who insult the insane *would* be liable for damages because others hearing the disparaging remark would understand it as an insult.[40] There are only a few such cases in which Jewish law would need to be changed, but looking at the world through the lens I am suggesting makes those areas that need to be changed crystal clear.

Epilogue

And now I want to pull what football players know as a "double reverse." We owe God daily thanks that most of us, for most of our lives, do not suffer from debilitating conditions that make living life hard. Because that is the case, and because we do need to work to ameliorate the difficulties faced by people who suffer from such maladies, the norm will inevitably—and properly—continue to be people with what we have come to expect as normal human abilities.

I have introduced this thought experiment to motivate readers more deeply concerning the disabilities in our society generally, and in Judaism in particular. Only when we walk in the disabled community's moccasins, at least in our imaginations, aided by what we can learn from what the disabled themselves tell us about what they face, can we begin appropriately to judge how we think about the disabled and how we treat them in society generally and in Jewish life in particular. In the meantime, may our journey into the world of the disabled—and into the upside-down world in which they are the vast majority—make us better, more sensitive people and Jews.

Tamara M. Green, PhD, was a founding member of the Jewish Healing Center and has written extensively about "being sick and being Jewish." In her secular life, she is professor of Classics and chair of the Department of Classical and Oriental Studies at Hunter College.

MISHEBERACH AND THE ADA: A RESPONSE TO ELLIOT DORFF

Tamara M. Green

My response to Rabbi Dorff is shaped both by my own understanding of the intersection of disability and Judaism and by my public role as ADA/504 coordinator at Hunter College where I have taught for the past thirty-six years. It is a response that has been shaped by what I have seen as the ambiguous meanings and ambivalent attitudes in Judaism about disability, and tempered by my personal experience of what it means to be disabled in the secular world of twenty-first-century America.

First, the personal story. For almost forty years I have lived with, most often now with acceptance, but sometimes with an amorphous sense of unease, and even occasionally with a great deal of rage, a debilitating chronic illness. It is not immediately life-threatening, although there have been moments when it has been, but it is life-encompassing; and one of the most painful lessons I have learned from this illness is that what is most difficult to come to terms with is not the possibility of dying from it, but the dailiness of living with it.

That is not to say that I have not thought about what it means not merely to look continually into the abyss of the unknown, but to feel myself losing my balance at the edge. Nevertheless, although chronic illness has had the virtue (I suppose) of allowing me to contemplate a great many things, not the least of which is the recognition of my mortality and of the fragility of human existence, of a life lived close to the edge, what I want to explain here are the ways in which my Jewish life has been affected by my illness, and the ways in which my disability has affected my understanding of what it means to be Jewish.

I was twenty-one when I became ill, newly married, beginning graduate school, my young head filled with plans for the future. I am now sixty-one years old, still married, and with that PhD, but this is not how I imagined my life would work out. I hasten to say that I have had—by and large—a very good time in these forty years, but it's not at all what I planned.

One of the very few lessons I have learned about the experience of illness is that there are very few lessons to be learned, but what I do know is that pain and suffering have not ennobled me in any way, and that I must struggle with the same thing that everyone with a disability or chronic illness faces: living with limitation—with what Eric Cassell labels as disorder, disharmony, and discord. But committed as I am to living a meaningful Jewish life, I have often given a Jewish spin to the many parts of my struggle with disability—not merely to shlep around on crutches, but to ponder what it might mean to be created *b'tzelmo*, in Adonai's image.

What does that mean to someone who is disabled? The rabbis say that the body is of value because it comes from Adonai, and therefore resurrection affirms that our physical existence is valuable in Adonai's eyes. What could be valuable about a physical existence that is marked by struggle and disability? If we all stood at Sinai at the moment of revelation, what about those of us who could not stand? And what does it mean to ask for *refuat hanephesh, refuat haguf* (a healing of spirit and healing of body)? There has always been the impulse to see my body as separate from who I really am, and yet there is the seeming inseparability of the two in the *misheberach*, the prayer for healing. How then does one become whole, when the healing of body seems to be an impossibility?

Paradoxically, the connections between my disability and being Jewish became more complicated for me over the years as my always active commitment to Judaism grew more intense. And so, impelled by some inchoate need to make Jewish sense out of what had happened to me, I explored the tradition, at first tentatively and then ferociously. Could I find a Jewish understanding of illness that would allow me to live within the traditions of Judaism while becoming increasingly disabled?

Certainly there is much to embrace within that tradition. Some of the first traditions I discovered were the injunctions concerning the remarkable mitzvah of *bikkur cholim*, visiting the sick, although the rabbinic discussions focus their attention not on the sick person, but on the performance of the mitzvah by those who are not sick. As both a frequent recipient and visitor, I have learned that it is, as the rabbis said, an act of *chesed*, lovingkindness that is gratifying beyond measure. Judaism, after all, is a religion that ultimately finds its spiritual center in concrete acts, but the ancient sages singled out certain deeds as having special importance. According to the Talmud, of all of Adonai's acts of *chesed* toward the creation that humans can imitate, one of the most important is the act of visiting the sick. It has been traditionally the Jewish way of embracing everyone within the community, a way of acknowledging the suffering of others. It is a way of recognizing our own fragility even while we try to give strength to another.

At the same time, however, I have also discovered that what many traditional Jewish texts have to say about the causes and consequences of illness is too often painful to read, even alienating, and I have found myself continuously wrestling with them, like Jacob with the angel. And like Jacob, I have found myself limping after the encounter. What follows is a brief summary of the various Jewish responses to illness that I have uncovered, and my own responses to them. Neither rabbinic interpretation nor personal response, I must warn you, is consistent.

1. *Illness is a punishment from Adonai.* If illness is a punishment, what did I do that was so terrible, and could I be forgiven?
2. *Illness is a way of making me spiritually aware.* I can state unequivocally that chronic pain and disability have not raised my level of spiritual awareness. And since I have not gotten any better, does that mean I haven't learned whatever lesson Adonai wanted to teach me? What happens if pain becomes a way of destroying faith, not strengthening it?
3. *Elucidation is beyond the grasp of the human intellect.* I would like to give it a shot; after all, I have a PhD. But if I concede that

the plans of Adonai for the creation are beyond my comprehension, what hope can I have of making sense of what has happened to me? And, most importantly, what intellectual and intuitive response can a person have to the mixed spiritual signals that the Torah seems to send to those who are less than physically whole?

Certainly all of us bring our own experiences when we try to find personal meaning in the words of the Torah and attempt to ferret out the spiritual and ethical messages that are embedded in the text. Rabbi Dorff and I have looked at the same texts, and yet we have profoundly different responses. For me, the intersection of the physical and the spiritual in traditional Judaism is much more complex, and the meaning of its message much more ambiguous than the portrait painted by Rabbi Dorff. Yes, it is true, as Rabbi Dorff writes, that Sarah, Rebekah, Rachel, and Hannah were all barren; but I took no comfort from the fact that Adonai "cured" them all, while I was struggling with the reality that I would never have a child. Yes, Isaac was blind in his old age; but it has always seemed clear to me that, despite the rabbis' attempts to explain his behavior, his inability to see is merely a symbol of his ethical blindness. Yes, Jacob limped after his wrestling match with the mysterious *ish* before his encounter with his estranged brother Esau; but the Talmud comments that he was immediately healed by the power of the sun, a power that will make whole at the end of days those who are physically impaired. I'm not sure I want to wait that long. And, even if I would be willing to wait, what does Judaism have to say to me in my present "unhealed" state?

One of the most powerful moments in all of Torah is the proclamation of Adonai to Moses at Sinai: "And you shall be a kingdom of priests, and a holy nation."[41] How exhilarating it is that we all have the potential to become *kohanim*, to become the link between the nation of Israel and Adonai. But it is difficult to reconcile that embrace of spiritual inclusion with the ritual exclusion from Temple service of those *kohanim* who are seen as deformed, those who have, as the sociologist Erving Goffman describes in his remarkable study *Stigma*, a "spoiled identity."[42] I would argue that it is not enough to say that these less than physically perfect *kohanim* were allowed their portion of the offerings, since they were barred from making them on behalf of the people.[43] From the perspective of someone who is disabled, this disbarment looks like a refusal of membership in that "kingdom of priests," and a denial of participation in the sacred; and the granting of the priestly portion sounds a lot more like condescension than an act of *chesed*. The menial task of cleansing the kindling wood of worms has always struck me as less than a second-best job, and no al- lotment of food is going to make that seem any better.

In its most extreme manifestations, that "spoiled identity" can lead to exile from the community. The Torah portion *Tazria* lists all the outward signs of leprosy in exacting clinical detail, and declares that after the diagnosis of leprosy is made, the leper's "clothes shall be rent, and the hair of his head shall go loose, and he shall cover his upper lip, and shall cry, Unclean, unclean. All the days wherein the plague is in him, he shall be unclean; he is unclean; he shall dwell alone; without the camp shall be his dwelling."[44] The isolation of the leper is complete and absolute and frightening, for he is forced to leave the camp, to live apart from the community. How must he feel, going through the rituals of mourning for himself, having been forced to de- clare himself before the entire community to be unclean? Judaism is supposed to be grounded in our collective responsibility toward Adonai and one another, is it not? How then, if we are enjoined to see the mitzvah of *bikkur cholim* as an emulation of Adonai's *chesed*, could we cast out someone who is suffering? What happens to the *chesed* we are supposed to demonstrate? What has happened to Adonai's *chesed*? Are we so horrified and so frightened by what has happened to the leper that we must banish him from our sight?

I think it was both this struggle to make "Jewish sense" out of what had happened to me and the recognition that I was increasingly "living with limitation" that led me to accept the position of ADA/504 coordinator at Hunter almost fifteen years ago. The Americans with Disabilities Act "prohibits discrimination against people with disabili- ties in employment, transportation, public accommodation, communi- cations, and activities of state and local government." I cannot say it is the Copernican revolution as envisioned by Rabbi Dorff, but for those who are disabled, it certainly has transformed the view of the land- scape, if not of the heavens. As coordinator, I am the first person con- sulted by Hunter faculty, staff, and students who are seeking "access" or a "reasonable accommodation" that will allow them, whatever their disability, to fulfill the responsibilities of study or work. The range of my duties is enormous: from ensuring double time for exams for students with learning disabilities to guaranteeing that deaf students and staff are provided with ASL interpreters; from making sure that entrances to the campus, classrooms, and bathrooms are wheelchair accessible to making sure that supervisors do not penalize a staff member who needs an adjustment in work schedules because sleep apnea keeps him up for most of the night; from convincing the college to provide an orthopedic chair for a staff member with osteoarthritis to speaking to future teachers at a Disabilities Awareness workshop.

Some of it is easy: I just say to a recalcitrant supervisor or teacher who is unwilling to grant an accommodation, "It's not a matter of doing someone a kindness or a favor. This is the law, and you just have to do it." And so they must do it, no matter how reluctantly. Some of it is very difficult and painful: it is not easy to help someone come to the realization that, even with an accommodation, she will not be able to meet the responsibilities of the job she holds and that she should begin to consider retirement or "going on disability" as an option. But perhaps the most challenging part of the job is "educating" those who are not disabled about their own perhaps unconscious perceptions of "differentness" and their often careless assumptions about the lives of those who are disabled, assumptions that allow them to suppress their fears about the "meaning" of disability.

I do this because I believe, as Goffman says, that attitudes toward those who are disabled reflect a particular social reality and that too often the disabled individual is reduced in our minds from a whole and usual person to "a tainted, discounted one," like the *kohen* whose perceived defects prevent him from participation in the Temple service. I do this because the ADA provides a means to call the leper back from exile, a means of providing "access and accommodation" in the wider world. And I do this because, while it is true that, as Rabbi Dorff says, "all the rest of us are *temporarily abled*," the deeper truth is that in the here and now the realities of those who are disabled and those who are "not yet" too often have no connection to each other. As Rosemarie Garland Thompson, the disability rights activist puts it, those who are disabled cannot create, on their own, "a world that wants me in it."

And so, as ADA coordinator, I must help to create that world. And this is the place at which I come back to the intersection of my own disability, my Jewish identity, and my secular life.

Goffman's disquisition of the meaning of stigma can provide one of those "aha!" moments in untangling the various threads of the Jewish response to disability. On the one hand, there are those texts with which I had wrestled that so often seem to see the individual who is disabled or ill as somehow, like the leper, "tainted and discounted." On the other hand, as Rabbi Dorff makes clear, there are other texts, other readings, that delineate the obligations of all Jews, disabled or "whole," thereby creating, perforce, a community that is inclusive. But on my journey to understanding the ambiguities of Jewish tradition about illness and disability, I discovered two that have had special meaning for me.

Considering the amount of education that had been poured into my head and the amount of time I have spent in front of a classroom, it took me a very long time and a lot of intellectual and spiritual exploration before it finally struck me that I was asking the wrong questions about Judaism and disability. The questions I really needed to ask had to be framed within the context of my own life: could I be spiritually healed even if I never got any better physically; and if I was not to be cured, what did Adonai expect of me? And since I am an academic, perhaps it is not surprising that the paths I explored, once I knew which questions to ask, led back once again to texts; and in the end I uncovered these two, one a midrash on the giving of the Torah at Sinai and the other in Lurianic Kabbalah, that have not only provided me with private images of enormous healing power but have also informed my understanding of what it means to be disabled in the here and now of secular America.

The first has as its starting point the episode of the Golden Calf. The Torah says that when Moses descended from Mount Sinai with the tablets of law inscribed by the finger of Adonai and found the people worshipping the Golden Calf, he smashed the tablets in anger. Although he returned to the mountain to receive new tablets of the commandments once again, the Talmud explains that the broken shards were not discarded, but were preserved and placed in the Ark along with the second set, to be carried by the Israelites everywhere, even into the Promised Land. Both the shattered tablets and the whole ones were together in the Ark of the Covenant. There must have been at Sinai some children of Israel who, like me, were physically broken, and saw themselves, as I did, in those fragments of the tablets, and who, like me, were relieved to find themselves included in the Covenant. They, too, could stand at Sinai.

That provided an answer to my first question, but the second—what does Adonai want of me?—was more difficult. An approach came from an unexpected source, when I discovered another image in the texts of the Jewish mystical teachings of Kabbalah. Whatever unease I might have felt about kabbalistic practices, its understanding of the nature of creation provided me with another metaphor that helped me find a spiritual path that I might take in order to make some sense of where I was physically.

Kabbalah, of course, takes many forms, but the teachings of the sixteenth-century Rabbi Isaac Luria declare that the spiritual world was the product of emanations that flowed from a transcendent Adonai. Adonai could be known only through these emanations, ten in number, wisdom, justice, and the like, that were contained in vessels. But the divine light contained in them was too powerful to be contained, and all but three vessels shattered as Adonai contracted to make room for the creation of the physical world, thus allowing the spiritual to mix with the material world. As a result, these divine emanations, most notably the *Shechinah*, the Divine Presence, are in exile in this world, the vessels that once held them now broken. And these divine sparks of light, trapped in matter, must be released from their prison; for only with the restoration of the spiritual world to its original completeness will redemption of Adonai's creation be possible.

It seems like an impossible task, but Rabbi Luria revealed the way to bring about the repair of the world: every person who acts in accordance with Torah brings home the fallen sparks; everywhere in the world a spark of the Divine Presence is waiting to be found, gathered, and restored; and Adonai holds out the possibility to each generation that it might be the one to redeem the world. Each one of us, then, has the potential to bring about *tikkun olam*, the repair of the world, not only through the performance of the commandments of Torah but through acts of *chesed*.

For those of us who are ill or disabled, the imagery of those broken vessels that have within them sparks of divine light, and the possibility that we have the opportunity to release them, is remarkably powerful and yet disturbing. The analogy to bodies shattered by disability is an irresistible one; and yet, how can we, if we are shattered physically, fulfill the obligation to set free those divine sparks, when pain and suffering, both physical and spiritual, seem to prevent us from even being aware of their presence in our lives?

Rabbi Luria offers the answer in his insistence that every person who acts in accordance with Torah brings home the fallen sparks.

Even for those of us who are ill, there still remains, I believe, the possibility of repair and restoration, even if we find it difficult or impossible to perform the multitude of commandments. Spiritual healing may be possible, even if we cannot be made whole again. *Tikkun olam* is, in some ways, easier than it seems, for the essence of Torah is *chesed*, as Rabbi Simlai taught: "The Torah begins with deeds of *chesed* and ends with deeds of *chesed.*" Torah, said Rabbi Luria, reveals the lovingkindness of Adonai toward his creation, and of each of us toward one another. By fulfilling the commandments of the Torah, we are able to restore our own spiritual structure, for our actions have both an interior and exterior effect: everything we do reacts somewhere and somehow, for ourselves and for others.

What have these images done for me? First of all, the shattered tablets that have their place in the Ark of the Covenant have helped me to see that I don't have to be physically whole to be part of the community of Israel. If ever I have difficulty remembering that, I look around at the *chevra* that is one of the centers of my life. Second, I have come to realize that spiritual repair, both of myself and of the world, is possible. It is a process that causes me to turn inward but also outward to the wider world as well. I may not be able to do much about the broken vessel that is my body, but certainly I can help to gather up the scattered light everywhere that I can. It's something I'm still working on, both for myself and for the wider world, because I would like to think that the regulations of the ADA and the words of the *misheberach* prayer are part of the same message that is sent to all of us.

5

OVERCOMING STIGMA

David I. Schulman, JD, is a pioneer in the field of HIV law and policy and in the Jewish health and healing movement. In 1981 he was one of the founders of the Jewish Hospice Commission of Los Angeles. In 1986 he became the world's first government AIDS discrimination attorney. In the late 1980s he served on Reform Judaism's national AIDS Committee. He is an advisor to the Kalsman Institute on Judaism and Health, and is the supervising attorney of the AIDS/HIV Discrimination Unit in the Los Angeles City Attorney's Office. B.A., Stanford 1973, J.D., U.C.L.A. School of Law 1978.

SPOILED IDENTITY AND THE SEARCH FOR HOLINESS: STIGMA, DEATH AND THE JEWISH COMMUNITY[1]

David I. Schulman

He not busy being born
Is busy dying.[2]

Introduction

By the time boys reach third grade, they know who has cooties and who does not. Yucky girls and weird boys. They know to stay away from them because cooties are catching, and they hope no one thinks that they have them. These cooties are not body lice. They are colorless, odorless, and tasteless. They have no material reality whatsoever. Yet they are powerful. Cooties confer high status on those with the power to declare who has them, and low status on those with them, and they bind the rest together in the knowledge of who is who. Eight-year-old boys know stigma. Stigma, sociologist Erving Goffman declared in his classic formulation, is spoiled identity.[3]

    Spoilage leads to rot and death. This essay interrogates stigma and death to understand how they are impediments to healing in the

Jewish imagination, and to explore what is needed to overcome their effects.

It does so first by considering the particular resonance that stigma bears for Jews. It then discusses the American Jewish experience within the recent shift in the human experience of death and dying. Finally, it looks at the way American law responded to AIDS stigma to argue for a similar halachic response to the stigma of illness and death.

Jews and Stigma

Our sacred texts are rife with distinctions between the spoiled and the whole, the *kasher* and the unclean. Jewish history, too, is awash with the signifiers of stigma imposed by others, sometimes pinned to our coats. So to proceed with a discussion of Jews and stigma is difficult.

If stigma is spoiled identity, it is useful to think of a spoiled self as a self ruined in the world, isolated from others. Many Jews come to the synagogue to retreat from that outside world, a world that cheapens and hides the lived, embodied truth of illness, and aging, and dying.

In response, congregations have begun holding healing services, sometimes as part of the main service, sometimes separately. Such services seek to create sacred space that can hold the fervent hope of recovery or the sadness of accommodation to loss. But such services can unconsciously replicate the outside world's isolation of those in need of healing; they can stigmatize the yearning of their heart.

For example, the rabbi might with all good intention ask everyone to shut their eyes to begin the following guided imagery exercise.

> Imagine your dearly departed one as a tree in the middle of a forest. The tree falls. The seasons change. The tree decomposes into rich nutrients that nurture the next generation of growth....

Such an exercise assumes that mourning should be peaceful and meditative. But is it always? What if there are those in the congregation for whom pleasant images obscure fresh, raw wounds, airbrush the biological mess of a loved one's death? Such well-meaning ritual may spoil the identity of such a mourner and set her outside the camp of normative Jewish experience.

A second injury, this one to the rest of the worship community, also occurs. By distancing the newly bereaved from the normative image of what is healing, the rest of the congregation achieves distance from their frightening presence. It can pretend through such peaceful images that healing has occurred for everyone when it has not.

This raises the question of just how welcome the seriously ill and the dying really are when their presence literally embodies all that is finite, mortal, frail, when they remind the community that everyone is always at risk for loss. And this is true not just for the ill and the dying, but for their caregivers and loved ones, as well. Are their lived truths well represented by peaceful imagery, or might they sometimes be better expressed through the image of the sackcloth and ashes that once animated Jewish consciousness? Are those who are suffering really always welcome at a healing service? Or does the community's unconscious belief that they are unclean, *tameh*, linger?

They are not required to announce their presence like biblical lepers, by wearing of bells, covering their mouths, and shouting, "Beware, beware!" But this essay suggests that those who dwell close to death may not be so welcome within the Jewish community, and that some healing rituals may, paradoxically, contribute to the further spoiling of their identity. To spoil the identity of the ill and the dying is to impose a social death before the actual one. How may the Jewish community resist pushing the sick and the dying, their caregivers and family, to the sidelines of congregational life? This essay proposes ways for the Jewish imagination to resist placing the very ill outside the encampment of normative community life.

American Jewish Life and Death

A season is set for everything,
a time for every experience under heaven:
A time for being born and a time for dying[4]

Americans seem to have forgotten this eternal truth. From time immemorial, death and dying were part of everyday life. People died at home, along the roadside, or on the battlefield. Animals were slaughtered in the backyard or at the village butcher shop. Death, while a mystery, was familiar to rich and poor, young and old, everywhere, at all times.

However, for the past few decades those who live with privilege are the first to live with death removed from daily experience. It is the specialized province of the clergy and the health care professional, the law officer and the soldier, the emergency worker and the mortician. It is removed to hospitals and nursing homes. While it remains a mystery, it is no longer familiar. Yet death and its denial leak out everywhere.[5] Broadcast television is flooded with police procedurals. Cosmetic surgery is a growth industry.

For American Jews there have been traumas during this same period that have made death and her handmaid, stigma, yet more complex. The Shoah melded stigma and technological efficiency. Anti-Semitism has always threatened the state of Israel's existence. And in the United States, there was a hysterical search for "communists," inordinately often Jews, in the early 1950s.

In the 1950s and 1960s, Jews shared further traumas with the rest of American society, each experienced through the peculiar heightening yet distancing of the new medium, television. The first was the spread of a new consciousness that life in an entire city could be incinerated with one nuclear bomb. The second was the quickening of the struggle of an entire group of Americans to throw off 350 years of stigma. The third was a string of assassinations of popular political heroes. And the fourth was a controversial war halfway around the world.

Liberal American Jewish institutions provided scant comfort in those years, perhaps because their primary mission was the negotiation of Jewish identity into the American experience, rather than religion's classic project of making meaning. That may be why sixties folksinger Phil Ochs's mordant observation packed such punch:

> [Liberals are] ten degrees
> to the left of center in good times,
> ten degrees to the right of center
> if it affects them personally.[6]

Liberal Jews could address injustices that did not affect them personally—the oppression of blacks or of Soviet Jews, for example—but they had trouble making religious meaning of their own subjective experience. It was not until the 1970s that the great movement of Jewish renewal began to reinvigorate Jewish meaning-making. The hospice movement emerged at the same time, resulting eventually in the Jewish healing movement.

The seeds of the hospice movement were planted in 1948 by a Holocaust survivor and his British nurse. As the patient lay dying of cancer, they pondered over why he should face such suffering after having suffered so much already. Inspired by their discussion, the nurse, Cecily Saunders, went to medical school to study better ways of controlling pain such as his. Her research documented that the pain faced by those dying of slow, degenerative illness was not just physical, but emotional, familial, communal, and spiritual. She crafted hospice as a response to all those levels.[7]

Saunders's pioneering work was timely. The average life span in Europe and America had improved significantly during the first half of the twentieth century because of such advances as vaccination, improved sanitation, and the advent of antibiotics. However, as people lived longer, their causes of death changed significantly. Instead of dying of such acute causes as infection, they died in stages of slow, degenerative, chronic illnesses. Saunders's work recognized that hospitals were geared toward the acute-care paradigm and ill-suited for chronic care.

Herman Feifel explored the challenges of this changing morbidity paradigm in 1959 in a landmark book, *The Meaning of Death*.[8] Feifel's work had impact in professional circles, as did the work of Zelda Foster, who published an article in 1965 in the *Journal of the National Association of Social Workers*.[9] But it was not until 1969, when Swiss-American researcher Elisabeth Kübler-Ross published *On Death and Dying*, that American society began to grapple with these issues. Among her findings, Kübler-Ross reported how none of the physicians she contacted believed that they had any dying patients for her to interview.[10]

By the late 1970s, Saunders's and Kübler-Ross's ideas had taken root in America, but they were pervaded by the former's Protestant Christian ethic and the latter's positivistic, five-stage schema for the "right" way to die. Neither addressed how Jewish or other religious, ethnic, or cultural values might differ. To address these shortcomings, the Council on Jewish Life of the Los Angeles Jewish Federation established the Jewish Hospice Commission of Los Angeles in 1981.

The Commission developed programs and materials that supplemented secular hospice care with specifically Jewish elements and practices. It also launched a companion effort to educate the Jewish community about the potential of Jewishly enriched hospice to deepen the meaning of Jewish dying: someone to help the dying light *shabbes* candles; someone to sing *niggunim*; someone to tell—or listen to—a Jewish joke; someone with whom to sigh, "Oy"; someone to look at pictures of the grandchildren, to help the dying give *tzedakah*.[11]

The Commission's short life presaged the emergence a few years later of a national Jewish healing movement committed to developing a Jewish praxis of health, care, and healing. That movement, however, has yet to develop a language for resisting stigma.

Stigma and Law, B'rit, and Remembering: On Jewish Healing

One of law's functions, whether halachic or secular, is to declare whose identities are spoiled. The Talmud worried about menstruating women. The Constitution held that a man of African descent was worth 60 percent of a European. Franklin Delano Roosevelt interned those of Japanese, but not German or Italian descent.

Law especially functions this way during times of disorder, when the need to bind normative society together is particularly great. Epidemics bring such times. For example, Jews and witches were drowned for "causing" the Black Death in thirteenth-century Europe. Unsurprisingly, it was those whose identities were already spoiled who were scapegoated and blamed, not noblemen and priests.[12]

Law performed a different function at the beginning of the AIDS epidemic in the United States. Instead of authorizing the wholesale tattooing and quarantining of gay men, as some had proposed, law worked closely with public health to create a climate of trust and respect to encourage those who feared stigma and discrimination to come forward to be tested.[13] AIDS civil rights laws required that people with AIDS be treated with dignity and respect. In doing so, they resisted the primitive stigmatizing impulse to construct a community of "us" by spoiling the identity of "them."[14]

There is something deeply familiar about the way AIDS civil rights laws resisted stigma. It recalls the ethic of Self and Other embedded in Halacha that requires justice and compassion in the treatment of the Other who is poor, or a stranger, or widowed, or an orphan "because remember, you too were once slaves in Egypt" (Exodus 23:0). AIDS civil rights laws remembered the humanity of persons with AIDS and brought them back from the place of spoiled identity to full membership in society.

An archaic form of the word "remember" is the antonym "dismember." Jews remember loved ones despite death's dismemberment. They are recalled at *yizkor* (memorial) services, on *yahrtzeits* (memorial anniversaries), at lifecycle events, and in countless private moments. At such times, those who are most dear are once again brought to heart and mind and soul. Healing must enable Jews to remember the ill and the dying, re-member them into the normative body of the Jewish people, remember the damage that modernity has done to the Jewish experience of illness and death.

Deep within the heart of every person is the fear of long, slow, degenerative illness and its corrosive effects on self and family. Jewish healing must name the peculiarly modern aspects of that fear using all of the meaning-making genius of the tradition—ritual and prayer, midrash and personal narrative, aggadic tales and case studies—until the community is surrounded by each other's stories. The central human drama of embodied life must be Jewishly remembered, so that society's images of airbrushed, eternal beauty can be resisted.

To do that, the Jewish imagination must grapple with how stigma operates subtly within community and robs it of meaning and integrity. Healing must resist how unconscious communal behaviors inflict a social death upon the seriously ill before their actual one. It must overcome how modernity obscures that humans decay, just as they dance, sing, love, and pray. But how?

Almost thirty years ago, a medical ethicist presciently called for covenantal relations in health care as the cure both for the paternalistic model out of which society was then emerging and for the contractual model into which it was even then rapidly plunging.[15] Jews know something about covenants. The *b'rit* that requires that the Other be seen as another Self is embedded more deeply within Jewish sacred texts than the stigma passages. Jewish healing should look to notions of *b'rit* for ways to re-member the ill and the dying, their families, and their caregivers.

Jewish healing must teach that those who sicken and die also reflect the image of God. Re-membering the stranger includes she whom the Jewish community has estranged, whom the community wants to forget, and who embodies the community's fear of death and unmaking. A Jew is not just made of the earth. She also consists of holy breath. Healing must bring the sick and the dying back into the holy place, the *makom kadosh*, which is the place of the communal *b'rit* relationship with God. This is the place where all Jews are re-membered.

Defining self and community by what is not, by what is spoiled, may be universal, but it is not immutable. Jewish healing must transform the primitive impulse to isolate the sick and the suffering from the congregational mainstream so that the congregation can pretend its identity is unspoiled. Jewish healing must not allow the ill and the dying, their caregivers and their families, to be a scapegoat for death. Death *is* the greatest spoiler of identity, the *tumah gedolah*. It is the spoiled rot at the root of life. But it is not only that.

Healing must resist the siren call of the secular culture to rely on technique instead of a person's Self, where God is embodied in human action. Jewish healing must resist the convenience of caring community *committees*, and instead insist that the praxis of the congregation be more caring. It must resist the impulse to allow congregations to distance themselves from the reality of the sick and the suffering by "sponsoring" special healing services instead of praying in a manner that is healing. Healing must redeem the American Jewish community from the stigmatizing behaviors that lead to the isolation and loneliness of the sick and the dying and their caregivers.

Jewish healing requires prayers and psalms and words of hope and comfort that address not just those who are sick or suffering, but the *entire* community. Jewish healing needs rituals and liturgy and places of study that allow all Jews—lay people and rabbis, doctors and nurses, alike—to strengthen the *b'rit* of the Jewish people with God. For *that* Jewish healing, however, Jews must unmake the unconscious communal behaviors that place outside the camp those who demonstrate that all humans are always near death.

Rachel Adler, PhD, is professor of Modern Jewish Thought and Feminist Studies at Hebrew Union College Los Angeles. She is the author of *Engendering Judaism: An Inclusive Theology and Ethics* and many articles on feminist approaches to Jewish theology and Halacha.

THOSE WHO TURN AWAY THEIR FACES: *TZARAAT* AND STIGMA

Rachel Adler

> As for the person with a leprous affection, his clothes shall be rent, his head shall be left bare, and he shall cover over his upper lip: and he shall call out, "Unclean! Unclean!" He shall be unclean as long as the disease is on him. Being unclean, he shall dwell apart; his dwelling shall be outside the camp. (Leviticus 13:45–46; JPS)

What is "a leprous affection?" The Hebrew word for this mystifying disease is *tzaraat*. *Tzaraat* does not correspond to any single disease familiar to Western medicine. Preceding our verses is an excerpt from a priest's diagnostic manual for *tzaraat* that identifies as symptoms phenomena we would not place together in the same category: human skin diseases, house fungus or mold, and mildews and molds on fabric. Not only human beings, but walls and houses, vessels and fabrics can contract *tzaraat*. Entities with *tzaraat* seem to have in common that their wholeness is being compromised. They are being eaten into, decayed, caused to come apart.

It has been usual for English translators to translate *tzaraat* as leprosy because leprosy is a degenerative disease that has been highly stigmatized. But the priestly diagnostics in Leviticus 13 do not match with leprosy. Moreover, leprosy does not afflict walls or fabrics. A better translation that has been suggested is "scale disease."[16]

Tzaraat is ancient Israel's version of what I am going to call radical illness, illness that strikes at the root of our being in the world, ravaging our communities, filling witnesses with fear. Radical illness erodes the body and often the self. It takes us and unmakes us. Radical illness seems to us arbitrary; either we do not know how to cure it or why it struck, or we do not know how to contain its spread. There is a dread about radical illness that is greater than the sum of its parts. If the illness is thought to be contagious as *tzaraat* was, communities may protect themselves formally by quarantine, isolating the diseased. Yet even an illness not known to be contagious may still bear a stigma so powerful that people shun the sufferer.

The paradigmatic radical illness of our own time is dementia, although AIDS, cancer, Ebola, and bird flu have been or are currently contenders for the title, too. There are now 4.2 million Americans with Alzheimer's disease alone, not counting cases of multi-infarct (ischemic vascular) dementia, Diffuse Lewy Body Disease, and late-stage Parkinson's disease, and it is predicted that the numbers will rise. The risk of Alzheimer's disease, for example, increases exponentially with age. Hence, the greater the life expectancy, the greater the rate of dementia a culture will have. Twelve percent of the American population is over sixty-five and thus at risk for dementia. Eighteen percent of American Jews are over sixty-five, making dementia a growing concern in the Jewish community. These diseases erase the personality. They destroy the ability to talk, walk, think logically, calculate, write, read, respond, and remember. Ultimately, those affected cannot swallow food or drink. Those at risk dread dementia, and sufferers are feared and shunned. Alive and breathing, they are being unmade before our eyes.

In this essay we will juxtapose *tzaraat* and dementia. We will try to think of *tzaraat* as a disease as feared as dementia and we will try to think of dementia as a plague as stigmatized as *tzaraat*. We will explore the nature of pollution thinking and the growth and transformation of stigmatized impurity in the Bible and later tradition. We will ask: how might we bring ourselves to reject the powerful call of pollution thinking and stretch out a hand to sufferers? Finally we will try to understand what purification can mean. Using corpse purification as a model, we will see how it is possible to reframe the meaning of a stigmatized condition and re-member the stigmatized Other as a whole self.

Pollution Thinking Persists in Cultures

In comparing *tzaraat* to dementia, I have begun to argue that some ancient social behavior toward the carrier of a feared disease ought to be recognizable to us. In the AIDS epidemic during the 1980s, apartment managers evicted tenants suspected of have AIDS. Employers told them to clean out their desks and never return. In the SARS epidemic of 2002, simply bearing an Asian face could cause others to recoil. Americans canceled performances by Asian troupes that had not been near SARS-affected areas of the world. They objected to being on airplanes with anyone who had been traveling from the East. A similar outsized dread motivates people's shrinking from those with Alzheimer's disease even though it is not contagious. Dread motivates ubiquitous jokes about having Alzheimer's.

In *Borrowed Time: An Aids Memoir*, Paul Monette offers an insight into the terror of pollution thinking by radical illness.[17] He describes the aftermath of a visit to his home by an AIDS-infected friend at the very beginning of the epidemic.

> I went in and spent a demented half hour airing and cleaning the guest room, stripping the bed to the bare mattress and wiping everything down with ammonia—a perfect frenzy of prophylaxis, almost a phobia…. Thankfully, that was the last time I was ever possessed by this particular madness, but it's why I have such an instant radar for the bone-zero terror of others. Those who a year later would not enter our house, would not take food or use the bathroom. Would not hold me.

What we observe in all these cases, ancient and modern, is purity and pollution thinking. Mary Douglas, an anthropologist whose work focuses on purity and impurity, argues that all cultures have notions of impurity, even our own, because all cultures organize reality into categories.[18] Disorders or anomalies disrupt the way we have systematized reality, the way we have organized the world so it will make sense. According to Douglas, notions of purity/pollution, cleanness/uncleanness function on two levels in a society. First, they are mechanisms that reinforce socially desired values and behaviors. Second, they are ways that societies image the "body politic" and its boundaries as a large-scale reflection of the human body.

By systematizing social categories, societies show where their boundaries are. Not crossing those dangerous boundaries, and thereby falling out of place and into chaos, ensures safety. In order to belong, we learn what or who is dirty, disgusting, or dangerous. Socialization means learning not to ingest poison or trash and not to play in the dirt. It is no coincidence that one of the first words a child learns is her society's version of *yuck* or *feh*. We want to know with certainty what the boundaries are that will keep us safe, let us know that we belong—and certainty is very hard to come by. People who cross the boundaries or seem to be teetering on their edges remind us of the fragility, the vulnerability of both society and self.

Societies dread invasion, attack, disintegration, and inundation. Hence the extremities and borders of our nations and our bodies are loci of concern, places where integrity may be breached and order overthrown. So the concrete or barbed wire fences separating the United States from Mexico or Israel from Palestine, the entrances and exits of airports, office buildings, mouths, vaginas, and anuses, are carefully monitored and passage through them is governed by rule and norm. Human skin is a long continuous boundary that demarcates the most basic of borders, the border between the human body and the world outside it. Breaches in the skin are attacks on the body's wholeness. They leave the raw flesh vulnerable to the external world or display flesh taken over by externalities: tumors, excrescences. This is what is frightening about *tzaraat*.

Also frightening is the therapeutic boundarylessness of the disease. There is no etiology, no cause, no therapeutic caution, or treatment recommendation in the priest's manual reproduced in Leviticus 13. The missing therapeutic boundaries are replaced by ritual boundaries. If, after days of quarantine and careful reexamination, the sufferer is diagnosed with *tzaraat*, he or she receives what Erwin Goffman would call a "spoiled identity," the stigmatized identity of a *tzaraat* sufferer, a *metzora*. (See David Schulman's essay.) He or she is banished, sentenced to a social death.[19] Overlaying the disease *tzaraat* is the stigma of *tzaraat*. The visible marks upon the *metzora* do not simply mean: this one is ill. They announce: this one threatens the priestly universe, that calm, pure world where death is present only in the choreographed slaughter of offerings.[20]

Shrink from him. Keep this dangerous one away, for *tzaraat* is identified with the very opposite of the priestly world: uncreation and death.

I theorized at the very beginning of this essay: "Entities with *tzaraat* seem to have in common that their wholeness is being compromised. They are being eaten into, decayed, caused to come apart." As selves we want to be whole, yet we are destined to fall apart. People whose bodily integrity has been breached, who are maimed or mutilated, remind us of our "disorganized" ultimate destination. People who are liminal or marginal—who have been pushed to the edges of social boundaries—also embody this anxiety-provoking place on the edge of the dangerous and the chaotic. This is where "normal" society puts those it stigmatizes as non-normal, such as people of color, the poor, and the aged. At times of social stress, those who represent the norm are greatly tempted to relieve their terrors by casting out or punishing these dangerous Others.

Pollution thinking did not begin nor did it end with the book of Leviticus. It is a form of dualistic thinking most cultures fall back on in times of crisis. However, the pollution thinking of Israelite religion is contained in Leviticus, and if we want to claim Leviticus as Torah, we must look at its painful text about people who hide their faces. That does not mean excusing the text. Instead, we must engage this text in conversation, confront it directly and hold it accountable. When I read Torah I retain a hope that even in the most forbidding passages redemptive meanings wait to be discovered.

Decoding Biblical Purity Law

What, then, characterizes biblical purity law? It is organized around a central dichotomy: life and death. The citadel of life is the Tabernacle or the Temple, the sacred space of the ever living God, the Creator of life. Into this place only the pure may come. The impure are forbidden to defile it with their presence. If purity is life, impurity represents death. It attests to the Creator's terrifying ability to uncreate, to melt form into formlessness, to erase the boundaries of the created world and return it to chaos.

The most intensely impure (and impurifying) entity is a corpse. It is the lifeless body soon to return to formlessness, flesh about to break down, liquefy, melt away. Second only to death in impurity is *tzaraat*, this non-Western, nonmedical category composed of things that are eaten into or have their integrity breached, comprising a group of skin diseases as well as fungi and mildews. Other categories of impurity include abnormal genital discharges, semen, and the blood of menstruation and childbirth, that is, liquids associated with begetting and birth and therefore occasions where departures or transferals of life force occur.[21] *Tzaraat*, however, is the paradigmatic visible impurity. It is, in one important respect, treated differently from all other impurities: only those who suffer from *tzaraat* are explicitly banished from society and commanded to hide their faces from those who encounter them. Only those for whom a final diagnosis of *tzaraat* is confirmed suffer an ongoing social death.

In Leviticus we glimpse the *tzaraat* sufferer only distantly, through a maze of priestly diagnostics. Much the way a hospital patient may be viewed as "the kidney in room 113" or "the colostomy in 224," the *tzaraat* carrier loses her full humanity to the diagnostician and becomes a condition of patches and rashes of different colors. Indeed, the priestly code does not even mention that this condition is likely to be irritating or painful. Pain is just another feature of the *metzora*'s overlooked subjectivity.

Scale Disease as "Death's Firstborn"

Professor Jacob Milgrom, author of the Anchor Bible translation and commentary on Leviticus, translates *tzaraat* as "scale disease."[22] Its features, he says, are reminiscent of psoriasis, vitiligo, and favus, all of which produce scales. In other words, the skin is no longer an intact body covering, but neither is it violated cleanly as in a knife wound. Parts of it are dying and flaking off. Milgrom quotes Elihu's description of Job's boils, characterizing them as a painful form of *tzaraat*: "His skin is eaten away by a disease. Death's firstborn consumes his limbs" (Job 18:13).[23] *Tzaraat* is death's firstborn. We see this connection with death in the other vivid biblical description of *tzaraat*, the puzzling incident in Numbers 12 in which Aaron and Miriam talk about Moses.

As the cloud withdrew from the Tent, there was Miriam stricken with snow white scales. When Aaron turned toward

Miriam, he saw that she was stricken with scales. And Aaron said to Moses, "O my Lord, account not to us the sin which we committed in our folly. Let her not be as one dead, who emerges from his mother's womb with half his flesh eaten away." (Numbers 12:10–12)

A stillborn infant's skin peels off in large sheets.[24] This peeling away or flaking off of the skin is the feature of *tzaraat* associated with death and disintegration. Indeed, the sloughing off of the skin is the initial stage of a corpse's decomposition. The terrifying aspect of "death's firstborn" was that the sufferer seemed to be disintegrating while still alive.

As the following chart illustrates, *tzaraat* is more explicitly similar to death in its definition, impurity conditions, duration, and purification than any other form of impurity. The *tzaraat* sufferer, the *metzora*, is like the corpse in the intensity of his or her impurity, but like the corpse-defiled in terms of ability to be purified and in the elaborateness of the purification ceremony. However, while the corpse-defiled need only wait the prescribed time to be eligible for purification, *metzoraim* must show signs that the disease has subsided. They must prove their recovery prior to purification. Purification should not be mistaken for a healing ceremony. A healing ceremony compensates for the trauma an individual has suffered; a purification ceremony undertakes to reverse the condition of impurity that causes an individual to imperil the orderly and the sacred.

The chart demonstrates that biblical religion regarded death and *tzaraat* as virulent and less virulent forms of impurities in which the human body becomes an object to be consumed and disintegrated. This human decay is a foundational source of shame; it is scandalous, even. Hence, it is a mitzvah to bury the dead so that their consumption and disintegration is not a public spectacle, and their bodies can become part of the earth in a single place rather than being torn apart and scattered by wild animals and birds, and they are covered rather than exposed to the eye.[25] The relatives of the dead, or if an anonymous corpse is found, anyone—even a priest if there is no one else— have an urgent duty to bury, even though they themselves will become impure in the process, and even if another mitzvah must be deferred. To the eyes of the priestly writers of Leviticus, the *metzora* seemed to trumpet the secret that culture tries to hide through burial: flesh decomposes and is eaten away. Small wonder that those who were not diseased should become uncomfortably aware that their own intactness is temporary. Turning away their own faces, they command that the *metzora* veil his.

Similarities Between Corpse and *Metzora* in Biblical Purity Law		
	Corpse	*Metzora*
As source of impurity	Impure forever.	Curable hence purifiable.
Diagnosis	No expert diagnosis for corpse or for those contaminated by it.	Diagnosis by Kohan.
Impurity conditions	May not enter sacred space; must rend clothes and dishevel hair.	May not enter sacred space; must rend clothes, dishevel hair, veil mouth, and warn passers-by of impurity; banished "outside the camp."
Durations of impurity	Corpse itself: infinite; corpse-contaminated person: seven days before purification.	*Metzora*: eight days minimum; if examination reveals no further deterioration: seven days before purification; *metzora*-contaminated person: one day until evening.
Transmission of impurity	Touch; overhang indoors contaminates entire enclosed space and those who enter; overhang outdoors contaminates directly above and below it vertically without limit ("up to the sky, down to *tehom* [the primal abyss]") unless blocked by a tent ceiling or a cave dwelling.	Touch; overhang indoors contaminates entire enclosed space and those who enter; overhang outdoors contaminates others who pass beneath any overhang that shelters the *metzora*, such as a tree.
Purification ritual	For corpse: none; for corpse-defiled: ceremonies require more than one day and sprinkling with "living water" containing cedarwood, scarlet thread, hyssop, and blood.	For *metzora*: ceremonies require more than one day and sprinkling with "living water" containing cedarwood, scarlet thread, hyssop, and blood.

We can compare the "uncreation" of the corpse and the *metzora* to the uncreation of the demented person through the failure of language. The language of the demented progressively deteriorates: first, word-retrieval problems and other memory blanks; then inappropriate word use, then inability to form coherent responses and full sentences; then word salad, disjointed words mixed with made-up words; and finally silence. As Elaine Scarry reminds us in her groundbreaking book *The Body in Pain*, the uncreation of language is the uncreation of the universe that is constituted by language, a world of relationships, a world of meanings.[26] All of these are unmade along with the demented.

Due Process but No Miracles

Despite the stigma, Torah law provides some protection for the *metzora*. It is significant that *tzaraat* can be diagnosed only by a priest. As Mary Douglas points out, this means that accusers with a grudge or panicked mobs, who in other societies are the usual source of witchcraft accusations, cannot make a determination of *tzaraat*.[27] The priest guarantees a ritual version of due process, and it is careful and lengthy. The suspected *metzora* is confined to home for a week and examined again. There is even a possibility for a second such week so that a harmless or fleeting rash is not mistaken for *tzaraat*. *Tzaraat*, moreover, is not always a life sentence. Leviticus assumes that some will be healed and provides a means of being definitively declared free of *tzaraat* and readmitted to the community and its most sacred places, a ceremony people today in remission from cancer might well envy.

Unlike other biblical books, Leviticus does not connect *tzaraat* or other impurities with sin. They are conditions that simply happen and could happen to anyone. Moreover, in contrast to the polytheistic nations around them, Israelite priests do not offer remedies or therapy. They can identify *tzaraat* but not cure it. Healing comes from God. Purification follows healing; it does not induce it. In this respect, priests claim more modest abilities than prophets. They do not claim the ability to make miracles or even the direct, spontaneous access to God that allows prophets to heal *tzaraat*. Moses, seeing Miriam's disease, implores, "Please God, heal her, please" (Numbers 12:13), the briefest and most powerful of healing prayers. Elisha not only heals *tzaraat,* but like his predecessor Elijah, he also brings the dead back to life.[28] But priests can only diagnose, observe, and purify according to instructions handed down to them.

These instructions are elaborate, especially for purification. A healed *metzora* goes through purification rituals at two separate sites. The first ritual is done outside the camp, prior to entering the encampment and the sanctuary, and resembles that for corpse-impurity. Red substances—blood, cedarwood, scarlet thread— are combined with "living water" to make a nexus fluid combining life and death, somewhat reminiscent of that in the Red Cow ceremony of Numbers 19. The two birds used in the ceremony are reminiscent of the two goats used in the scapegoat ceremony on Yom Kippur (Leviticus 16). One is slaughtered as a sacrifice. The other bird is used to sprinkle the nexus fluid on the *metzora* and then is released into the wild, perhaps carrying the *tzaraat* away as the scapegoat carried the impurities and sins of the Israelites away.[29, 30] After this ceremony, the *metzora* must shave off all his hair as a Nazirite does. He is the Nazirite's opposite, however. The Nazirite shaves off all his hair because it has been grown under conditions of purity and is offered in the sanctuary. The *metzora's* hair grew under conditions of impurity. Hence, Baruch Levine explains, the extreme nature of the shaving: usually shaving the beard and sidelocks is forbidden.[31]

After seven days the *metzora* bathes and washes his clothes and is pure. Then there is another purification. The ex-*metzora* takes his sacrifice to the priest at the entrance of the Tent of Meeting. The priest puts first the blood of the offering and then some of the oil of offering on the ridge of the *metzora's* right ear, the thumb of his right hand, and the big toe of the right foot. This treatment is similar to the ritual described in Exodus 29:20 and Leviticus 8: 23–24 for the installation of the Aaronite priesthood. The *metzora* is the only nonpriest who receives this ritual anointing.

What has occurred is remarkable. The former *metzora,* the death-devoured one who could be considered the antithesis of the priest of the ever living God is made to resemble the priest more closely than any other nonpriest. It is a paradox for which I have found no satisfying explanation other than the one I am going to suggest: that the ritual is subversive. It offers a way to undercut the polarization of purity and impurity and to undermine the hierarchies of Leviticus. When we read our text closely we will see how *tzaraat* is identified with death. Then we will look at a custom that, like the priestly purification of the *metzora,* subverts and transcends the dichotomies and hierarchies of Leviticus. Priest, *metzora*, and corpse are one in holiness.

A Close Reading of Our Text

Let's now return to Leviticus 13:45–46 and parse it more closely, phrase by phrase.

> As for the person with a leprous affection, his clothes shall be rent, his head shall be left bare, and he shall cover over his upper lip; and he shall call out, "Unclean! Unclean!" He shall be unclean as long as the disease is on him. Being unclean he shall dwell apart; his dwelling shall be outside the camp.

His head shall be left bare. Jacob Milgrom prefers to translate this as, "His head shall be disheveled," the translation preferred by the rabbis.[32] Baring the head and covering the upper lip are expressions of shame according to Baruch Levine, that signal others to avoid the *metzora*. But Hyam Maccoby observes:

> [These requirements] seem more related to expressing grief over his predicament than with avoiding human contacts. This ritualized grief is very similar to that prescribed for mourners. Torn clothes, disheveled hair and covered face are all characteristics of mourners.[33]

This reading concurs with Rashi, who understands covering the lips as a sign of mourning for the dead. We thus return to the theme of the *metzora*'s association with the dead. "Four are accounted as dead," says a talmudic passage (*Nedarim* 64b), "A pauper, a *metzora*, a blind person, and a childless person." A passage in the talmudic tractate *Moed Katan* (15a–b) lists the many similarities between the *metzora* and the mourner, who is like the corpse at one remove.

The mourner is akin to the corpse as a pollutant because the mourner has corpse-impurity second in intensity only to that of the corpse itself. In rabbinic law, especially in the early stages of mourning, the mourner could be said to mirror the corpse, identifying with it as if loath to relinquish the relationship.[34] The ascetic behaviors practiced by mourners or fasting penitents—not working, not wearing shoes, not bathing or anointing, not having sexual intercourse—may be viewed as imitations of the dead. In this connection, many commentators have pointed to the ascetic practices of Yom Kippur as a mimesis of death.[35] Moreover, like the [male] corpse, the [male] mourner does not pray or study; he is in these respects asocial, isolated, exempt from the activities that distinguish the rabbinic male as a social being.[36]

The person with *tzaraat*, second in impurity only to the corpse, acts out a similar charade of death. According to tractate *Moed Katan* (15a–b) both *metzora* and mourner wear torn clothes; the mourner rends his clothes in imitation of the corpse's no longer intact body while the *metzora* tears his clothes to advertise his own fragmenting body. Both *metzora* and mourner have unshorn hair, do not give ordinary greetings, and isolate themselves, all signs of desocialization. The only difference is that the *metzora*'s social death is indeterminate in length while the mourner's is time-limited.

He shall cover over his upper lip. Fearing contagion from the *metzora*'s breath,[37] the biblical text commands that he veil his upper lip and proclaim his impurity to warn others away, but under his veil, his eyes can still call out wordlessly for compassion, for connection. The contemporary philosopher Emmanuel Levinas teaches that the face of the Other upturned to our own face is the primary locus of ethics.[38] Faces are infinitely varied, the most individualized of our body parts. The face is bare, vulnerable. It expresses pain, need, and loneliness. The face is also the primary locus of Otherness. The Other's face is different from mine. The face demands our attention. The eyes, delicate and unprotected, communicate without sound. Levinas would say that we must meet those eyes, that we are ethically bound to provide comfort. In the face of radical illness, Levinas would argue that our ethical obligation is to do what is counter-intuitive, what is the very opposite of pollution thinking: to stay rather than to flee, to comfort rather than reject. As I shall soon argue, this requires us to transcend pollution thinking; and the most powerful means of transcending it is to subvert it.

And he shall call out, "Unclean! Unclean!" A more correct translation would be "Impure! Impure!" Even if his disease is not contagious, his impurity is contagious and can pollute those who share an enclosed space with him. Hence he must warn them to avoid pollution. Paradoxically, he is given the responsibility of warning others against his own dangerousness.

Outside the camp is outside civilization. Ancient peoples did not romanticize wilderness as we do. To be outside civilization was to inhabit a universe unmade—unboundaried, unfrequented, disordered, chaotic—a place of unsafety.[39] In the narrative in Numbers 12, the people wait for Miriam to be healed and purified of *tzaraat* before resuming travel because she is greatly respected. It is possible that an ordinary *metzora* might have simply been abandoned. In a story in II Kings 7, four *tzaraat* sufferers are outside the besieged city of Jerusalem, exposed to the enemy. Ironically, their exposed position enables them to be the first to find that the enemy has decamped and the first to allay their hunger with the Aramean army's abandoned provisions, but they take the risk of approaching the enemy camp because they are so desperate that they don't care whether they live or die.

Before we become shocked at this inhumanity, we should consider that hospitals and nursing homes in our culture are dwellings outside the camp. People who are well are notoriously disinclined to visit them. Nursing-home residents, and the demented in particular, suffer social stigma and isolation. And unlike some *tzaraat* sufferers, the demented who enter do not emerge to regain their places in society. If their dementia proves temporary, due to depression or incorrect medication, and they are released from the nursing home, there is no reentry ritual to inform everyone of their complete recuperation as there is for the healed *metzora*. The demented, like the *metzora*, remind others of brokenness, decay, the inevitable descent into the dust that awaits priest and king, scientist and senator, as well as leper and beggar. "O let me kiss that hand," cries blind Gloucester to demented King Lear. "Let me wipe it first," says Lear, "It smells of mortality" (*King Lear* IV, iv).

He shall be unclean as long as the disease is on him. The Torah, concerned that the unpurified *metzora* not pollute the camp, sends the priest outside the camp to reevaluate the *metzora* and, if he can be declared free of disease, do the initial purification ritual (Leviticus14:1–8). What an outreach program! "The priest must go out to the very antithesis of his home territory, from the shrine of the ever living God to the realms of chaos and disorder outside the camp to perform the initial ritual. But what if the *metzora* turns out not to be healed? What does the priest say to the *metzora* then? The text does not tell us. Would he quickly pronounce him impure and hasten away? Would he give the *metzora* some word of hope or the priestly benediction only he can offer? Would he remind the sufferer that he is only a priest, and not a prophet, and has no gift of healing to bestow? And would he feel then his smallness and his helplessness before the *metzora*'s distress? Would he know, as a prophet would know, that God is outside the camp with the Other and not just in his golden shrine?

What do doctors and nurses do in confronting the inexorable uncreation of the dementia patient, given that they, too, are unable to work any miracle of healing? Do they try to say some words of comfort or tenderness? Do they work on the patient's physical systems as if functioning could be mechanically maintained without considering the well-being of the whole person? And what about rabbis and visitors from the synagogue? Do they reach out to the demented who were once members of their own community? Do they find God in the company of the broken and the silent, or only in the grandeur of their congregations?

Tzaraat *in Other Biblical Books and in Rabbinic Literature*

Although Leviticus depicts impurities as part of the human condition, like death itself, many other biblical books associate *tzaraat* with the sins of arrogance and presumption. David curses the descendants of his nephew Joab with *tzaraat* and other misfortunes because Joab murdered Abner ben Ner of the House of Saul after David had gotten his allegiance (II Samuel 3:28–29). The foreign general Naaman is cured when he humbles himself (II Kings 5:9–15). Elisha's arrogant disciple

Gehazi is cursed with *tzaraat* (II Kings 5:26–27). King Uzziah gets *tzaraat* for arrogantly taking on a priestly function in the Temple (II Chronicles 26:16-21). Miriam is the only woman in the Bible who gets the disease, for her presumption in talking about Moses (Numbers 12:9).

Some scholars have expressed astonishment that a disease so common in Second Temple times would have disappeared by the rabbinic period. But *tzaraat* has not disappeared, as talmudic and even Gaonic references attest. Instead, first in Babylonia and eventually in Israel, it simply ceases to be labeled deviant and becomes a socially tolerated difference.[40] Perhaps it is because, as I will soon demonstrate, death itself was beginning to be regarded differently. By this time, there is no longer a Temple or a ritual means of purification for corpse impurity or *tzaraat*. Mishnaic tractate *Negaim*, it has been pointed out, deals with only one of the biblical types of *tzaraat*. The tractate of *Mishnah* has no Gemara, which generally indicates that a subject once of concern within the land of Israel is no longer relevant. *Tzaraat* does not disqualify men from attending synagogue or study hall. It has become an arcane study for designated experts. When Rabbi Akiva delivers a particularly clumsy *aggadic* midrash, his colleague advises him tartly to confine himself to studying *tzaraat* (Sanhedrin 67b).

Once the affliction itself has become academic, rabbinic literature's most common explanation is that *tzaraat* is a punishment for gossiping, and the most common association is with Miriam. In *Leviticus Rabba* the word *metzora* [leper] lends itself to the pun *motzira, motzi shem ra*, slanderer. Once it is definitively moralized by the rabbis, *tzaraat* also acquires gender: the *metzora* is a gossiping woman or a man like a gossiping woman.

Paradoxical Purity: Purification of the Dead

Corpse impurity ceases to have behavioral consequences after the destruction of the Temple, but this does not mean that corpses automatically become destigmatized. From the Mishnaic period onward, Jewish tradition attests to a process of preparing the dead for burial that by medieval times is called *taharah*, purification. It is worth our while to investigate this transformation of meaning. If a corpse can be regarded as pure, perhaps a *metzora* as well can attain purity and shed the terrible stigma of radical illness. What mysterious process occurs in the *taharah* ritual that removes the old stigmas and brings new purity to birth? And how can we reproduce it in other cases?

The *taharah* ritual is unlike the purification ritual for a healed *metzora* because the subject of the ritual is not healed of impurity. To call the corpse-preparation ritual *taharah* is, first of all, oxymoronic. The corpse is the Levitical pollutant par excellence. It pollutes everyone or thing that shares a room or an overhang with it. Even when buried in the ground, it pollutes vertically without limit ("up to the sky, down to the primal abyss") unless blocked by a ceiling of some sort interposing itself. It pollutes when reduced to a bone the size of a barleycorn or flesh the size of an olive (*Moed Katan* 5b). What, then, does it mean to have a corpse undergo a process called "purification"?

The purifiers of the corpse are volunteers who are not mourners. The Talmud references the term *chavura* for a burial association, but its context makes clear that such an organization was a rarity (*Moed Katan* 27b). By the end of the medieval period, these volunteers are usually formalized into an organization structured like the medieval guilds of non-Jewish European craftspersons and called a *chevra kaddisha*, the "holy fellowship" of those who prepare the dead for burial.[41]

The oldest features of burial preparation that we know about are washing the dead and clothing them in burial garments. Washing is attested in the Mishnah and there are references to it in tractate *Shabbat*.[42] Water is, of course, a powerful transformative medium. Most biblical purification rites, including that of the *metzora*, entail immersion in "living water," water that is fresh or running or spring-fed, rather than standing and stagnant. The flow of life that has been interrupted by the impurity is unblocked by immersion. If impurity is a form of death, immersion enacts birth, emergence out of the amniotic fluid or the sea or the "cosmic soup" from which life on earth first originated.[43] It dissolves old forms and creates them anew. By the time there are recorded *taharah* liturgies, the *chevra kadisha* is accompanying its final pouring of water on the corpse with the declaration, "She is pure! She is pure!" In some rites, the corpse is even immersed in a *mikveh*.[44]

The dressing of the corpse also became associated with Levitical imagery. In the second century CE, Rabban Gamliel decreed that rich and poor alike should be buried in plain linen garments. As the ritual evolves in the medieval period, these garments come to correspond to those of the Aaronite priesthood: *mitznefet* (mitre), *michnasayim* (breeches), *kutonet* (tunic), *avnet* (girdle). The appropriate passages from Leviticus about clothing the priest are recited while dressing the corpse. When the mitre is set on the corpse's head, the verse recited, Zachariah 3:5, refers to the reclothing of Joshua the high priest in pure garments: "And they placed the pure diadem on his head and clothed him in [priestly] garments as the angel of Adonai stood by." The corpse, which in Levitical law is the epitome of impurity, is thus clothed as a priest and likened to the high priest, the epitome of purity. All of this washing and enrobing is done with the utmost tenderness and respect.[45]

Reframing the Meaning of Radical Illness

The *taharah* ritual draws on Leviticus to build a counter-Leviticus that wholly reframes the meaning of the corpse. It divests the corpse of impurity and invests it with purity. How can we divest the radically ill of stigma and invest them with purity? The very center of the book of Leviticus, the core from which all else radiates, is Chapter 19, whose center, the eighteenth of thirty-seven verses, is *v'ahavta l'reacha kamocha*: "love your fellow as yourself."[46] The chapter prescribes specifically how to act lovingly toward particular others: the poor, the laborer, the deaf, the blind, the aged, the stranger. But the chapter begins with a general statement: "You shall be holy, for I Adonai your God am holy." To invest the other with purity, we must invest ourselves with holiness. To invest the other with holiness, we need courage and purity of heart.

I am remembering a family celebration I attended with my mother and her partner when my mother had become demented. For several hours we sat at a table by ourselves and no one approached us. There were present two generations of parents who had often turned to my mother for her expert professional advice, two generations of children she had played with and whose birthdays she never forgot.

But no one sat down to talk to my now-diminished mother or her caregivers. We were silently shunned.

Lamentations describes a terrible reversal in which bloodstained prophets and priests blindly wander the streets of the captured city, while people shout at them " 'Away! Unclean!' 'Away! Away!' ' Touch not!' " (4:14). Suddenly those who represented holiness, purity, and contact with the divine become personifications of the abhorrent and the abject. Pollution thinking allows the bystanders to separate from their own horror and their own fears, projecting them onto those whose holiness is now broken and defiled. What frees us from the trap of pollution thinking is what we saw in the quasi-priestly installation of the purified *metzora* or the rabbinic and postrabbinic construction of *taharah*, a transfiguration into paradoxical purity.

What does it take to see a leper as a son of Aaron? A corpse transfigured as a high priest? What does it take to see the devastated bodies or brains of radically ill people as exemplars of holiness, even when only the rags and tatters of personhood remain? It requires accepting our fear and our revulsion but allowing compassion for the other to override them. "Human is not whole," I once wrote. "Human is full of holes."[47] Everyone is full of holes. That is what a body is: *nekavim, nekavim, chalulim, chalulim*, as the morning prayer Asher Yatzar says. No one is unperforated, not even the healthy, not even the young. We cherish one another in our imperfection, in the brevity and contingency of our lives. Human holiness results when our *holey* fragments are gathered together with awe and reverence, with compassion, with the care of outstretched hands, when we see in the radically ill or the radically disempowered the Other that Leviticus 19 asks us to love. That is the only way we can be whole—not perfect, but *shalem*, complete.

Albert J. Winn's (MA) photographs are in the permanent collections of the Library of Congress, the Jewish Museum, the Museum of Fine Arts (Houston), and the International Center of Photography, and he has shown nationally and internationally. He has received fellowships from the NEA/WestAF and the Memorial Foundation for Jewish Culture and his work has been published in the *Jewish Quarterly Review*, *Zeek*, *ZYZZYVA*, and on FreshYarn.com. He lives in Los Angeles.

THE NEW MAN, ILLNESS, AND HEALING

Albert J. Winn

The image of an "AIDS *Halutznik*" first appeared as a "Heal the World ... Tikkun Olam" poster on a *tzedakah* box in 1999 for an exhibition at the Jewish Museum of San Francisco entitled "Making Change: 100 Artists Interpret the *Tzedakah* Box." It is a self-portrait, digitally enhanced and altered. It grew from my previous autobiographical work and from a desire to raise the issue of AIDS within the Jewish community, to seek social action and justice, and to address the issue of AIDS as stigma. Although I am a photographer, the museum curators asked me to participate because I had created other installations—"Blood on the Doorpost ... The AIDS Mezuzah" and a set of "AIDS Dreidels"—that were not photographic in nature. The *tzedakah* box was made of clear Lucite, resembling a letter holder for the top of an office desk. Titled the "*Tzedakah* OUT Box," it contained letters addressing the problems people with AIDS encountered with their Social Security benefits.

Visitors to the exhibition were encouraged to take the letters and send them to their representatives in Congress.

AIDS made its appearance in the United States in 1978, when gay men in San Francisco, Los Angeles, and New York began presenting unusually disabling and mystifying physical symptoms that progressed rapidly to morbidity and death. In 1982, when the Centers for Disease Control and Prevention (CDC) labeled the illness AIDS (Acquired Immune Deficiency Syndrome), it was determined that the illness was blood-related and was now seen in hemophiliacs, intravenous drug users, and heterosexuals, but the overwhelming number of people in the United States who were sick and dying from the disease continued to be gay men. In 1983, the Institut Pasteur in Paris identified HIV (human immunodeficiency virus), which caused AIDS. In 1987, AZT, the first FDA-approved drug to treat AIDS was released. Although there were further drug advances in the intervening years, it was not until 1995 that the "cocktail" was introduced. The cocktail had the first real impact in stopping the progression of the illness. Still, in 1995 alone there were 34,947 people who died of AIDS according to the CDC, and by 2004, the cumulative number of AIDS deaths in the United States was 529,113, with more than 900,000 people infected.

My photographs and stories chronicle my life and struggles with identity and illness. When I began the autobiographic work, I was very much in the throes of the disease. I was diagnosed in 1990, when AIDS was still considered a death sentence, and my main concern was to leave a record of my life, a way to make my life visible. Previous photographic studies of AIDS patients had always concentrated on bodily signifiers of illness, presenting the infected as sickly in an environment in which the illness was the sum total of their lives. I resented this kind of stigma and objectification. AIDS was not all that defined me, and it became imperative to leave a more encompassing story, so I began photographing myself and writing stories that weaved together memory with daily experiences. The work was never meant to be a documentary project, but rather a series of vignettes of text and image that would blend the various identities to which I ascribed: gay, Jewish, male, son, brother, lover, and person with AIDS.

By the time the Jewish Museum of San Francisco contacted me, I had begun a new regimen of medication, a variation of "the cocktail," revolutionary in the treatment of AIDS, which in a very short time restored me to good health, or at least the appearance of good health. After all, the illness was still incurable, but the virus was now held in check and my body responded. After years of being weak and ill, dependent on others for my welfare, I was able to return to work, but I couldn't without losing my government-provided health insurance and health care. The government assistance program into which I had entered, Supplemental Security Income (SSI), allowed me to receive health care for free as long as I remained sick and impoverished but would be revoked as soon as I earned a dollar over the very low income and asset threshold required to avail myself of the service. The same was true for many people with AIDS (and, incidentally, people with other disabilities) across the country. I felt trapped and enslaved. Now able-bodied, willing to become a contributing member of society, I was being stopped, forced to remain poor and dependent so I could continue to receive life-saving drugs. The physical manifestations of illness had vanished but the stigma of illness was being perpetuated. The *tzedakah* box project offered me the opportunity to address this dilemma.

Tzedakah encourages us to do something more than the disassociated practice of putting coins in a box. It teaches us to be involved and to perform in a prescribed escalating manner of ways. The highest form is to right a wrong by anonymously helping people in need become self-sufficient so that they may help themselves. These parameters helped me formulate my message encouraging social change and addressing the issue of AIDS as stigma. The box would contain a stack of sample letters delineating the problems that people with AIDS faced. Visitors to the exhibition were instructed to take the letters from the "out box." By sending them to our elected representatives in Washington, D.C., they would encourage changing the Social Security rules so that people with AIDS and other disabilities could return to work without losing their medical benefits. This would be the anonymous act to help people help themselves. The venue, a Jewish museum, would naturally direct my message to Jews, who had not responded strongly as a community to the AIDS crises.

When the AIDS epidemic appeared in 1978, the government and the population at large were mainly silent. As a blood-born disease that was transmitted by sexual contact, it was almost impossible to separate AIDS from sexuality. That it centered on gay sexuality in particular, a topic that made many people uncomfortable, seemed the reason for the silence. The disease was first known as the gay cancer, the gay plague, and GRID (gay-related immune deficiency). Gay people, hemophiliacs, and intravenous drug users were on the margins of society, and it would take until 1987 for President Ronald Reagan to address the issue publicly. AIDS Project Los Angeles (APLA) and the Gay Men's Health Crisis (GMHC) in New York, both opened in 1982 by gay people, were founded in reaction to the low level of governmental response to the epidemic.

Jewish communal response was also slow, even though many Jewish men, and some women, were infected and dying. With homosexuals not accepted in the Jewish community, AIDS was not considered an issue for Jewish communal organizations. Their sexuality a stigma in and of itself, gay men and lesbians were often alienated from their tradition, so they did not turn naturally to Jewish organizations for help. The first synagogues with specifically gay outreach were organized in 1972 and 1973 and were not officially recognized by most of the mainstream Jewish religious movements. AIDS affected these congregations in high numbers, so it fell to Beth Chayim Chadashim in Los Angeles, Congregation Beth Simchat Torah in New York, and Congregation Sha'ar Zehav in San Francisco to provide social services to those who wanted a Jewish component to their care.

Kosher meals, pastoral counseling, and support groups were offered, but these small, underfunded and understaffed organizations were not equipped to provide the level and volume of care needed in the early years of the epidemic. Jewish men and women turned to GMHC and APLA. When Jewish communal organizations finally did respond, it was late in the progress of the epidemic and the services could never replace those of the major AIDS organizations. By the time I was asked to make the *tzedakah* box, the epidemic was in yet another phase. People were living longer, healthier lives and I saw an opportunity for the Jewish community to participate. Acting in a Jewish context, giving by taking and doing would become an overtly social, political, and communal act.

The image needed for the *tzedakah* box to inspire the reaction I desired had to resonate with Jews, one with which everyone could identify. In modern Jewish culture, there is perhaps no more venerated figure than the Zionist pioneer, the *halutz*. Images of the *kibbutznik*—rugged, citizen-soldier, optimistic, heterosexual, and healthy—were pervasive in everyone's visual vocabulary. According to Bezalel Narkiss, professor emeritus of the Center for Jewish Art at the Hebrew University in Jerusalem, "The concept of the 'the new Jew' as a rugged pioneer in the Land of Israel became key in the renovation of Jewish culture and the creation of a new national identity." The main source of this propagandistic art was the Bezalel school in Jerusalem, opened in 1906, although by the 1920s and 1930s, Bezalel artists had come under international influences, adapting Art Deco, Dadaism, and other art styles. Considering the background of many Zionists who came from Russia and eastern Europe, it seems only natural that the iconography of Zionism was influenced also by the Social Realism of the Soviet Union, art that was supposed to glorify the political and social ideals of the state. Kibbutzim were a form of communism, and the Labor government of the early years of the state was closely aligned with international socialism. In the Soviet Union, art was meant as a glorification of the proletarian revolution, while in Israel it translated as idealization of the return to the land and a revitalization of Jewish national aspirations. The state-sponsored art of Israel fostered these same ideals. It was an art meant to ennoble and inspire participation, a kind of Zionist Realism.

The AIDS *Halutznik* was modeled after one of the figures on the Israeli ten-lira note of 1952, an example of Zionist Realism. In that scene, a young couple, a boy and a girl, stand upright, looking slightly to the left and upward into the sun as hope, heroism, and confidence in the future radiate from their faces and their stance. The point of view of the observer is reverential, looking up from slightly below. It is an inspiring presence. It engenders the confidence of the new state and inspires the viewer to be a part of their world. It is a given that they are heterosexual and healthy. It is an archetype that we in the Diaspora have seen in multiple guises, and if we cannot actually be a part of their world, we long to be associated with them, wish them success, and contribute in some fashion, be it social, political, or financial.

The AIDS *Halutznik* is taken directly from that scene. Photographed from below, it is reverential. Skin toned, arms and shoulders pumped up and buff, the figure has a look of confidence, optimism, hope. The stance and look is heroic. Like the pioneers who have conquered the land, restoring themselves and the Jewish People, I was conquering AIDS, restoring my health and reinventing the image of a person with AIDS. Even the background references the Israeli scene in that it is a hillside dotted with trees and small houses. Rather than portray a person with AIDS in an urban or interior setting, scenes usually associated with AIDS, the background is, if not agrarian, at least suburban. In that way perhaps, it is more American than Israeli and speaks more directly to the American audience.

The AIDS *Halutznik* was meant to inspire righteous acts, to correct an injustice of silence, and to remove the stigma of illness. Like so many others, I remember those Zionist images from childhood. They inspired and influenced me in profound ways. I traveled to Israel and lived there for many years, yet I also knew I could never measure up to the ideal. For me, those images created great longing but also great alienation and pain, because there was an essential part of me that could not conform to the ideal. Creating a "new" Jew with AIDS as a way to affirm and unite my Jewish, gay, and AIDS identities, I was also attempting to heal myself and emerge from the stigma.

The image was also a call to the Jewish community to acknowledge that there were Jews with AIDS, people who resembled our ideal notions of ourselves, who needed the help and healing that community involvement could bring. The image is surrounded by words in Hebrew and English, "*Tikkun Olam*, Heal the World." Across the image is a statement: "Help Him Help Himself. Help People with HIV/AIDS and Other Disabilities Go Back to Work." Across the bottom of the image, it reads, "Please take a sample letter from the *Tzedakah* Box and send it to your representatives in Washington, D.C." A simple act of sending a letter could be an act of righteousness.

The idea of a Zionist pioneer with AIDS may seem ludicrous, blasphemous to some, irreverent at least, but the AIDS *Halutznik* is meant to make us stop and think and to question. Can it be that the ideal imagery we create, which we then model ourselves after, can also separate us from ourselves? By using one of our most iconic images, I had hoped to question assumed notions of Jewish identity, notions that stop us from seeing difference, illness, otherness within our midst, and cause us to be ashamed or silent. It is ironic when the imagery that fuels our mythology turns out to be something completely different than what we envision, or even turns us against ourselves. The subversion of that notion can cause us to question, demand change, and offer acceptance and help. In American popular culture it was the image of Rock Hudson, the matinee idol, dying from AIDS, who turned out to be gay in real life. His death catapulted the AIDS epidemic into the mainstream. His friends the Reagans were forced to acknowledge the illness publicly. Or it might be the lush photographs of Israeli photographer Adi Ness whose images of Israeli soldiers exude a sensual homoeroticism and call us to question the archetype of masculinity and the Israeli soldier. And, because of the unfortunate circumstance that homosexuality and AIDS are linked, we have to imagine that some of those Israeli soldiers may be infected.

Interestingly, in spite of the religious establishment, homosexuals enjoy many legal protections in Israel that are still contended in the United States. The Supreme Court in Israel has ruled favorably on spousal equivalency rights for gay couples, and discrimination in military service is forbidden. But in AIDS issues Israeli society has done no better than the United States. The silence and shame associated with AIDS are still pervasive. Treatment options are limited. As recently as the year 2000, the Israeli pop singer Ofra Haza died of AIDS. Her illness was kept secret and denied after her death. The Israeli media was complicit in the silence. Haza, of Yemenite background, may not have been the "new" Jew of early Zionist propaganda, but she was a "new" Jew nevertheless. A Sabra, she was the voice of the new Jewish culture that Israel represents. She became an international pop star, selling millions of records throughout the world, spreading Israeli culture to a wider audience than any other previous Jewish or Israeli personality. Yet when she was ill and dying, infected, many believe, by her drug-addicted husband, the cause of death was kept a secret. To many in the AIDS community, this was seen as an act of shame, reinforcing the notion of AIDS as stigma. If nothing else, it was seen as a missed opportunity for education, to acknowledge the presence of AIDS.

There will always be reasons to stigmatize illness. Perhaps even the circumstances of Haza's illness brought out people's prejudices. The image I created was for a small exhibition of limited duration that had limited exposure. I have no idea if it changed the mind of even one person. Some people took letters from the *tzedakah* box and perhaps those few decided to act. I will never know. I can only hope that had a Zionist pioneer become infected with AIDS, he or she would have been embraced by the Jewish world, not isolated. My experience causes me to believe otherwise. Many of the Jewish communal organizations that eventually started AIDS services have now disbanded them. As the epidemic has appeared to wane, even the gay synagogues have scaled back their programs. The need appears no longer to be there.

I think that AIDS has made the Jewish world uncomfortable in another way. AIDS is a blood-born disease, and Jews know the stigma of blood accusations. To embrace AIDS in our midst would mean we would have to acknowledge our fears and be secure in ourselves as a community, to embrace difference. All social and political movements need imagery to inspire a following. It seems only natural to create an ideal. My image also represents an ideal, but one with a twist that deliberately undermined the stigma of AIDS, the stigma of difference. It was art meant to ennoble and inspire participation, a kind of new Jewish Realism.

6

JEWISH BIOETHICS IN
STORY AND LAW

Rabbi Peter Knobel, PhD, is rabbi of Temple Beth Emet—the Free Synagogue in Evanston, Illinois, and holds a PhD in Bible from Yale University. He has chaired numerous major commissions of the Reform Movement and is prominent as both a rabbinic leader and a scholar. He is especially interested in applying Jewish ethical principles to the life of the Jewish community. Most recently he chaired the liturgy committee of the Reform Movement as it produced its newest Siddur, *Mishkan Tefillah*.

AN EXPANDED APPROACH TO JEWISH BIOETHICS: A LIBERAL/AGGADIC APPROACH

Peter Knobel

This essay is part of my larger effort to address the limitations of traditional halachic thinking on behalf of patients, families, and doctors. My thinking will move in a direction that some would call "liberal." On an earlier occasion I addressed a primarily Reform Jewish discussion by enumerating a set of principles that were essential for liberal discourse that expands boundaries. I include here many of these: (1) I seek an approach in which patients and their families may feel empowered; (2) I privilege greater flexibility in decision making so that more choice will be available to the agents of critical life and death situations; (3) I urge more consideration of "virtue"—that is, the explicit seeking of good and noble behavior in every ethical decision we make; (4) I contend that Jewish bioethics has not paid adequate attention to the person at the center of a specific ethical decision, and that those who make the decisions or who decide how to enact ethical principles are often not adequately "person-centered"; and (5) I believe that most of our Jewish constituents—even those committed to a Jewish way of life—pay little attention to classic halachic discourse as a way of addressing ethical issues, and especially the crucial bioethical issues that everyone faces at one or another time in life.

There are, traditionally, three primary methods for doing Jewish ethics: legal (halachic), covenantal, and narrative. Louis Newman provides us with a useful description of each of these methods in his important volume *An Introduction to Jewish Ethics.*

Advocates of the legal model analyze questions and Jewish ethics in light of precedents found in traditional legal sources. Given a moral problem, legalists cite classical Jewish sources and, through analogical reasoning and other means, attempt to distill the principles behind the precedents and apply them to questions at hand.

Covenantal ethicists find guidance not so much in the substance of legal tradition as in the character of the relationship between God and Israel and between God and the world. In the final analysis, in this system, Jewish moral obligations are not determined by legal processes but by living in a covenantal relationship with God and attending to the responsibilities that are imposed by the character of that relationship.

Narrative ethics looks to the stories within Jewish tradition for a kind of moral guidance and suggests that there are aspects of stories that can guide us into different *ways* of looking at a problem, and not just for a different result. Jewish narrative ethicists believe that Jews learn to see the world in a distinctively religious way through stories. They argue that the reading of narratives exposes the ethical agent to aspects of a situation that are not always clear when utilizing more conventional, legalistic models.[1]

The standard model for conducting Jewish bioethics has been the halachic model, which is act-centered. Using legal precedents, the ethicist determines what is permitted or prohibited in a particular case. Since most contemporary Jews are not halachic in their approach to Judaism, we must—at the very least—supplement this approach with aspects of the other systems I describe above. At the most, we might find the halachic system inadequate on intrinsic grounds. Surely our Jewish people ought to be guided by Jewish tradition and a history of opinions from the legal community, but a non-halachic approach is more suited to their understanding of themselves and their lives. A method that combines a greater measure of the covenantal and narrative models will focus more on the person in any ethically relevant case, and it will help everyone involved in the care of the ill deal with the new realities of current medical practice. It is also a way to enhance the spiritual potential in people's lives as they face very concrete and practical issues. Finally, narrative models—using Jewish narratives—may be a way of keeping the tangents on discourse within a Jewish framework.

Any Jewish approach to decision making will require reflection on Jewish texts, but I do not believe that these texts need to have been developed as part of halachic decision making. Indeed, to the contrary, I believe a contemporary Jew will be more comfortable with stories that have been of universal importance and impact.

Therefore I begin my ethical work with a reading of three primary narratives: the Creation, the Covenant at Sinai, and the Exodus from Egypt. Each of these stories involves a basic understanding of the role of humankind in the world and the role of Jews as exemplars of that understanding.

The Creation narrative provides us with a definition of personhood that is rooted in the relationship between God and the human being. The Exodus narrative provides us with a definition of Jewish personhood that is rooted in our identification with the experience of slavery and liberation and assigns us the task of creating a just and compassionate world *because* we were slaves. The gift of Torah at Sinai (*Matan Torah*) provides us with a definition of Jewish personhood that is rooted in the binding covenant between God and Israel and it obligates us to do (what we determine to be) God's will, but with the full participation and consent of the covenanted human being.

Each of these narratives requires the reader to interpret their meanings and to derive the richest possible personal meaning, and thus I am proposing that a liberal Jewish approach ought to be a conversation between the texts of our people and the texts of our lives. Our lives and the texts we read must be open to interpretation and to a free understanding of their implications, in the same way in which we approach any literary text that we experience. The classic texts of the biblical and rabbinic tradition, Mishnah, Talmud, Midrash, codes, and responsa, by now must be amplified by the more philosophical writings of an ever-unfolding modernity, and even by the historical evidence about the way in which people have lived and interpreted those texts over time. [Editor's note: see the essay by Professor Ruderman within.]

I will discuss the Creation narrative first because not only does it occur first in the public consciousness, but it also offers one of the most interesting examples of human responsibility and even freedom. Judaism's understanding of the role of humankind in the world is encapsulated in two different stories of creation. In the first account we are created in the divine image and we are given dominion over the natural world; in the second account we are made from the dust of the earth and animated by the divine breath. In the first story, dominion is emphasized, whereas in the second story we are introduced to the notion of stewardship. If we juxtapose these two stories we discover that there is a necessary tension between domination and stewardship. This tension is elegantly described by Yitzchok Breitowitz, who reminds us that we have the power to redeem the world and to destroy it. Being formed in the image of God (Genesis 1) connotes "autonomy, power, and the ability to make moral judgments." It enhances partnership in improving the world and in conquering illness. But Genesis chapter 2 offers a strikingly different vision of human beings—we are given the mission of preservation and protection.

In that tension, Breitowitz's argument leaves a much wider berth for the interpretation of the individual as he or she faces the living situation and tries to apply principles and norms to a particular situation. To summarize Breitowitz's position in his own words:

> Therefore, in effect, human beings must live in a perpetual state
> of tension and contradiction between realizing their divinity by
> the exercise of power, wisdom and control, while at the same
> time recognizing the need to submit to that which is greater and
> all knowing.[2]

Jewish ethics begins with an assumption that there is a duty to God, while secular ethics tends to rely on human autonomy and the consideration of that autonomy in light of modern philosophical reasoning. The duty to God within Jewish tradition is implied when at Mount Sinai the Jewish people responded to God's covenant with the words: We will perform, and we will hear (*Naaseh venishma*)—in that order. Jewish life is centered on the performance of commandments (*mitzvot*), deeds that are obligatory in nature. We are asked to imagine

that we will be called to account for what we do. Therefore it ultimately matters what choices we make because our choices have an effect on our destiny and on the destiny of the human race. We seek a
just society through these *mitzvot*. Therefore a pure autonomy (autonomy being one of the most salient developments of the last century and
a half) is modified by the harness of obligation. But it is autonomy,
nonetheless, and it is usually absent from halachic reckoning—at least
as an explicit value.[3]

At the heart of modern secular bioethics, according to physician
Benjamin Freedman (himself an involved Jew), is "the principle of free
and informed consent, the right of every competent person to decide
about proposed medical treatments after receiving the information that
person finds necessary." In large measure this concept developed because of the horror of the Nazi medical "experiments." The goal is to
permit patients to become health care decision makers in partnership
with medical professionals. Secular bioethics uses the language of
rights rather than the language of duty. Freedman reframes the discussion on autonomy by linking duty with autonomy:

> Judaism supports self regarding duties.... The ultimate source
> of all obligations, including duties to the self, is to be found
> within the self, through a covenant with God. [But] ... if in-
> formed consent means that one has the right to decide about
> medical care, ... it is in conflict with the view that one is duty
> bound to act toward the self in certain ways.[4]

Thus ours is an embedded or relational autonomy. In Judaism, while individuals are of inestimable value, our range of choices is harnessed by
the fact that we are embedded in community and family and that we are
governed and limited by our obligations both to the self and to others.

Eugene Borowitz, prominent Reform theologian, has sought this
balance between autonomy and obligation and has proposed the concept of the Jewish autonomous self. His method assumes that the individual seriously identifies with the Jewish narrative and accepts the
reality of a covenant between God and the Jewish people. Therefore,
even in a framework of autonomy, what Jewish tradition teaches will
affect our decisions. For Borowitz the Jewish autonomous individual

remains rooted in relationship, rooted in history, and sensitive to the present through the people and tradition.[5]

Thus autonomy seems to be both legitimated and limited by Jewish tradition, just as it is by some of the Jewish feminist thought that has also emphasized relationship, narrative thinking, and awareness of the "other."[6] But even Leon Kass, well-known conservative ethicist, who is generally regarded as encouraging caution in our invocation of autonomy, points out the following:

> Every human encounter is an ethical encounter, and occasion for the practice and cultivation of virtue and respect, between doctors and patients, for the exercise of responsibility and trust on both sides.[7]

No guidelines can cover all real cases, much less touch the critical nuances that distinguish one case from another.

Three Stories About Life and Death

In this section, I present three classic texts that deal with the death of a prominent individual. Each has a long history in Jewish reflections on the end-of-life decisions. My aggadic analysis leads to conclusions that are generally rejected by those who use the halachic approach.

The Story of King Saul

When mortally wounded in battle, King Saul requests that his armor bearer kill him, and the armor bearer refuses. Saul and the armor bearer both commit suicide to prevent torture and humiliation by the Philistines. The biblical text condemns neither Saul nor his armor bearer for an act that is (halachically, although this is prehalachic) prohibited. While some of the subsequent rabbinic discussions (i.e., the post-talmudic responses) equivocate about the special conditions of being a king, it is clear that his biography requires that his end have some dignity. When we apply this situation to the terminally ill, continued medical treatment may be construed as constituting abuse or torture. It is Saul who initiates the request for help in killing himself. The analogy to physician-assisted suicide seems easy to draw. The dilemma of patient and the dilemma of physician are clearly etched. Both subjects are, arguably, subject to torture or abuse in the continuation of life (I Samuel 31:10).

The Story of Hananiah b. Teradion

This fairly well-known talmudic story reports that an executioner eased the passing of Hananiah by raising the flames and taking away a wool mat that was keeping the process moving more slowly. Torture was reduced and both men—according to the legend—acquired eternal life as a result of this act of mercy (B. *Avodah Zarah* 18ab).

The Hananiah story has been subjected to a great deal of analysis and is often used to demonstrate that active euthanasia is prohibited, and that death can be hastened if it is part of the natural course of things. What we have here is a situation of assisted suicide in which the person is unable to act for emotional or moral reasons but is able to permit another to help him. In this story, according to one possible reading, hastening death in certain circumstances is even meritorious.

Rabbi Judah's Servant

Perhaps the most interesting and best known story for our purposes is the much-analyzed story about the death of Rabbi Judah haNasi, the editor of the Mishnah. In this aggadah, the mortals, including the servant, pray that the rabbi's life be extended and that he live beyond the suffering his illness causes him. But the servant actually pays attention to the suffering—marked by repeated acts of removing his tefillin to resort to the privy—and she finally comes to see that he must die. She throws a jar from the rooftop and startles the mortal out of prayer. And when the prayers on behalf of Rabbi Judah stop, his soul departs (B. *Ketubot* 104a).[8]

The fact that the servant cares deeply for Rabbi Judah (and, indeed, takes notice of his plight, which is part of the narrative strength of the episode) makes this story especially instructive. She puts his interests above hers (her wish for him to live) and above the interests of the current norms, in defiance of a presumed rabbinic norm. She comprehends that the rabbi's disciples have lost sight of their master's needs and are consumed with their own needs—the preservation of norms that support extending his life.

There is a preference in Judaism and in general medical ethical literature to suggest that what makes her act morally acceptable is that the act is indirect. She removes an impediment to dying (*mesir monea* in the tradition that followed) rather than hastening his death. From a psychological point of view it may be easier to deal with indirect rather than direct action, and the concept of enabling the natural process of dying has greater appeal than killing. But it is difficult to maintain this distinction. Ironically, God is powerless in this story to terminate the rabbi's life as long as the other rabbis continue to pray. The analogy to modern medical techniques is not at all far-fetched. We could remove certain kinds of artificial support from a patient presumed to be dying. (I am avoiding the term *goses*—a person about to die—as a technical category that has fragile standing today.) We should further note that once the rabbis' prayers no longer constitute therapy in any meaningful sense, they become a form of abuse and torture.

William Cutter has argued that the crucial factor in making decisions may seem to be the law, whereas it is often the suffering of patients that brings about a shift, which then encourages people to reread the law in any event. He argues that knowing the narrative of people has helped many rabbis respond more tolerantly to the stickier questions with which they are faced. Further, he suggests that one way of preserving outdated norms is to avoid paying attention to individual suffering as an active influence in shaping attitudes and opinions.[9]

Each of these stories requires greater analysis than space here allows. In each story we would have to ask: who is the central character? Then we would have to read the story in direct relationship to the specific case with which we are concerned. Do the characters in the story help us find analogies to the individuals in our particular case? Do the stories provide a range of possibilities? Each story requires us to confront the role of compassion in decision making, and each story has a unique form whose elements may assist us in decision making (surprise, character development, context, and so on).

Philip Cohen, a Reform rabbi who devotes considerable time to pastoral duties, argues that aggadic reasoning is important as a hermeneutic act that can tolerate multiple views simultaneously.[10] As such, it can be the means through which we enter into dialogue with each other as a community consisting of multiple views.

Although Cohen may not be a classic halachic decisor, or a bioethicist, this simple position captures one of the most important shifts that must take place within Jewish discourse: the community carries multiple views and that principle must be preserved as part of our ethical discourse.

Louis Newman's Contribution

I now want to consider a position enunciated by my partner in this encounter, Louis Newman. Professor Newman has suggested that:

> the rhetoric of Jewish ethics should change from what Judaism teaches to what we, given our particular interpretive assumptions and our particular way of constructing the coherence of tradition as a whole, find within the traditional sources.

Further, he proposes:

> that contemporary Jewish ethics be conceived as a dialectical relationship in which finally no sharp distinction can be made between classic rabbinic voices and ours.[11]

Thus even though Professor Newman is generally regarded as being more closely linked to halachic norms and their methods of discovery, he clearly embraces some of the concerns that my essay tries to address.

Additional Arguments to Support Narrative Thinking

Benjamin Freedman uses the ethics consultation as a model of a non-halachic approach to Jewish bioethics. His description of the patient, the family, and the physicians provides the beginning of a narrative model. The narrative that is constructed as part of the decision-making process should reflect the life of the patients and the motives as well as the values of the family and caregivers. In this model, I would add that the ethics consultant or chaplain serve as a translator; and, as with all translations, the conversation is enriched by this distillation and interpretation of the ethical literature into pastoral form.

Laurie Zoloth, prominent ethicist and feminist thinker, provides a model for using narrative to discuss issues of justice. Her "ethics of encounter" is decidedly person-centered. Drawing on the insights of feminism and the Jewish prophetic pursuit of a just society, she uses the Book of Ruth to argue that meaningful discourse "starts with the recognition of the other, and that justice is prior to any human freedom. The text insists on the radical recognition of primary responsibility as calling into being a community that is prior to and responsible for the just flourishing of any human self."[12]

There are, of course, other examples of the primary responsibility of one person for another—particularly in the case of David and Jonathan whose story demonstrates that a person may act against his or her own interests to save a life. And finally, for this part of the discussion, Melissa Raphael in her book *The Female Face of God*, urges:

> relational care as the most important medium of God's power in the world ... not to ask why God did not protect us at the time [of the Holocaust] ... rather it should be asked how we could and can protect God's presence as it is this which makes it possible to know God in the "other."[13]

I argue that aggadic modes of discourse enhance the potential for a sense of the presence of the divine.

Notes of the Prophetic

Ultimately a Jewish bioethical approach must include the prophetic voice. The Hebrew prophets condemn the wealthy and the powerful for ignoring the needs of the poor and the weak. They decry both the callousness of the wealthy and their lack of justice and compassion. The prophets assume that the bounty of this earth must be justly shared. Modern leaders may be loath to level that criticism at our lay leaders and Jewishly committed wealthy. When the prophet Nathan condemns King David for arranging Uriah's death, he sets the example of speaking truth to power. Our narrative of slavery and liberation sets a framework for discussing a just society that—when applied to this essay's context—means the just distribution of health care. This is not to say that halachic modalities are opposed to this prophetic value but—rather—to suggest that the prophetic consciousness makes equity the highest priority and adds it to the ethical decision-making process.

Toward a Conclusion

We live in a time when we face social problems that we have never before been able to imagine. It is not only the individual or "intimate" bioethical decision that can best be addressed by aggadic modes of thinking and discourse. The larger issues having to do with our self-definition, the potential to create life, genetic questions, and our very definitions of humanity are already with us. Other macro-issues are on the horizon. We will soon have the ability to be God's partners in completing and perfecting creation or to dethrone God and destroy creation. Yesterday's science fiction has become today's reality. Therefore I believe that what is required of us is an ethic of "imagination" and "anticipation."

Thus far our ethical systems have been reactive; and so we have not been proactive regarding the opening of Pandora's box. Narrative thinking, I believe, gives us the best chance to act as cocreators with God as we seek to recreate humankind and remove the flaws in creation. How do we reflect on commodification? How shall we assess physical prowess? Where will the lines be drawn between removing a blemish (the possibility of a genetic flaw) and a glib enhancement of a person's ability to perform? Shall we be as concerned as Leon Kass, in his anticipation of something like Huxley's Brave New World? Kass believes that unless we radically limit some technologies and, more importantly, prohibit others, we will forget the most important values of human dignity:

> Everything depends on rejecting the rationalist and utopian dream of perfecting human beings by recreating them, and on remembering that richer vision of human liberty and human dignity that informs the founding of our polity.[14]

While I may not agree entirely with Kass, his note and Huxley's vision are not vain concerns. Even Kass emphasizes our need to understand "fully the meaning and significance of proposed actions." And, as a corollary to this emphasis, he warns us that we must look at individual ethical decisions in context with their broader implications for society and humankind as a whole. Byron Sherwin, Jewish theologian and ethicist, asserts that Judaism will insist on the responsibility of the scientist to determine the ethical implications of his or her work.[15] Thus narrative thinkers do not all reside on the permissive side; what they do contribute, however, is a deepened sensitivity to the implications of our actions on a macro-scale. Finally, we might revert to another fundamental biblical tale—the Tower of Babel. That story, as interpreted by the rabbis, warns us that when we lose our humility before God, we care more for the bricks that fall than the people who are killed in our attempt to supplant God (Genesis 11).

Conclusion

My argument has been that an aggadic ethic can bring us closer to addressing the macro-issues we face as a Jewish society that needs to think way ahead of the immediate circumstances of any specific ethical decision; and that aggadic discourse is the best way to enhance flexibility, to ennoble the individual, and to engage the citizens of our contemporary Jewish polity. Our stories suggest how we may think about our values and our life projects, and permit more imaginative constructions of ethical possibility. The stories are nuanced and open to multiple readings. In addition, as Jews we participate in a narrative reconstruction of our relationship to Jewish history, the Jewish people, and God. Only when embedded in the primary narrative do norms make sense. Where we locate ourselves and which version of a narrative we accept as determining our decisions affect how we read and understand Jewish texts. The stories of our lives and the stories of our people are sacred texts along with the texts that have heretofore been identified by the term "texts." Only when they are read together will they help us act and create more meaningful lives, a more comprehensive discourse, and perhaps even a better world.

Louis E. Newman, PhD, is the John M. and Elizabeth W. Musser Professor of Religious Studies and the director of the Program in Judaic Studies at Carleton College in Northfield, Minnesota. He is the author of *Past Imperatives: Studies in the History and Theory of Jewish Ethics* and *An Introduction to Jewish Ethics*, as well as co-editor (with Elliot Dorff) of *Contemporary Jewish Ethics and Morality* and *Contemporary Jewish Theology*. His current work is on the concept of *teshuvah* (repentance) in Judaism.

The Narrative and the Normative: The Value of Stories for Jewish Ethics

Louis E. Newman

Stories have the power to shape our lives, and especially our moral lives, in dramatic ways—by providing a model of a virtuous life, a framework for moral development, and a vision of the purpose and direction of human life. In recent years many ethicists (secular, Christian, and Jewish) have argued that stories are uniquely capable of capturing the essence of moral life, precisely because they most closely parallel and capture lived human experience. Our lives, after all, are "stories in progress," and so the nature of the moral life is conveyed most richly and accurately through narratives. Such an approach, of course, stands in sharp contrast to an alternative approach to ethics that emphasizes the centrality of rules and principles. Such a "rule-based" ethic is abstract and (in theory) universally applicable, focused on the discrete moral decision rather than the whole person, on acts rather than character. From the perspective of narrative ethics, an inordinate (still more, an exclusive) focus on moral rules overlooks important dimensions of moral life and may even distort those aspects of life that it addresses.

Peter Knobel stands with many other religious ethicists (most notably Stanley Hauerwas among Christians and Laurie Zoloth among

Jews) who favor a narrative approach to ethics. In addition to the reasons adduced above, he cites the fact that most modern Jews are "non-halachic" and so will not respond positively to a Jewish ethic that speaks to them in the language of moral rules. Given that the halachic system presupposes the authority of a divine lawgiver (as well as the derivative authority of the rabbinic legal decisors), modern Jews no longer feel compelled by a halachic ethic. Moreover, this halachic discourse is highly technical and largely inaccessible to contemporary Jews, most of whom do not have the requisite skills to read and analyze the complex halachic literature that has developed over two millennia. Hence, for both substantive and pragmatic reasons, contemporary Jewish ethics should turn its attention to narrative.

I

There is much to commend this narrative approach to Jewish ethics, not least the fact that much of Torah and rabbinic literature is, in fact, aggadic, or narrative, in nature. The Torah begins, after all, with the story of Creation. And, as Knobel notes, the stories of the patriarchs and matriarchs, of the Exodus, of the giving of the law at Sinai, and even of the ultimate redemption predicted by the prophets are all central features of the biblical text. Torah, which in its most basic sense means "instruction," surely provides many forms of guidance—stories no less than laws—grand, sweeping visions of the beginning and the end of the world no less than injunctions about the penalties for theft and the proper treatment of the poor and the stranger. Moreover, rabbinic literature is replete with the stories of famous rabbis, some of which (like the martyrdom of Hananiah b. and Rabbi Judah's servant) can be mined for their ethical guidance. Knobel, then, is surely on solid ground in advocating a narrative approach to Jewish ethics.

But I wish to suggest that the benefits of such an approach are mitigated by a number of limitations, some of which Knobel notes and others of which he overlooks. We cannot escape the need for moral principles and rules, and if this is true of ethics generally, it is truer still of Jewish ethics. The challenge faced by contemporary Jewish ethicists, I suggest, is to see narrative and law as complementary and ultimately interdependent aspects of any authentic Jewish ethic. In the sections that follow, I will try to defend the need for such a two-dimensional approach to Jewish ethics and to illustrate how it might be applied to at least one question in bioethics.

II

For all its merits, a narrative ethic has some significant limitations. As Knobel notes, an aggadic (narrative) ethic provides a range of acceptable choices based on the collective Jewish narrative as applied to the story of individuals. Stories are rich and ambiguous and subject to multiple readings. They offer a range of responses depending on what details are emphasized and the point of view of actors in the narrative. Narratives are intrinsically ambiguous in a number of respects. They are open-ended and subject to multiple interpretations. What, precisely, does the creation story in Genesis teach us? What moral guidance does it provide? Perhaps that human life is infinitely precious, since we were created "in the image of God." Perhaps that we should have lots of children, since we are told to "be fruitful and multiply and fill the earth." Perhaps that men and women are equal, since it says, "male and female, God created them." All these messages and many more *could* be extracted from the story, depending on our particular point of view.

But there is yet another ambiguity intrinsic in narratives. Suppose that we can agree on an interpretation of a given story, for example, that Genesis teaches us to value life as a gift from God. How, exactly, are we to operationalize this value? What specific actions does it permit, or require, or prohibit? At best, the story provides us with a value, or a goal to be pursued, but it does not clearly prescribe the means for achieving it. And, as we all know, well-intentioned and deeply moral people can agree on a goal (e.g., world peace) but disagree radically on the best way to achieve it. Narratives, then, provide only a very general moral direction, not a course of action to follow.

In addition, the fact that our tradition includes many different narratives makes this approach to ethics problematic in yet another way. As Knobel notes, there are central stories in Jewish tradition, which I would argue are the Creation story, the stories of the patriarchs and matriarchs, the Exodus story, stories of the conquest of

Canaan, stories about the judges, kings, and prophets, and stories about the end of days. If we factor into the equation the narratives of individuals, in addition to the "master" narratives of the biblical text, as Knobel wishes to do, the multiplicity of potential perspectives becomes staggering. There is no single unified Jewish narrative to provide us guidance; instead, we find many narratives, each with its own (very ambiguous) prescription for behavior. And precisely because narratives and the interpretation of them are unsystematic, they do not demand to be reconciled. When different narratives point in different directions, we are left without even the (relatively ambiguous) moral guidance that a single story can provide.

Halacha, by contrast, is by nature systematic. If two rulings conflict, religious authorities will feel compelled to reconcile them, since a legal system that does not provide clear guidance about what is forbidden and permitted is self-defeating. Halachic ethics, whatever its deficiencies, has the merit of providing a consistent system of moral guidance.

Finally, Knobel's argument that an aggadic ethic is preferable to a halachic one for modern Jews is not entirely compelling. To be sure, most modern Jews, especially in America, are "post-halachic." The traditional notion that Jews are bound to a system of divinely ordained laws has been maintained only among a relatively small group of Orthodox Jews. But much the same point could be made about the plausibility of the biblical narratives. Many biblical stories emphasize first and foremost God's power to intervene in nature and to control the course of human history. If we believed those stories and made them the framework for our ethics, we would be advising Jews to rely on God's supernatural powers to save them from adversity, and we would be advocating the Jewish right to settle the whole land of Israel as a divine mandate—positions that are rejected by the very liberal Jews to whom Knobel wants to appeal.

Moreover, just as most liberal American Jews have rejected the divine authority behind Halacha, they have similarly rejected the same authority behind the aggadah. Why, given that the Torah is not of divine origin, should modern Jews be guided by these biblical stories, rather than by Greek myths, or Shakespearean heroes, or American folktales? The fact is that some Jews find the aggadah inspirational and meaningful for their lives and look to it for moral guidance, despite the fact that they have long since abandoned any notion of "Torah from Sinai." But, of course, the same could be true for Halacha, which similarly may not depend on divine authority to be a source of meaning and guidance for modern liberal Jews.

So, narrative ethics has its problems, but so, too, does a halachic ethic, as Knobel correctly notes. Yet the benefits of a legal ethic are worth recalling, if only briefly. As many, including Knobel, have noted, a halachic ethic is "act-oriented," or "decision-oriented." Rather than looking to the larger context of an individual's life (or the life of the community to which that individual belongs), Halacha looks to the individual deed. While narrative ethicists will focus on what this approach ignores, it is important to consider what it captures, as well. For most of the time, we experience our moral lives as a series of discrete decisions: Should I give money to this beggar on the corner? Should I report this co-worker (or supervisor) who is charging personal expenses to her employer? Should we have our infirm parents move in with us, where they will get better care, or place them in a nursing home, which will cause less family friction? Moral life, in large part, is about making myriad such decisions; indeed, hardly a day goes by when we do not make moral decisions, for every interpersonal encounter brings with it the potential for conflicting interests and the opportunity for acts of kindness and generosity. If narrative ethics provides us with an overarching story to guide our lives, we must still have direction at the "micro" level, for our moral lives are lived one decision at a time.

But if this is true of ethics in general, there are yet other reasons for preferring rules to narratives as the cornerstone of Jewish ethics. In the realm of ethics, Jewish tradition places more value on the concrete deed than on the intention. If I fulfill my obligation to give 10 percent of my income to *tzedakah*, it is not a matter of great concern to the rabbis if I did so out of a motivation to be recognized and honored in my community, or even if I did so grudgingly. It is preferable, of course, but not essential to have a generous spirit; what is essential is that those in need be supported by the community. The fact that the poor are fed is more important to Halacha than what brought me to the fulfillment of this obligation. (Interestingly, the converse is true in matters of ritual law, when no other person's interests are at stake; performing the mitzvah with proper intention is essential.) Narrative approaches to ethics emphasize intention and motivation over mere performance—the quality of a person's moral deeds over the conformity to prescription—are not in keeping with a tradition that gives priority to moral actions and concrete results.

In fact, Jewish tradition sees morality as part of a system of holiness, as evidenced by the appearance of the most elevated moral rules in Leviticus 19, in the midst of the priestly "holiness code." Like the rest of the priestly injunctions, these moral principles ("love your neighbor as yourself," "do not stand idly by the blood of your neighbor," etc.) are meant to be part of a pattern of sacred deeds that honor the Creator of all life. Compassion for your fellow human being, no less than offering the proper sacrifices and observing the rules of ritual purity, defines a holy community. This community demonstrates its devotion to God by behaving in prescribed ways, so that the very daily life of the community testifies to God's presence in their midst. This is the point of the refrain, "You shall be holy because I, the Lord your God, am holy." The Israelite community's behavior is to be a mirror that captures and reflects God's holiness. To place moral life in this context is to see it as defined by specific behaviors, which are woven together as part of a larger fabric of religious life.

For all these reasons, Jewish ethicists dare not minimize the value of Halacha. Not only is it the most significant repository of our tradition's moral wisdom, but it responds to our need for specific, decision-based, moral guidance, and it places those moral norms in the larger context of ritualized practices that infuse the community with holiness. By the same token, I take seriously the suggestion of Knobel and others that narrative approaches to ethics have much to offer us by focusing on the person and on the trajectory and context of an individual's life story. Indeed, it could be argued that Halacha is, at least in part, an attempt to concretize the values embedded in the great stories of our people and its relationship to God. So, in principle, narratives and rules need not be diametrically opposed. They are, after all, both part and parcel of Torah, and so, one might surmise, they must point us ultimately in the same direction. The question before us, then, is how we can draw equally from both of these sources of moral instruction.[16] What might a Jewish ethic look like that is equal parts Halacha and aggadah?

III

Let us turn to one of our great contemporary teachers of Torah, Abraham Joshua Heschel, who was both a brilliant theologian and an exemplary moral leader. In his *God in Search of Man*, he addresses this issue with characteristic insight and sensitivity.

> Halacha represents the strength to shape one's life according to a fixed pattern; it is a form-giving force. Aggadah is the expression of man's ceaseless striving which often defies all limitations. Halacha is the rationalization and schematization of living; it defines, specifies, sets measure and limit, placing life into an exact system. Aggadah deals with man's ineffable relations to God, to other men, and to the world. Halacha deals with details, with each commandment separately; Aggadah with the whole of life, with the totality of religious life.... Halacha teaches us how to perform common acts; Aggadah tells us how to participate in the eternal drama. Halacha gives us knowledge; Aggadah gives us aspiration.
>
> Halacha gives us the norms for action; Aggadah, the vision of the ends of living. Halacha prescribes, Aggadah suggests; Halacha decrees, Aggadah inspires; Halacha is definite; Aggadah is allusive....
>
> To maintain that the essence of Judaism consists exclusively of Halacha is as erroneous as to maintain that the essence of Judaism consists exclusively of Aggadah. The interrelationship of Halacha and Aggadah is the very heart of Judaism. Halacha without Aggadah is dead, Aggadah without Halacha is wild.[17]

Heschel's exploration of the relationship between Halacha and aggadah occurs in the context of his discussion of religious observance in general, not ethics in particular. But his insight points us toward a solution to the problem we face in creating a modern Jewish ethic that is both authentic to our tradition and responsive to our situation. There is a dialectical tension between these two elements of Judaism. Though they seem to arise from different impulses and lead in opposite directions, ultimately they are complementary—allies, not antagonists. Translated into the realm of ethics, Heschel's view suggests that we need to combine the specificity of Halacha with the open-endedness of aggadah. We need an ethic that focuses equally on both individual deeds and whole lives, for either approach alone will fail to provide a well-rounded and comprehensive guide to Jewish moral living.

To get a clearer sense of how such a Jewish ethic might look, we can consider the oft-discussed issue of medical treatment at the end of life. One of the earliest halachic sources on this issue, which is reiterated in various forms throughout the subsequent legal codes, comes from *Mishnah Semahot* 1:4:

> One may not close the eyes of a dying person (*goses*); one who touches him so as to move him is a murderer. R. Meir would say: "It is to be compared to a sputtering candle which is extinguished as soon as a person touches it—so too, whoever closes the eyes of a dying person is considered to have taken his soul."

At first glance, the rule makes little sense. A *goses*, after all, is a person who is in the final stages of dying. As such, we might wonder why the extraordinary concern about closing her eyes or moving him. What could be wrong with hastening by a matter of minutes or hours the inevitable end?

Though the Mishnah is characteristically silent about the reasoning behind this rule, the point is not difficult to discern. Life is not ours to end. Even life in extremis, on the verge of death, belongs to God, not to us. Anything we do to take control of the process of dying betrays a presumptuous attitude toward God, who alone is the author of life and death. Hence, even when death is approaching, Halacha tells us, we must not trespass into realms where we do not belong.

This rule is especially difficult for many modern Jews to follow, for we have become accustomed to controlling our lives, and especially our medical care, to an extraordinary degree. We readily assume that our autonomy is inviolable, and that we are rightfully the "masters of our fate." But the wisdom of our tradition is otherwise. We may do things that either prolong or shorten life, but we cannot engage in an act that definitely ends it. Determining the moment when life ends is God's prerogative, not ours.

But this halachic rule must be supplemented by the story of Rabbi Judah's servant that Knobel cites. There it is clear that the woman who experiences Judah's suffering up close understands that the time has come to quit praying for his recovery. By shattering the jar and interrupting the other rabbis' prayers, she is not acting to end his life but to end the activity that is artificially keeping him alive. By the same token, the story of the martyrdom of Hanina ben Tradyon, which is also routinely cited in Jewish discussions of these issues, underscores the fact that it is acceptable to wish for, and even to facilitate, a speedy end to a life racked with pain and suffering. Under these circumstances, removing the impediments to the dying process is acceptable.

Taken together, the Mishnaic law and the talmudic narratives provide a more complete and subtle picture of how to think about care for the dying. The Mishnah provides the prohibition that defines the outer limit of what is acceptable—we must not be the proximate cause of death. But short of that, our narratives tell us, we can do a number of things that will cut short the period of suffering by removing impediments to the dying process. To let nature run its course without our interference is the ideal. But so long as we do not "pull the plug," we may do what is within our power to facilitate the process that is already under way. Translated into specific terms, this suggests that we are not allowed to kill the dying individual directly, as Dr. Kevorkian was famous for doing, but we are permitted to withhold medicine and even nutrition and hydration from the dying. Where Halacha defines the boundary of what is prohibited, aggadah explores the nuances of what is permissible. In Heschel's words, "Halacha prescribes, Aggadah suggests."

But Heschel's insight could be applied even more broadly, for our moral obligations toward the dying are not restricted to the actions that cause, prolong, or hasten death. The most complex and subtle issues in end-of-life care concern the quality of attention that the dying receive. If Heschel is right, aggadah will focus our attention on the quality of relationships, not only on the permissibility of specific acts. The moral challenges of caring for the dying take many forms:

- How can we continue to view and treat a patient as being "in the image of God" when the person has lost so many of his or her healthy human capacities?
- How can we facilitate the process of "letting go," for both the patient and his or her loved ones?
- How can we make the final days and hours a sacred time for all concerned?
- How can we encourage the dying and those around them to be open to the possibility of forgiveness and reconciliation in relationships that have been conflicted?

These are the sorts of questions that, by their nature, are not readily susceptible to halachic regulation. They belong, instead, to the realm of aggadah, where we can be inspired by the stories of our tradition and seek to emulate the values embedded in them. Imagine how we might address these issues if we were inspired by Esau's conciliatory spirit toward Jacob, or by the psalmist's quiet confidence in God's protection, or by the resignation of Ecclesiastes? Clearly there are many sources of wisdom in our tradition, apart from Halacha, that might guide us as we care for the dying.

A Jewish ethic that combines halachic and aggadic approaches is both more authentic and more comprehensive than an ethic that relies exclusively on either aspect of the tradition. It is able to address a wider range of moral questions, since it can accommodate both the concern for specific deeds and the desire to strive for certain lofty goals. It can both direct and inspire, insofar as it both defines a set of behaviors that we need to observe and shapes a set of values that we need to internalize. It concerns both the concrete decisions that we make each day and the building of moral character that unfolds over many decades. Such an ethic, I think, is most likely to appeal to modern Jews because, unlike a narrative or legal approach, it is neither "dead" nor "wild," but a source of authentic, dynamic moral guidance.

CONCLUSION

Looking Back, Moving Forward

Rabbi David B. Ruderman, PhD, is the Joseph Meyerhoff Professor of Modern Jewish History and Ella Darivoff Director of the Center for Advanced Judaic Studies at the University of Pennsylvania. He has taught at the University of Maryland (1974–1983) and Yale University (1983–1994). He is the author of many books and articles, and recently won the Koret Award for the best book in Jewish History in 2001, *Jewish Enlightenment in an English Key*. He is the immediate past president of the American Academy for Jewish Research. In 2001, the National Foundation for Jewish Culture honored him with its lifetime achievement award for his work in Jewish history.

THE HISTORY OF INVENTION: DOCTORS, MEDICINE, AND JEWISH CULTURE

David B. Ruderman

We tend to view ourselves, our victories and achievements as well as our failures and frustrations, from the overly narrow perspective of the present. In reflecting on our Jewish challenges and commitments, we often suffer from a kind of historical amnesia, a predicament the late Rabbi Morris Adler once called "standing naked before the immediate," without a clear sense of what preceded us and how we might be connected to a legacy of the past. In considering the subject of healing and medicine in the Jewish tradition, most of our reflections are similarly orientated toward the here and now. When we actually search for earlier Jewish answers to our current bioethical or spiritual dilemmas by consulting older texts, be they halachic or aggadic, philosophical or mystical, we often do so mechanically, seeking primarily to justify our positions on the basis of traditional precedents we can locate. But, to my way of thinking, such efforts are often too impersonal, too detached, and too programmatic to actually permit an intimate engagement with the creative people of past eras that wrestled with similar challenges, arrived at thoughtful and carefully constructed responses, and authored these texts in the first place. Instead, the sources we select are primarily props, necessary resource tools to confirm our moral judgments and to demonstrate their Jewish pedigree, but they serve as no more than that.

Being a cultural historian fascinated with the history of Jewish doctors and medicine in their own right, I would like to evoke in this essay a different way of dealing with the past in relation to the present. I seek a more intimate and personalized connection with the history of our Jewish preoccupation with healing. I seek more than merely to collect halachic or homiletical data to bolster our specific medical positions. I would like to know more about the actual men and women who devoted their lives to medicine and healing in previous generations, their motivations, their accomplishments, and most significantly, how they saw themselves and their professional activities as Jewish in the first place.

What is at stake is the discovery of a broader and deeper perspective in which to situate medicine and healing at the very core of our Jewish identity. It is no coincidence that doctors, over a remarkably long time, were at the center of the Jewish cultural experience. Understanding their vital role in shaping Jewish culture, in engaging in the larger world as creative and inventive human beings, should be our first priority in studying medicine from a Jewish perspective. Jewish doctors, nurses, and other health care professionals need to examine the vital historical links between their professional and cultural identities. When a Jewish person chooses a career in health care, she is consciously connecting herself to a *shalshelet hakabbalah*, a chain of tradition, and participating in an experience that her ancestors always considered to be a vital part of what Jews do and how they engage with the societies in which they live. Viewed historically, Jewish physicians are in many ways comparable to rabbis in their relation to the Jewish communities they served. Like rabbis, they were always cultural intermediaries connecting high with low culture, Jewish with non-Jewish life, and humanity with the natural and spiritual worlds they inhabited. And often, rabbis and doctors were even the same persons, serving their Jewish constituencies with professional expertise both in

Jewish law and in medicine. I would like to illustrate these claims by offering some historical examples.

This is not the place to present a cursory history of Jewish medicine or even a brief inventory of Jewish doctors and their lives through the ages. Such a history is almost coterminous with the history of Judaism itself, comprising the medical dimension of biblical civilization; the preoccupations of the rabbis in Palestine and Babylonia with healing and the human body; the medical careers of Jewish luminaries under medieval Islam from Hasdai ibn Shaprut to Moses Maimonides; the high percentage of Jews among doctors, surgeons, midwifes, and other health care professionals under medieval Christendom; the entrance of a sizable number of Jewish students into medical schools in early modern Europe and their significant impact on the Jewish communities they served; and the dominant and conspicuous role of Jewish doctors in medical theory and practice both in Europe and in North America throughout the modern era.[1]

Instead, I offer a sampler of three succinct portraits to illustrate my point that the activity of healing in Jewish communities and particularly the interrelations between Judaism and medicine were profound and mutually fructifying over many centuries from rabbinic antiquity well into the modern age. My examples are taken from the period I know best, that of early modernity, a period in which the so-called scientific revolution emerged. But many examples could easily be located in other epochs to demonstrate repeatedly how significant and how wide ranging the connections between Jewish culture and medicine actually were. By presenting my three case studies, I hope to offer a model of how the study of Jewish physicians and medicine in the past might enrich and fortify our contemporary efforts to pursue medicine within the framework of our religious and cultural traditions.[2]

My first example comes from the late sixteenth and seventeenth centuries and focuses on the life experiences of two Hamburg physicians, conversos on the way to reclaiming their Jewish identities. The first was Rodrigo de Castro (1550–1627), and the second, his son Benedict (1597–1684). Rodrigo was born in Lisbon and lived as a Catholic, even baptizing his children. After publishing an important study of gynecology in 1603 in his newly adopted city of Hamburg, he completed another work called *Medicus Politicus* some eleven years later, which he describes in the title as a:

> Treatise of Medical Political Skills ... in which not only are the mores and virtues of good doctors explained and the frauds and impostures of bad ones unveiled ... A work very useful for doctors, patients, and nurses and for everyone interested in letters and politics.

It was about the same time that Rodrigo affiliated himself publicly with the Jewish community, coinciding as well with the rise of an affluent community of Portuguese conversos alongside the poorer Ashkenazic one already inhabiting the city of Hamburg-Altona.[3]

The *Medicus Politicus* is fascinating as testimony of Rodrigo's first embrace of his new Jewish identity. The centerpiece of his Jewish self-reflections is his eloquent commentary on Ben Sira 38, extolling the physician and his moral and religious role in the community. He regularly cites biblical passages, speaks of the divine origin of medicine, repudiates the notion of an exclusive Christian ministry of medicine, and even refers to the Kabbalah. His kabbalistic citations are surely the most interesting, compensating for his lack of rabbinic sources, and often presented through Christian Latin translations. For Rodrigo, Solomon best exemplified the political and social role of the physician. It was clear to Rodrigo that his professional responsibility extended into the social realm; physicians had the moral responsibility to lead their communities; and thus he promoted the notion of a "political physician." That Rodrigo could anchor this role in biblical and Jewish sources apparently made his transition into Judaism all the easier.[4]

Rodrigo's son, Benedict de Castro, also known as Baruch Nehamias, was already practicing medicine in Hamburg by 1622. He attained considerable success like his father and was eventually named physician-in-ordinary to Queen Christina of Sweden. Benedict was also fascinated by kabbalistic mysteries and became an avid supporter of the messianic figure Shabbetai Zevi in 1666. Even more so than his father, he was exceedingly public and confident about his Jewish identity and appreciated the unique role Jews, specifically Sephardim like him, played in the practice of medicine.

In 1631 he published in Latin an apologetic defense of Jewish physicians against an unnamed author who had recently published a vilification of them. By Benedict's time, there had already existed a long-standing tradition of anti-Semitism especially directed to the Jewish medical profession in Germany and specifically aimed at the newly arrived Sephardic doctors. Benedict sought to counter these charges by offering a general defense of the loyalty and piety of Jewish citizens, extolling the diagnostic abilities of Jewish physicians in his day and offering an honor roll of great Jewish physicians beginning with Moses and Solomon.

Like his father, Benedict extolled the divine function of the physician who holds power over life and death, grasps nature's secrets, and applies them practically: "Not for the sake of money, nor for the sake of honor, nor, finally, for the sake of ambition for their minds are only bent upon the expectation of better human health."[5] Benedict, like his father, defined medicine as a profession having moral and spiritual dimensions. But even more than his father, he explicitly underscored the holy task of the physician as a Jewish enterprise. Despite the paucity of his Jewish sources other than the Bible and Josephus, Benedict nevertheless displayed a powerful sense of Jewish pride, transforming the debasement and stigma of the converso doctor into a badge of honor. He closed his work with a moving elegy to the Jewish martyrs Eleazar and Hannah as described in II Maccabees, a transparent reference to the martyrs of the Inquisition. By recalling their memory, he linked his own fate with that of the Jewish community. Being a Jewish doctor ultimately came to be for him the primary expression of his evolving Jewish identity.[6]

My second portrait is that of Isaac Lampronti (1679–1756), the celebrated rabbi and physician of the city of Ferrara, memorialized until this day by a street named in his honor and by an inscription affixed to the building where he once lived.[7] Lampronti was trained by another distinguished Italian Jewish physician, Isaac Cantarini, matriculated in the medical school of Padua, and completed his rabbinical studies in Mantua. Having successfully pursued the dual tracks of rabbinics and medicine, he was hired to teach young Jewish students at the Italian Talmud Torah of Ferrara traditional Jewish subjects along with Hebrew grammar, Italian, and mathematics. His academic and homiletic interests soon consumed much of his time, so it appeared natural to him to involve his students in his other activities, first by translating his sermons delivered orally in Italian into Hebrew, and then by collecting materials for an ambitious project of creating a talmudic encyclopedia.

Lampronti's idea of using his students as assistants in his research was deemed unacceptable by the directors of the school who had hired him and he was ordered to stop employing them for his own purposes. He nevertheless persisted and succeeded in publishing three issues of the first journal devoted to Jewish law, the *Bikkurei Kezir Talmud Torah*, meant to be an initial forum, prepared in installments, for the eventual publication of his monumental encyclopedia, the *Pahad Yizhak*. Lampronti succeeded in completing part of the work before his death, although the entire set of volumes, the first work of its kind, appeared only later. He eventually headed the yeshivah in Ferrara while continuing to function as a physician, as is evidenced by his extensive medical correspondence with his teacher Cantarini and other Jewish physicians, much of which was included within the volumes of the encyclopedia itself.[8]

The *Pahad Yizhak* can be accurately described as a digest of halachic opinion, arranged in encyclopedic form according to the letters of the Hebrew alphabet, but it would be fair to describe it as a medical encyclopedia as well. In his discussion of halachic matters, Lampronti never missed the opportunity to discuss medical and scientific aspects of the law, to refer to contemporary medical opinions, to cite medical texts, and to enlist the opinions of other contemporary Jewish practitioners of medicine. But his inclusion of medical learning in a work purporting to deal with Jewish law is only a small indication of the revolutionary nature of his massive project. Both the social and educational setting in which the encyclopedia was created and the final product of the many tomes eventually appearing in published form suggest the novelty of his accomplishment.

In the first place, Lampronti's yeshivah resembled a scientific academy. The publication of his findings, first in the form of an academic journal and eventually in a scientific encyclopedia, indeed suggests the formation of an academic community of scholars and their students engaged in publishing papers and linking their individual findings in a collective publication. The final result of this undertaking

was a book unprecedented in Jewish legal history, a talmudic encyclopedia. The latter represented nothing less than a radical reorganization
of knowledge, assembling the scattered *sugiyot* (coherent units of discourse) of the Talmud and later medieval and contemporary responsa
in a new order according to subject matter and even organized chrono-
logically to some extent.

We could suggest that Lampronti had fully integrated his rabbinic
and scientific training in envisioning and carrying out this undertaking.
Rabbinical culture was now subjected to the mindset of contemporary
science and medicine, to the culture of the university. Like the basic
textbook of medicine, the medical encyclopedia, rabbinic knowledge
could now be structured along similar paths to make it more accessible
to the scholar accustomed to approaching unwieldy knowledge
through reference guides.

Lampronti had not merely functioned along two parallel professional paths, that of the doctor and the rabbi. In his mind, they were
one: medical ideas flowed freely and naturally from halachic discourse
and vice versa. And rabbinic literature could be more effectively presented and studied by organizing it in the manner in which other scientific disciplines were studied and mastered. The process of integrating
his two professional preoccupations seems innocent and uncontrover-
sial on the surface; the *Pahad Yizhak* was to become the progenitor of
the widely used *Encyclopedia Talmudit* of our own day. But surely
Lampronti's daring act was more radical and subversive than it might
first appear. The two worlds he inhabited, that of Halacha and medicine, not only stood side by side in a harmonic mode of coexistence;
they were amalgamated into one. Being a rabbi, for Lampronti and his
colleagues, required medical expertise, and being a doctor required rabbinic knowledge. The two disciplines could not be segregated or com-
partmentalized into Torah and *maddah* (non-Jewish learning, science),
for Torah was identical with *maddah*, and thus rabbinics and medicine
were indispensable to and intrinsically fused with each other.

Lampronti's achievement constituted the culmination of a peda-
gogic and cultural practice that had begun several centuries earlier
with the creation of Jewish preparatory schools that had dual curricula
for students wishing to enter medical schools such as that in Padua. As
far back as the late fifteenth century Judah Messer Leon, the

rabbi/physician of Mantua, offered his students a similar program. In the sixteenth century he was followed by David Provençal who actually proposed a Jewish school where Judaism and the sciences would be taught together. In the late seventeenth and early eighteenth centuries his ideal was fully implemented by yet another Jewish physician Solomon Conegliano in Padua. By the time Conegliano was running his school, hundreds of Jewish students had successfully completed the dual tracks of rabbinics and medicine, assuming medical or rabbinic posts, or both, throughout the Italian peninsula but also throughout Europe. For them and their descendents, Lampronti's rabbinic encyclopedia was a welcome and natural outcome of their educational and cultural aspirations.[9]

The most illustrious graduate of Solomon Conegliano's preparatory school was surely Tobias Cohen (1652–1729), our third and final portrait. Tobias was born in Metz, growing up in the home of a physician and rabbi who had fled Poland during the Chemelnicki pogroms of 1648. He studied in the yeshivah in Cracow before entering the medical school of the University of Frankfurt an der Oder in 1678 under a special arrangement. Tobias and his friend Gabriel Felix of Brody found it impossible, however, to study in Frankfurt as Jews so they traveled south to the more tolerant surroundings of the University of Padua. There both Tobias and Gabriel received support from Conegliano and matriculated as doctors of philosophy and medicine in 1683. Upon graduation Tobias pursued a distinguished medical career in the Ottoman Empire, finally settling in Jerusalem where he died.

The primary source for understanding Tobias and his world is his *Ma'aseh Tuviyyah*, surely the most influential early modern Hebrew textbook of medicine and the sciences, published first in Venice in 1707 and then repeatedly republished, most recently in Brooklyn in 1974. I have treated this author and book more extensively elsewhere. Here I will focus primarily on the connection between Tobias's self-image as a doctor and purveyor of the sciences and his Jewish identity. Tobias's work is, to my knowledge, the most self-conscious effort of any premodern physician to link his Jewish identity with his medical knowledge.[10]

In the introduction to his medical work, Tobias articulates his desire to present the latest medical information to doctors and laypersons in a simple and accessible manner, even utilizing diagrams and pictures throughout. But there is more at stake than simply disseminating knowledge, as the reader immediately appreciates when Tobias inserts his life experiences that led up to this publication. He writes, first and foremost, with a deep-seated sense of cultural inferiority, surely stemming from the negative experiences he encountered as a Jew among the student population of Frankfurt. He is obsessed with the need to respond to those gentiles—

> who vex us, raising their voices without restraint, speaking haughtily with arrogance and scorn, telling us we have no mouth to respond, nor a forehead to raise our heads in matters of faith, and that our knowledge and ancient intelligence have been lost, as I heard the slander of many from the surrounding den during the days of my youth. The truth of the matter is that because of our many sins men of learning are lost and we have no one who knows how to answer [our adversaries] with an appropriate winning response.[11]

Tobias's text is thus his own attempt to construct "a winning response," to reply to those who ridicule Jews for their lack of up-to-date knowledge, who consider their culture inferior to all the rest. There is clearly a sense of urgency that Tobias conveys. He lives in a world where the learning of non-Jewish culture has overtaken that of the Jews, in which the Jewish minority feels more inferior than ever before. And lack of scientific knowledge is apparently a sign of theological deficiency as well. Since the knowledge of Jews has been lost, they have proved incapable "to raise our heads in matters of faith." Tobias's effort to demonstrate to the world that Jews are not as stupid as they appear is just as much about religious apologetics as it is about imparting medical knowledge.

Of course Tobias composed his work not in the languages most Christians could read but in Hebrew. The book was obviously addressed to Jews, to reassure them of their cultural worth, and to demonstrate, by providing the latest and most reliable scholarship in the medical sciences, that they had not fallen so far behind as they had imagined. Tobias himself was the living embodiment of how a Jew deprived of the opportunities available to others could overcome his limitations to produce a work equal to and even surpassing any equivalent work written in other European languages. In other words, writing on medicine in Hebrew fully confirmed the label long associated with his coreligionists of still being "a wise and discerning people" (Deuteronomy 4:6). It also provided the direct link he sought between his medical texts and earlier defenses of the Jewish faith such as those of Saadia Gaon, Judah Halevi, Isaac Abravanel, and the Maharal of Prague.

The most revealing testimony about Tobias's motivation in composing his sophisticated treatise comes in a section that surprisingly discusses a phenomenon having nothing to do with medicine or healing at all: the pathetic obsession of some contemporary Jews with false messiahs. Although he had opened his textbook in the style of similar Latin works, with a brief theological section on God, creation, and revelation, a discussion of the messianic idea of Judaism in general and of Shabbetai Zevi in particular, the quintessential false messiah of his generation, might certainly seem bizarre and out of place in such a work. The inordinate amount of space he devotes to this subject indeed requires a satisfying explanation.

In recent years, scholars have noted to what degree Shabbetai Zevi was known in the Christian world and was especially held up for derision as an example of the lunacy and barbarity of Jewish belief and practice. Christian polemicists saw the Jewish enthusiasts of Shabbetai Zevi as easy prey in encouraging them to approach the baptismal font and in removing the blinders of their allegedly inferior faith. Several of Tobias's Jewish contemporaries fully appreciated the vulnerability of Jews to Christian missionaries and noted the communal disintegration the Sabbatean movement had wrought throughout the European continent. Tobias shared intensely the same anxiety, believing that the messianic obsession and the particular frenzy surrounding Shabbetai Zevi "gave our enemies an opportunity to make fun of us and to defame us, almost providing a sword in the hands of the Gentiles to kill us."[12]

We should recognize immediately the similarity between the opening lines of Tobias's preface to his text with those uttered about the phenomenon of messianic delusion. They underscore a common obsession with both the self-image and the external representation of Jewish culture to Jews and non-Jews alike. For Tobias, medical and scientific knowledge is the perfect antidote to messianic self-deception and enthusiasm. Being "a wise and discerning nation" meant for him a repudiation of irrational and delusional messianic behavior, on the one hand, and an appropriation of the latest and most sophisticated medical data on the other. Jewish doctors, in Tobias's eyes, armed with their scientific knowledge and their consequent theological sophistication, were the only ones qualified to lead Judaism out of its present morass. They were the only ones capable of reclaiming the proper image of Jewish culture tarnished by the messianic pretenders and of setting it on the right rational and enlightened course. Tobias was apparently unfamiliar with the aforementioned converso doctor, Benedict de Castro, who, despite his scientific background, had still become an avid follower of Shabbetai Zevi!

In fact, Tobias had no doubt whatsoever regarding the unique leadership role and the elite status university-trained doctors held within the Jewish community:

> Don't the unintelligent realize that a person is not called a scholar without knowledge, nor a doctor without a doctorate, nor distinguished or ordained without rabbinical ordination? Moreover, no Jew in all of Italy, Poland, Germany, and France would ever consider studying the science of medicine without first stuffing himself with the written and oral Torah as well as the other sciences, as is the case for the large number of students of my teacher ... Solomon Conegliano, as I can personally testify, among them those who become rabbis and physicians to kings and great nobles. And among all of them, I am the least significant.[13]

Notwithstanding his expression of false modesty at the end, Tobias well articulates in this passage the intimate connection between medicine and rabbinic learning, between scientific knowledge and piety, and between the status of the university physician and the positive image the Jewish community needed to project. Being a Jewish doctor thus meant considerably more to him than healing the sick; it meant providing a proper model of Jewish leadership to a community in desperate need of rehabilitation and repair.[14]

How refreshing and how inspiring are the profiles of Rodrigo and Benedict de Castro, Isaac Lampronti, and Tobias Cohen to our generation in search of our Jewish moorings. For each of them, being a physician was a striking demonstration of Jewish advocacy and Jewish commitment. They could never imagine their professional status to be unrelated to their religious and cultural concerns. There is something humbling and profoundly moving in each of their life stories, in the creative ways they integrated their medical careers into the very matrix of their Jewish identities, and in their own self-awareness that being a doctor was an obvious way of living their lives Jewishly and working on behalf of the community they loved. It is that merger between the medical profession and Jewish religion and culture that the historical study of Jewish doctors reveals time and time again in variegated periods and contexts. These three portraits thus illustrate how the rich resources of our historical past might invigorate our own attempts to reconnect the links between medicine and Judaism in the unique and challenging world we inhabit.

NOTES

The following abbreviations have been used in the notes: M. = Mishnah (edited c. 200 CE); T. = Tosefta (also edited c. 200 CE); J. = Jerusalem (Palestinian) Talmud (edited c. 400 CE); B. = Babylonian Talmud (edited c. 500 C.E.); M.T. = Maimonides' *Mishneh Torah* (1177 CE); and S.A. = Joseph Karo's *Shulchan Aruch* (1567 CE), with glosses by Moses Isserles.

1. The Importance of the Individual in Jewish Thought and Writing

1. By modern Jewish thought I, following Eliezer Schweid, mean the body of (more or less) systematic reflection by Jews informed with knowledge of their people's history and tradition upon the situation of Jews and/or Judaism in the modern political, economic, social, and cultural orders, with the aim of securing the survival (and if possible the thriving) of Jews and/or Judaism. Schweid is justly driven by this definition to count Spinoza's *Theologico-Political Treatise* as part of the prehistory of modern Jewish thought but not the actual "corpus" itself, since that work does not see much point in the survival of Judaism as a distinct religious tradition, and therefore does not see much point in the survival of Jews. See Eliezer Schweid, *A History of Jewish Thought in Modern Times* (Hebrew; Jerusalem: Keter, 1977): pp. 7–30.

2. For a valuable introduction in English to Kook's writings, see Benjamin Ish-Shalom, *Rav Avraham Itzhak HaCohen Kook: Between Rationalism and Mysticism*, trans. Ora Wiskind-Elper (Albany: SUNY Press, 1993). A good selection from Kook's huge oeuvre is available in Abraham Isaac Kook, *The Lights of Penitence* [and other works], trans. Ben Zion Bokser (New York: Paulist Press, 1978). Kook's psychological acuity (and so his relevance to our concern with health and healing) is particularly evident in chapters 8–9.

3. See for example Martin Buber, *I and Thou*, trans. Walter Kaufmann (New York: Charles Scribner's Sons, 1970), especially Part I; "Dialogue Between Martin Buber and Carl R. Rogers," in Martin Buber, *The Knowledge of Man*, trans. Maurice Friedman and Ronald Gregor Smith (New York: Harper Torchbooks, 1965): pp. 166–84; and Rollo May, "The Origins and Significance of the Existential Movement in Psychology," in *Existence*, ed. Rollo May, Ernest Angel, and Henri F. Ellenberger (New York: Simon and Schuster, 1958): p. 16n.

4. Abraham Joshua Heschel, "The Patient as Person," in *The Insecurity of Freedom* (Philadelphia: Jewish Publication Society, 1966): pp. 24–38; Joseph B. Soloveitchik, "A Halakhic Approach to Suffering," in *The Torah U-Madda Journal* 8 (1998–99): pp. 3–24; and "Catharsis," in *Tradition* 17.2 (Spring 1978): pp. 38–54.

5. Abraham J. Heschel. "The Individual Jew and His Obligations" in *The Insecurity of Freedom* (repr., New York: Schocken, 1987): p. 191.

6. Heschel might have been expressing wariness of Ben Gurion's bid to appropriate both religious language and the Jewish agenda in the attempt to build up the young state he headed; Heschel might also have been critiquing Mordecai Kaplan's conception of Judaism as "civilization" rather than religion and Kaplan's attendant emphasis on Jewish group life rather than on the spiritual well-being of the individual. See the patent critique of Kaplan's view of prayer in Abraham Joshua Heschel, *Quest for God* (New York: Crossroad, 1986): p. 54. Ironically, Kaplan faulted his mentor Ahad Ha'am for focusing exclusively on the Jewish people to the exclusion of concern with the individual. See Mordecai M. Kaplan, *Judaism as a Civilization* (Philadelphia: Jewish Publication Society, 1994): p. 282.

7. Franz Rosenzweig, *The Star of Redemption*, trans. William W. Hallo (Boston: Beacon Press, 1972): p. 3.

8. Franz Rosenzweig, *Understanding the Sick and the Healthy: A View of World, Man, and God*, ed. N. N. Glatzer (Cambridge, MA: Harvard University Press, 1999): pp. 39–41.

9. See Rosenzweig's important and related essay, "The New Thinking," conveniently available in *Franz Rosenzweig's "The New Thinking,"* ed. and trans. Alan Udoff and Barbara E. Galli (Syracuse, NY: Syracuse University Press, 1999).

10. Ibid., p. 89.

11. Ibid., p. 93.

12. Hilary Putnam compares Rosenzweig's thought on truth and philosophy to that of Ludwig Wittgenstein and William James. See his introduction to *Understanding the Sick and the Healthy*, pp. 1–20.

13. Abraham Joshua Heschel, "The Sabbath: Its Meaning for Modern Man," in *The Earth Is the Lord's;* and *The Sabbath* (New York: Harper Torchbooks, 1966); and *Man Is Not Alone* (New York: Harper Torchbooks, 1966): pp. 71, 77.

14. Joseph B. Soloveitchik, *The Lonely Man of Faith* (New York: Doubleday, 1992): p. 103. Soloveitchik's essay has pronounced affinities to Buber's depiction of the two sorts of self that consist in two sorts of relation: one (It) in which we treat the world (and human beings, and God) as means to our own ends, while in the other (You) we open ourselves, make ourselves fully present, and engage in relationships.

15. Jürgen Habermas, *The Philosophical Discourse of Modernity*, trans. Frederick Lawrence (Cambridge, MA: The MIT Press, 1991).

16. It should be noted, however, that Kaplan's critique of American society—and particularly of capitalism—in his great work, *Judaism as a Civilization* (Philadelphia: Jewish Publication Society, 1994; originally published 1934) was remarkable. See for example the discussion of "economic justice" on pp. 471–78.

17. Michael Wyschogrod, *The Body of Faith: Judaism as Corporeal Election* (New York: Seabury Press, 1983): pp. 1–9.

18. See the groundbreaking essay by Hava Tirosh-Rothschild, "Dare to Know": Feminism and the Discipline of Jewish Philosophy," in *Feminist Perspectives on Jewish Studies*, ed. Lynn Davidman and Shelly Tenenbaum (New Haven, CT: Yale University Press, 1994): pp. 85–119.

19. Shulamit Magnus, "Pauline Wengeroff and the Voice of Jewish Modernity," in *Gender and Judaism: The Transformation of Tradition* (New York: New York University Press); and Marion A. Kaplan, *The Making of the Jewish Middle Class* (New York, NY: Oxford University Press, 1991).

20. Arnold Eisen, "Re-reading Heschel on the Commandments," in *Modern Judaism* 9:1 (Febuary 1989): pp. 1–33.

21. On Heschel's debt to Hasidism, see Arthur Green, "Three Warsaw Mystics," in *Jerusalem Studies in Jewish Thought* 13 (1996): pp. 1–58.

22. I draw here on Nietzsche's brilliant and well-known distinction between "Apollonian" and "Dionysian" in his analysis of Greek tragedy. See Friedrich Nietzsche, *The Birth of Tragedy*, trans. Walter Kaufmann (New York: Vintage Books, 1967).

23. Rosenzweig, *The Star of Redemption*, pp. 324–27.

24. I owe this insight into one possible meaning of sacrifice to Wyschogrod, *Body of Faith*, pp. 17–21. No recent scholar has done more to further understanding of Leviticus than Jacob Milgrom. See his commentaries on *Leviticus* in the Anchor Bible series (New York: Doubleday, 1991, 2000).

25. I owe the notion of sacred order to conversation with my teacher Philip Rieff.

26. Heschel, *Man Is Not Alone*, pp. 294–96.

27. Rosenzweig, *Understanding*, pp. 32, 103. Zachary Braiterman has perceptively critiqued Rosenzweig's preoccupation with death in "'Into Life'? Franz Rosenzweig and the Figure of Death," in *AJS Review* 23:2 (1998): pp. 203–21.

28. Neil Gillman, *The Death of Death: Resurrection and Immortality in Jewish Thought* (Woodstock, VT: Jewish Lights Publishing, 2000).

29. For more on this theme, see Arnold Eisen, *Rethinking Modern Judaism: Ritual, Commandment, Community* (Chicago: University of Chicago Press, 1998): ch. 7.

30. Emil Fackenheim. *God's Presence in History: Jewish Affirmations and Philosophical Reflections* (New York: Harper Torchbooks, 1970): pp. 20–21.

31. Martha Nussbaum, *Poetic Justice: The Literary Imagination and Public Life* (Boston: Beacon Press, 1995): pp. xvi, 2, 4, 8.

32. Saul Bellow, *Humboldt's Gift* (New York: Penguin Books, 1996). All page numbers given in the text refer to this edition.

2. Health and Healing among the Mystics

1. From his "Tale of the Seven Beggars." Translation from my discussion in *Tormented Master: A Life of Rabbi Nahman of Breslov* (Birmingham: University of Alabama Press, 1979).

2. The reader is referred to a more extended discussion in my book *EHYEH: A Kabbalah for Tomorrow* (Woodstock, VT: Jewish Lights, 2002), especially the chapter on the *sefirot*, pp. 39–60.

3. This nexus between spiritual centeredness and physiological balance has been developed with nuance in several contemporary works on the meditative practice of mindfulness. Representative among these are: Thich Nhat Hanh, *The Miracle of Mindfulness: An Introduction to the Practice of Meditation* (Boston: Beacon Press, 1976); Jack Kornfield, *The Path Is the Heart: A Guide Through the Perils and Promises of Spiritual Life* (New York: Bantam Books, 1993).

4. This work was published in Benson's *The Relaxation Response* (New York: Random House, 1992 [first published by HarperTorch, 1975]).

5. Consider the potent and knowledgable integration of these dimensions in Melinda Ribner, *Everyday Kabbalah: A Practical Guide to Jewish Meditation, Healing, and Personal Growth* (Sacramento: Citadel Press, 1998).

6. See, for example, Moshe Cordovero, *Pardes Rimmonim*, 17:4; Isaiah Horowitz, *Shnei Luhot ha-Brit*, Commentary on *Masekhet Pesahim*, 6:8.

7. The classic source for this tradition is *Genesis Rabbah*, 1:1, but it was preserved as well through the Aramaic translation and interpretive paraphrase of the Hebrew Bible, the *Targum Yerushalmi*.

8. It is important to note the clear correlations between this early Jewish exegesis and that of early Christianity in the opening lines of the *Gospel of John*: "In the beginning was the Word, and the Word was with God." In the Christian interpretation, the pre-existent Word was the spiritual nature of Jesus Christ, and the metaphysical word of God became manifest in the physical world through the incarnation of the Christ—and thus Word became flesh. It would not be much of a stretch to see the parallel exegeses of *Genesis Rabbah* and the *Gospel of John* as competing interpretations of the correlation between Genesis 1 and Proverbs 8. To frame the matter in the discourse of Late Antiquity: was the wisdom that antedated the world and accompanied God in primordial times the spiritual and pre-existent Torah (the rabbinic-midrashic view), or was it the spiritual and preincarnational Christ (the Judaeo-Christian view of the New Testament)? Both of these views reflect a logos-oriented theology. For more extended reflection on this relationship, and on the *Gospel of John* as a text of Judaeo-Christian

Midrash, see Daniel Boyarin, *Border Lines: The Partition of Judaeo-Christianity* (Philadelphia: University of Pennsylvania Press, 2004).

9. See, for example, William Collinge, *The American Holistic Health Association Complete Guide to Alternative Medicine* (New York: Warner Books, 1997).

3. Hope and the Hebrew Bible

1. As W. H. McNeill points out in his book *Plagues and Peoples* (Garden City, NJ: Doubleday, 1976): p. 284, disease has always been more lethal than enemy weapons among premodern armies. See also Carol Meyers, *Discovering Eve: Israelite Women in Context* (New York: Oxford University Press, 1988): pp. 64–71 for specific applications to the biblical world.

2. Mary Douglas, *Leviticus as Literature* (New York: Oxford University Press, 1999).

3. Jocee Hudson, "D'var Torah" (Los Angeles: unpublished paper, 2003).

4. Douglas, *Leviticus*, p. 45.

5. Ibid., p. 46.

6. Hector Avalos, *Illness and Health Care in the Ancient Near East: The Role of the Temple in Greece, Mesopotamia and Israel*, Harvard Semitic Monographs (Cambridge, MA, 1995).

7. Arthur Kleinman, *Patients and Healers in the Context of Culture* (Berkeley: University of California Press, 1980): p. 72. Cited in John Dominic Crossan, *The Birth of Christianity: Discovering What Happened in the Years Immediately after the Execution of Jesus* (San Francisco, CA: Harper, 1998): p. 294.

8. Arthur Kleinman and Lilias H. Sung, "Why Do Indigenous Practitioners Successfully Heal?" *Social Science and Medicine* 13B (1979): pp. 7–26.

9. McNeill, *Plagues and Peoples*.

10. F. Brown, S. Driver, and C. Briggs, *The New Brown-Driver-Briggs Hebrew and English Lexicon* (Peabody, MA: Hendrickson Publishers, 1996).

11. The expression comes from the title of Phyllis Trible's book, *Texts of Terror: Literary-Feminist Readings of Biblical Narratives*, Overtures to Biblical Theology (Philadelphia: Fortress Press, 1984).

12. *The New Oxford Annotated Bible* (New York: Oxford University Press, 2001).

13. JPS translation with one modification: I render "person" instead of "woman" to represent Koheleth's message in a gender-neutral fashion. Koheleth throughout seems to be specifically addressing a young man (see 11:9).

14. The lecture format, the original setting of this essay, did not allow enough time to develop this section on Esther and other parts of the Megillot in great detail. For a fuller exposition, see my forthcoming book, *The Bible and the Seasons of Life*.

15. On Esther as a book of "laughter and liberation," see Chapter 3, "Liberation and Laughter: Exodus and Esther," in J. William Whedbee's book, *The Bible and the*

Comic Vision (New York: Cambridge University Press, 199; and repr. Philadelphia: Fortress Press, 2002), pp. 129–91. I dedicate this essay to Bill Whedbee, my husband, who died in 2004, and who even in illness was able to demonstrate the celebrative vision of life in the midst of sorrow and loss.

16. All quotes from Tamara Eskenazi are from her May 14, 2003, address, " 'Is there no balm...? Is there no healer?' (Jeremiah 8:22): Biblical Reflections on Holiness, Health and Hope."

17. Ibid.

18. The translations of passages in Genesis and I Samuel originate with Robert Alter, *Genesis: Translation and Commentary* (New York: W. W. Norton, 1996) and *The David Story* (New York: W. W. Norton, 1999). Those for Ruth are mine or taken from the *Hebrew English Tanakh* (Philadelphia: 1999). I will note my own translations. These include the literal "the opening of eyes" translated both by Alter (p. 220) and the JPS as "the entrance to Enaim."

19. Note that one of the ways in which this story can be read in comparison and in contrast with that of Ruth and Boaz is that unlike Judah's second son, Boaz is quite willing to fulfill the levirate responsibility on behalf of Ruth's dead husband, even though his is a far more distant family tie.

20. Alter, ibid., p. 221.

21. Due to constraints of length, I cannot discuss Hannah's wonderful poem found in I Samuel 2, a poem that introduces the major themes of the stories of the first two kings of Israel, Saul and David. Hannah's unusually vocal presence in the text as well as the fact that she initiates the sacrifice at the time of Samuel's entry to the Temple service are both discussed in a very interesting article by Carol Meyers, "Hannah and Her Sacrifice," in *A Feminist Companion to Samuel and Kings*, ed. Athalya Brenner (Sheffield, UK: Sheffield Academic Press, 1994): pp. 68–104. Within the biblical context, barren women most often conceive because of God's intervention on their behalf. We know too well that in our time, infertility is a real and grievous situation for many couples who sadly will not experience the relief afforded a biblical Sarah or Hannah.

22. Brown, Driver, and Briggs, *Hebrew and English Lexicon*, p. 630.

4. From Disability to Enablement

1. Genesis 15:2–4; 18:1–15; 25:21; 30:1–8, 22–24; 35:16–20; I Samuel 1:1–20.

2. Isaac: Genesis 27:1; Jacob: Genesis 48:10.

3. Genesis 32:25, 31–32.

4. Exodus 4:10.

5. Nahum of Gimzo: B. *Ta'anit* 21a. Dosa ben Harkinas: B. *Yevamot* 16a. Rav Joseph and Rav Sheshet: B. *Bava Kamma* 87a. There were also a number of anonymous, blind scholars: B. *Haggigah* 5b; J. *Pe'ah*, end.

6. Genesis 1:27; 5:1; 9:6.

7. Deuteronomy 21:22–23.

8. M. *Oholot* 7:6.

9. Leviticus 19:14.

10. Leviticus 21:17–21.

11. Maimonides, *Guide to the Perplexed* 3:45.

12. Deuteronomy 23:2; see commentary on that verse in *Etz Hayim* (Philadelphia: Jewish Publication Society, 2002): p. 1122.

13. *Heresh* as deaf-mute: M. *Terumot* 1:2. *Heresh* as deaf but not mute, with *ileim* describing a mute: B. *Haggigah* 2b.

14. B. *Megillah* 24a–24b; S.A. *Orah Hayyim* 69:2.

15. M.T. *Laws of Fringes* 3:7.

16. I am drawing this list from the work of Carl Astor, *Who Made People Different: Jewish Perspectives on the Disabled* (New York: United Synagogue of America, 1985): chapter 4, a book that I heartily recommend in its entirety. In the Talmud, whether the deaf are obligated to recite the *Shema* is disputed (B. *Berakhot* 15a), but the codes rule that a deaf person can fulfill the commandment: M.T. *Laws of Reading the Shema* 2:8; S.A. *Orah Hayyim* 62:3.

17. That the Torah must be read: B. *Gittin* 60b. That blind people are therefore excluded from reciting it for the congregation: S.A. *Orah Hayyim* 53:14; 139:4. That the blind may be called to recite the blessings over the Torah: Moses Isserles, gloss and the commentary of the *TaZ (Turei Zahav)* by Rabbi David ben Samuel Ha-Levi there.

18. Astor, *Who Made People Different*, pp. 75, 107–109.

19. S.A. *Orah Hayyim* 53:14.

20. B. *Megillah* 19b; S.A. *Orah Hayyim* 689:2. M.T. *Laws of the Megillah* 1:2, however, leaves out the *heresh* as an excluded category.

21. B. *Peshaim* 116b.

22. M.T. *Laws of Slaughter* 4:5; see, however, B. *Hullin* 2a, where this special circumstance permitting the animals that they slaughter for consumption is not mentioned.

23. S.A. *Orah Hayyim* 589:1–2 with the glosses of R. Moses Isserles and the *Magen Avraham* there.

24. M.T. *Laws of Acquisition (Zekhiyah)* 4:6–7.

25. M.T. *Laws of Inheritance (Nahalot)* 6:1; 10:5. As for inheritance from a spouse, marriage to a deaf-mute or insane person is valid only by rabbinic, and not by biblical authority, because such people could not be presumed to be of sound mind and could not pronounce the blessings with the proper intent. Therefore the usual biblical laws of inheritance, where property is passed on automatically to relatives in a prescribed order, do not apply, and the property is treated as gifts. A deaf-mute cannot give gifts but can receive them. Thus a woman who is deaf cannot transfer property to her husband, but a man who is deaf can receive property from his hearing wife (M.T. *Laws of Marriage* 22:4).

26. M.T. *Laws of Sale* 29:1.

27. B. *Gittin* 59a, 67b.

28. M.T. *Laws of Sale* 29:3–4.

29. M.T. *Laws of Sale* 29:5.

30. B. *Gittin* 59b.

31. M.T. *Laws of Testimony* 9:9.

32. B. *Gittin* 71a.

33. M.T. *Laws of Testimony* 9:11.

34. M.T. *Laws of Testimony* 9:12.

35. B. *Niddah* 50a.

36. B. *Yevamot* 112b.

37. B. *Yevamot* 81a.

38. B. *Bava Kamma* 86b.

39. Deuteronomy 8:17–18; see verses 11–18 to understand the context.

40. B. *Bava Kamma* 86b.

41. Exodus 19:6.

42. Erving Goffman, *Stigma: Notes on the Management of Spoiled Identity* (New York: Simon and Schuster, 1963).

43. Leviticus 21:16.

44. Leviticus 13:45.

5. Overcoming Stigma

1. An earlier version of this article, "Thinking About Stigma: What the Health and Human Rights Movement and the Jewish Health and Healing Movement Can Learn from Each Other," was the opening plenary presentation at the Partners' Gathering of the Kalsman Institute on Judaism and Health, Hebrew Union College–Jewish Institute of Religion, Los Angeles. The text of that presentation and a video excerpt were available on the Internet at www.huc.edu/kalsman/ projects/p2 as of Nov. 2, 2011. My thanks to William Cutter for joining me in the conversation.

My thanks, as well, to Rachel Adler of Hebrew Union College, Los Angeles, for her careful reading of the texts discussed in her companion essay, and for the conversation we began nineteen years ago. When I asked whether she was familiar with Mary Douglas's work on contagion and pollution, she demurely replied that she had found it of great help to an article she had once written on *mikveh*. I was grateful for her forbearance then, and for so much more ever since.

2. Bob Dylan, "It's All Right Ma (I'm Only Bleeding)," (1965; 1993).

3. Erving Goffman, *Stigma: Notes on the Management of Spoiled Identity* (New York: Simon and Schuster, 1963).

4. Ecclesiastes 3:1–2, *JPS Hebrew-English Tanakh* (Philadelphia: Jewish Publication Society, 1999).

5. See, for instance, Ernest Becker, *The Denial of Death* (New York: Free Press, 1973).

6. Spoken introduction to "Love Me, I'm a Liberal," *Phil Ochs in Concert* (1966), available on *There but for Fortune* (1989).

7. Nicky James, "From Vision to System: The Maturing of the Hospice Movement," in *Death Rites: Law and Ethics at the End of Life,* ed. Robert Lee and Derek Morgan (New York: Routledge, 1994): pp. 102–130.

8. Herman Feifel, ed., *The Meaning of Death* (New York: McGraw Hill, 1959).

9. Dennis Hevisi, "Zelda Foster, 71, Pioneer in Hospice Care," obituary, *New York Times,* July 13, 2006.

10. Elisabeth Kübler-Ross, *On Death and Dying* (New York: MacMillan, 1969).

11. Jewish Hospice Commission of Los Angeles (hereafter "JHCLA"), *A Hospice Guide for Care of Jewish Patients and Families* (1983); JHCLA, *The Hospice Guide for Jewish Families* (1984); JHCLA, *Let Me Help You: The Hospice Guide for Jewish Patients* (1985).

12. See generally, William H. McNeill, *Plagues and People* (Garden City, NY: Doubleday, 1976).

13. For a simple, current description of this law and public health partnership, see David I. Schulman, "Making a Difference with HIV Legal Checkups," *Human Rights* 31:4 (2004): 18, a civil rights quarterly published by the American Bar Association. Available as of Nov. 2, 2011, at www.abanet.org/irr/hr/fall04/checkups.htm.

14. David I. Schulman, "AIDS Discrimination: Its Nature, Meaning and Function," *Nova Law Review* 12:3 (1988): 1113 (expanded version of testimony before the Presidential Commission on the Human Immunodeficiency Virus Epidemic, Vanderbilt University, Nashville, TN, March 16, 1988). Available as of Nov. 2, 2011, at www.aegis.org/law/journals/1988/alaw0003.html. See also, David I. Schulman, "AIDS, the Law and Society: Fact vs. Fear," *Los Angeles Lawyer* 11:6 (September 1988): 19. Available as of Nov. 2, 2011, at www.aegis.org/law/journals/1988/alaw0019.html.

15. Dr. Jack Provonsha (Loma Linda School of Medicine) speaking at a Los Angeles–area conference on death and dying sponsored by the National Conference of Christians and Jews, April 1977.

16. Jacob Milgrom, Leviticus 1–16, in *The Anchor Bible,* vol. 3. (New York: Doubleday, 1991): p. 803.

17. Paul Monette, *Borrowed Time: An AIDS Memoir* (San Diego: Harcourt Brace Jovanovich, 1988): pp. 45–46.

18. Mary Douglas, *Purity and Danger: An Analysis of the Concepts of Pollution and Taboo* (New York: Routledge Classics, 2002).

19. Goffman, *Stigma.*

20. In a conversation, Tamara Eskenazi remarked that Leviticus was the least violent book of the Torah.

21. Rachel Adler, "Tum'ah and Taharah: Ends and Beginnings," in ed., Michael Strassfeld, Sharon Strassfeld, and Richard Siegal, *The Jewish Catalogue* (New York: Jewish Publication Society, 1972).

22. Milgrom, Leviticus 1–16, p. 817.

23. Milgrom, ibid., p. 819.

24. Ibid.

25. On *Met Mitzvah*, the unclaimed corpse, see Adin Steinsaltz, *The Talmud: A Reference Guide*, trans. Rabbi Israel V. Berman (New York: Random House, 1989): p. 225.

26. Elaine Scarry, *The Body in Pain: The Making and Unmaking of the World* (Oxford: Oxford University Press, 1985).

27. Mary Douglas, "In the Wilderness: The Doctrine of Defilement in the Book of Numbers," *Journal for the Study of the Old Testament Supplement Series* 158 (Sheffield, England: JSOT Press, 1993).

28. I Kings 17:17–24; II Kings 4:8–37, 5, 13:21.

29. Milgrom, Leviticus 1–16, pp. 837–38.

30. The *nazirite* who has incurred impurity shaves all his hair and discards it like the *metzora*, however.

31. Baruch Levine, *Leviticus JPS Torah Commentary* (Philadelphia: Jewish Publication Society, 1989): p. 86.

32. Milgrom, Leviticus 1–16, p. 803.

33. Levine, ibid., p. 82. Hyam Maccoby, *Ritual and Morality: The Ritual Purity System and Its Place in Judaism* (Cambridge: Cambridge University Press, 1999): p. 125.

34. Saul M. Olyan, *Biblical Mourning: Ritual and Social Dimensions* (Oxford: Oxford University Press, 2004): pp. 39–43.

35. Irving Greenberg, *The Jewish Way* (New York: Summit Books, 1988): p. 208.

36. Women also mourn but their mourning is a deviation from the male norm in that certain restrictions do not apply to them because they did not have those *mitzvot* in the first place.

37. Milgrom, Leviticus 1–16, p. 803. Ibn Ezra, Leviticus 13:45, loc. cit.

38. Emmanuel Levinas, "The Face" in *Ethics and Infinity: Conversations with Philippe Nemo*, trans. Richard A. Cohen (Pittsburgh: Duquesne University Press, 1985): pp. 85–92.

39. It is not, however, impure in its entirety or the first purification ritual for the *metzora* could not be efficacious. Milgrom, Leviticus 1–16, p. 262.

40. B.T. *Berakhot* 5b.

41. Sylvie-Anne Goldberg, *Crossing the Jabbok* (Berkeley: University of California Press, 1989): pp. 75–99.

42. B. *Shabbat* 151a.

43. Mircea Eliade, *The Sacred and the Profane* (New York: Harcourt, Brace and Company, 1959): pp. 130–31.

44. Samuel Heilman, *When a Jew Dies* (Berkeley: University of California Press, 2001): p. 55.
45. Ibid., pp. 31–71.
46. Mary Douglas, *Leviticus as Literature* (New York: Oxford University Press, 1999).
47. Rachel Adler, "In Your Blood, Live," *Tikkun.*

6. Jewish Bioethics in Story and Law

1. Louis E. Newman, *An Introduction to Jewish Ethics* (Upper Saddle River, NJ: Pearson Prentice Hall, 2005): p. 139.
2. Yitzchok Breitowitz, "What's So Bad About Human Cloning?" *Kennedy Institute of Ethics Journal* 12, no. 4 (2002): pp. 325–41.
3. For an interesting current treatment of autonomy, see Alfred I. Tauber, *Patient Autonomy and the Ethics of Responsibility* (Cambridge, MA: The MIT Press, 2005). See also the curricular work of Thomas R. Cole, University of Texas Medical School, Houston: "Sacred Vocation."
4. Benjamin Freedman, *Duty and Healing Foundations of Jewish Bioethics* (New York: Routledge, 1999): p. 140.
5. Eugene Borowitz, "Jewish Autonomous Self," in *Exploring a Jewish Ethic: Papers on Covenant and Responsibility* (Detroit: Wayne State University Press, 1990): pp. 182–83.
6. Melissa Raphael, *The Female Face of God in Auschwitz: A Jewish Feminist Theology of the Holocaust* (New York: Routledge): pp. 86–106; and Laurie Zoloth, *Health Care and the Ethics of Encounter: A Jewish Discussion of Social Justice* (Chapel Hill: University of North Carolina Press, 1999): pp. 193–220.
7. Leon Kass, *Life, Liberty and the Defense of Dignity: The Challenge for Bioethics* (San Francisco: Encounter Books, 2002): pp. 62–63.
8. William Cutter, "Rabbi Judah's Handmaid," in Walter Jacob and Moshe Zemer, ed., *Death and Euthanasia in Jewish Law: Essays and Responsa* (Pittsburgh: Rodef Shalom Press, 1994): pp. 61–87.
9. William Cutter, "Do the Qualities of Story Influence the Quality of Life? Some Perspectives on the Limitations and Enhancements of Narrative Ethics," in Noam Zohar, ed., *Quality of Life in Jewish Bioethics* (Toronto: Lexington Books, 2005): pp. 55–66.
10. Philip Cohen, "Towards a Methodology of Reform Jewish Bioethics," *CCAR Journal* (Summer 2005): p. 5.
11. Louis E. Newman, "Woodchoppers and Respirators: The Problem of Interpretation in Contemporary Jewish Ethics" in *Contemporary Jewish Ethics and Morality: A Reader* (Elliot Dorff and Louis Newman, eds.) (Oxford: Oxford University Press, 1995): p. 154.
12. Zoloth, *Health Care and the Ethics of Encounter*, pp. 193–220.

13. Raphael, *The Female Face of God in Auschwitz*, pp. 86–106.

14. Kass, *Life, Liberty and the Defense of Dignity*, pp. 62–63.

15. Byron Sherwin, "Moral Implications of the Golem Legend," in *Partnership with God: Contemporary Jewish Law and Ethics* (Syracuse, NY: Syracuse University Press, 1990): pp. 181–204.

16. See Robert Cover, "Nomos and Narrative" for probably the fundamental theoretical expression of this dialectic. *Harvard Law Review* 97:4 (1983): pp. 1–5.

17. Abraham Joshua Heschel, *God in Search of Man* (New York: Farrar, Straus and Giroux, 1955): pp. 336–37.

Conclusion: Looking Back, Moving Forward

1. Some of this is treated in my book, *Jewish Thought and Scientific Discovery* (New Haven: Yale University Press, 1995; Wayne State University Press: Detroit, 2001). The later paperback edition lists some additional works on some of these subjects published after 1995. Mention should also be made of the new annual publication edited by Gad Freudenthal called *Aleph: Historical Studies in Science and Judaism* (Bloomington: Indiana University Press), which contains essays on medicine. Four issues have already appeared from 2001–2004. *Rambi*, the bibliographical index of the National and University Library of Jerusalem, lists hundreds of recent articles under "medicine." See also John Efron, *Medicine and a History of the German Jews* (New Haven, CT: Yale University Press, 2001). For a popular history of Jewish doctors, see Michael Nevins, *The Jewish Doctor: A Narrative History* (Northvale, NJ: Aronson Press, 1996), and by the same author, *Case Reports: Short Stories about Jewish Doctors* (no place of publication mentioned, 1997).

2. Most of this is based on the discussions in my book *Jewish Thought and Scientific Discovery in Early Modern Europe*. Full documentation can be found there. I list below only some more recent bibliography.

3. Ibid., pp. 295–96.

4. Ibid., pp. 297–99.

5. Ibid., p. 305.

6. Ibid., pp. 299–307. The most up-to-date information on Rodrigo and Benedict de Castro can be found in Michael Studemund-Halévy, *Biographisches Lexikon der Hamburger Sefarden: die Grabinschriften des Portugiesenfriedhofs an der Königstrasse in Hamburg-Altona* (Hamburg: Christians Verlag, 2000), index.

7. The inscription reads: "*medico teologo tra I dotti celebratissimo.*" The formulation "physician-theologian" is a precise description of the fusion of medical and rabbinic expertise that I am emphasizing here.

8. Ruderman, *Jewish Thought*, pp. 256–58.

9. Ibid., pp. 258–60. On Lampronti, see most recently David Malkiel, "Creation and Subject of Study [*Sugiyah*] in Italian Halachic Literature in the Modern

Period [Hebrew]," *Pe'amim* 86–86 (2001): pp. 258–96; David Gianfranco Di Segni, "*Il problema della storione secondo Rabbi Yitzhaq Lampronti nello Ferrara del 700*," *Zakhor* 4 (2000): pp. 115–25.

10. Ruderman, *Jewish Thought*, pp. 229–55; David Ruderman, "Medicine and Scientific Thought: The World of Tobias Cohen," in *The Jews of Early Modern Venice*, ed. Robert C. Davis and Benjamin Ravid (Baltimore: Johns Hopkins University Press, 2001): pp. 191–210. See also Shaul Massry, Miroslaw Smogorzewski, Elizur Hazani, Shaul M. Shasha, "Jewish Medicine and the University of Padua: The Contribution of the Padua Graduate Toviah Cohen to Nephrology," *American Journal of Nephrology* 19 (1999): pp. 213–21.

11. Cited in Ruderman, *Jewish Thought*, p. 236.

12. Ibid., p. 243.

13. Ibid., p. 238.

14. The portrait of Tobias is based on ibid., pp. 229–44.

Bible Study/Midrash

The Book of Job: Annotated & Explained
Translation and Annotation by Donald Kraus; Foreword by Dr. Marc Brettler
Clarifies for today's readers what Job is, how to overcome difficulties in the text, and what it may mean for us. Features fresh translation and probing commentary.
5½ x 8½, 220 pp (est), Quality PB, 978-1-59473-389-5 **$16.99**

Masking and Unmasking Ourselves: Interpreting Biblical Texts on Clothing & Identity *By Dr. Norman J. Cohen*
Presents ten Bible stories that involve clothing in an essential way, as a means of learning about the text, its characters and their interactions.
6 x 9, 240 pp, HC, 978-1-58023-461-0 **$24.99**

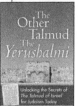

The Other Talmud—*The Yerushalmi*: Unlocking the Secrets of The Talmud of Israel for Judaism Today *By Rabbi Judith Z. Abrams, PhD*
A fascinating—and stimulating—look at "the other Talmud" and the possibilities for Jewish life reflected there. 6 x 9, 256 pp, HC, 978-1-58023-463-4 **$24.99**

The Torah Revolution: Fourteen Truths That Changed the World
By Rabbi Reuven Hammer, PhD A unique look at the Torah and the revolutionary teachings of Moses embedded within it that gave birth to Judaism and influenced the world. 6 x 9, 240 pp, HC, 978-1-58023-457-3 **$24.99**

Ecclesiastes: Annotated & Explained
Translation and Annotation by Rabbi Rami Shapiro; Foreword by Rev. Barbara Cawthorne Crafton
5½ x 8½, 160 pp, Quality PB, 978-1-59473-287-4 **$16.99**

Ethics of the Sages: Pirke Avot—Annotated & Explained *Translation and Annotation by Rabbi Rami Shapiro* 5½ x 8½, 192 pp, Quality PB, 978-1-59473-207-2 **$16.99**

The Genesis of Leadership: What the Bible Teaches Us about Vision, Values and Leading Change *By Rabbi Nathan Laufer; Foreword by Senator Joseph I. Lieberman*
6 x 9, 288 pp, Quality PB, 978-1-58023-352-1 **$18.99**

Hineini in Our Lives: Learning How to Respond to Others through 14 Biblical Texts and Personal Stories *By Rabbi Norman J. Cohen, PhD* 6 x 9, 240 pp, Quality PB, 978-1-58023-274-6 **$16.99**

A Man's Responsibility: A Jewish Guide to Being a Son, a Partner in Marriage, a Father and a Community Leader *By Rabbi Joseph B. Meszler* 6 x 9, 192 pp, Quality PB, 978-1-58023-435-1 **$16.99**

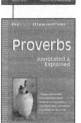

The Modern Men's Torah Commentary: New Insights from Jewish Men on the 54 Weekly Torah Portions *Edited by Rabbi Jeffrey K. Salkin*
6 x 9, 368 pp, HC, 978-1-58023-395-8 **$24.99**

Moses and the Journey to Leadership: Timeless Lessons of Effective Management from the Bible and Today's Leaders *By Rabbi Norman J. Cohen, PhD*
6 x 9, 240 pp, Quality PB, 978-1-58023-351-4 **$18.99**; HC, 978-1-58023-227-2 **$21.99**

Proverbs: Annotated & Explained
Translation and Annotation by Rabbi Rami Shapiro
5½ x 8½, 288 pp, Quality PB, 978-1-59473-310-9 **$16.99**

Righteous Gentiles in the Hebrew Bible: Ancient Role Models for Sacred Relationships
By Rabbi Jeffrey K. Salkin; Foreword by Rabbi Harold M. Schulweis;
Preface by Phyllis Tickle 6 x 9, 192 pp, Quality PB, 978-1-58023-364-4 **$18.99**

Sage Tales: Wisdom and Wonder from the Rabbis of the Talmud
By Rabbi Burton L. Visotzky 6 x 9, 256 pp, HC, 978-1-58023-456-6 **$24.99**

The Wisdom of Judaism: An Introduction to the Values of the Talmud
By Rabbi Dov Peretz Elkins 6 x 9, 192 pp, Quality PB, 978-1-58023-327-9 **$16.99**

Or phone, fax, mail or e-mail to: **JEWISH LIGHTS Publishing**
An imprint of Turner Publishing Company
4507 Charlotte Avenue • Suite 100 • Nashville, Tennessee 37209
Tel: (615) 255-2665 • www.jewishlights.com
Prices subject to change.

Congregation Resources

A Practical Guide to Rabbinic Counseling
Edited by Rabbi Yisrael N. Levitz, PhD, and Rabbi Abraham J. Twerski, MD
Provides rabbis with the requisite knowledge and practical guidelines for some of the most common counseling situations.
6 x 9, 432 pp, HC, 978-1-58023-562-4 **$40.00**

Professional Spiritual & Pastoral Care: A Practical Clergy and Chaplain's Handbook
Edited by Rabbi Stephen B. Roberts, MBA, MHL, BCJC
An essential resource integrating the classic foundations of pastoral care with the latest approaches to spiritual care, specifically intended for professionals who work or spend time with congregants in acute care hospitals, behavioral health facilities, rehabilitation centers and long-term care facilities.
6 x 9, 480 pp, HC, 978-1-59473-312-3 **$50.00**

Reimagining Leadership in Jewish Organizations: Ten Practical Lessons to Help You Implement Change and Achieve Your Goals
By Dr. Misha Galperin
Serves as a practical guidepost for lay and professional leaders to evaluate the current paradigm with insights from the world of business, psychology and research in Jewish demographics and sociology. Supported by vignettes from the field that illustrate the successes of the lessons as well as the consequences of not implementing them.
6 x 9, 192 pp, Quality PB, 978-1-58023-492-4 **$16.99**

Empowered Judaism: What Independent Minyanim Can Teach Us about Building Vibrant Jewish Communities
By Rabbi Elie Kaunfer; Foreword by Prof. Jonathan D. Sarna
6 x 9, 224 pp, Quality PB, 978-1-58023-412-2 **$18.99**

Building a Successful Volunteer Culture: Finding Meaning in Service in the Jewish Community
By Rabbi Charles Simon; Foreword by Shelley Lindauer; Preface by Dr. Ron Wolfson
6 x 9, 192 pp, Quality PB, 978-1-58023-408-5 **$16.99**

The Case for Jewish Peoplehood: Can We Be One?
By Dr. Erica Brown and Dr. Misha Galperin; Foreword by Rabbi Joseph Telushkin
6 x 9, 224 pp, HC, 978-1-58023-401-6 **$21.99**

Finding a Spiritual Home: How a New Generation of Jews Can Transform the American Synagogue
By Rabbi Sidney Schwarz
6 x 9, 352 pp, Quality PB, 978-1-58023-185-5 **$19.95**

Inspired Jewish Leadership: Practical Approaches to Building Strong Communities
By Dr. Erica Brown 6 x 9, 256 pp, HC, 978-1-58023-361-3 **$27.99**

Jewish Pastoral Care, 2nd Edition: A Practical Handbook from Traditional & Contemporary Sources
Edited by Rabbi Dayle A. Friedman, MSW, MAJCS, BCC
6 x 9, 528 pp, Quality PB, 978-1-58023-427-6 **$30.00**

Jewish Spiritual Direction: An Innovative Guide from Traditional and Contemporary Sources
Edited by Rabbi Howard A. Addison, PhD, and Barbara Eve Breitman, MSW
6 x 9, 368 pp, HC, 978-1-58023-230-2 **$30.00**

Rethinking Synagogues: A New Vocabulary for Congregational Life
By Rabbi Lawrence A. Hoffman, PhD 6 x 9, 240 pp, Quality PB, 978-1-58023-248-7 **$19.99**

Spiritual Community: The Power to Restore Hope, Commitment and Joy
By Rabbi David A. Teutsch, PhD
5½ x 8½, 144 pp, HC, 978-1-58023-270-8 **$19.99**

Spiritual Boredom: Rediscovering the Wonder of Judaism
By Dr. Erica Brown
6 x 9, 208 pp, HC, 978-1-58023-405-4 **$21.99**

The Spirituality of Welcoming: How to Transform Your Congregation into a Sacred Community
By Dr. Ron Wolfson 6 x 9, 224 pp, Quality PB, 978-1-58023-244-9 **$19.99**

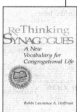

Holidays/Holy Days

Prayers of Awe Series

An exciting new series that examines the High Holy Day liturgy to enrich the praying experience of everyone—whether experienced worshipers or guests who encounter Jewish prayer for the very first time.

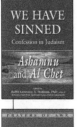

We Have Sinned—Confession in Judaism: *Ashamnu* and *Al Chet*
Edited by Rabbi Lawrence A. Hoffman, PhD
A varied and fascinating look at sin, confession and pardon in Judaism, as suggested by the centrality of *Ashamnu* and *Al Chet*, two prayers that people know so well, though understand so little.   6 x 9, 250 pp (est), HC, 978-1-58023-612-6 **$24.99**

Who by Fire, Who by Water—*Un'taneh Tokef*
Edited by Rabbi Lawrence A. Hoffman, PhD 6 x 9, 272 pp, HC, 978-1-58023-424-5 **$24.99**

All These Vows—*Kol Nidre*
Edited by Rabbi Lawrence A. Hoffman, PhD 6 x 9, 288 pp, HC, 978-1-58023-430-6 **$24.99**

Rosh Hashanah Readings: Inspiration, Information and Contemplation
Yom Kippur Readings: Inspiration, Information and Contemplation
Edited by Rabbi Dov Peretz Elkins; Section Introductions from Arthur Green's These Are the Words
Rosh Hashanah: 6 x 9, 400 pp, Quality PB, 978-1-58023-437-5 **$19.99**
Yom Kippur: 6 x 9, 368 pp, Quality PB, 978-1-58023-438-2 **$19.99**; HC, 978-1-58023-271-5 **$24.99**

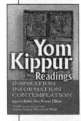

Reclaiming Judaism as a Spiritual Practice: Holy Days and Shabbat
By Rabbi Goldie Milgram 7 x 9, 272 pp, Quality PB, 978-1-58023-205-0 **$19.99**

The Sabbath Soul: Mystical Reflections on the Transformative Power of Holy Time
Selection, Translation and Commentary by Eitan Fishbane, PhD
6 x 9, 208 pp, Quality PB, 978-1-58023-459-7 **$18.99**

Shabbat, 2nd Edition: The Family Guide to Preparing for and Celebrating the Sabbath
By Dr. Ron Wolfson 7 x 9, 320 pp, Illus., Quality PB, 978-1-58023-164-0 **$19.99**

Hanukkah, 2nd Edition: The Family Guide to Spiritual Celebration
By Dr. Ron Wolfson 7 x 9, 240 pp, Illus., Quality PB, 978-1-58023-122-0 **$18.95**

Passover

My People's Passover Haggadah
Traditional Texts, Modern Commentaries
Edited by Rabbi Lawrence A. Hoffman, PhD, and David Arnow, PhD
A diverse and exciting collection of commentaries on the traditional Passover Haggadah—in two volumes!
Vol. 1: 7 x 10, 304 pp, HC, 978-1-58023-354-5 **$24.99**
Vol. 2: 7 x 10, 320 pp, HC, 978-1-58023-346-0 **$24.99**

Freedom Journeys: The Tale of Exodus and Wilderness across Millennia
By Rabbi Arthur O. Waskow and Rabbi Phyllis O. Berman
Explores how the story of Exodus echoes in our own time, calling us to relearn and rethink the Passover story through social-justice, ecological, feminist and interfaith perspectives. 6 x 9, 288 pp, HC, 978-1-58023-445-0 **$24.99**

Leading the Passover Journey: The Seder's Meaning Revealed,
the Haggadah's Story Retold *By Rabbi Nathan Laufer*
Uncovers the hidden meaning of the Seder's rituals and customs.
6 x 9, 224 pp, Quality PB, 978-1-58023-399-6 **$18.99**

Creating Lively Passover Seders, 2nd Edition: A Sourcebook of Engaging Tales,
Texts & Activities *By David Arnow, PhD* 7 x 9, 464 pp, Quality PB, 978-1-58023-444-3 **$24.99**

Passover, 2nd Edition: The Family Guide to Spiritual Celebration
By Dr. Ron Wolfson with Joel Lurie Grishaver 7 x 9, 416 pp, Quality PB, 978-1-58023-174-9 **$19.95**

The Women's Passover Companion: Women's Reflections on the Festival of Freedom
Edited by Rabbi Sharon Cohen Anisfeld, Tara Mohr and Catherine Spector; Foreword by Paula E. Hyman
6 x 9, 352 pp, Quality PB, 978-1-58023-231-9 **$19.99**; HC, 978-1-58023-128-2 **$24.95**

The Women's Seder Sourcebook: Rituals & Readings for Use at the Passover Seder
Edited by Rabbi Sharon Cohen Anisfeld, Tara Mohr and Catherine Spector
6 x 9, 384 pp, Quality PB, 978-1-58023-232-6 **$19.99**

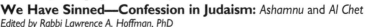

Life Cycle

Marriage/Parenting/Family/Aging

The New Jewish Baby Album: Creating and Celebrating the Beginning of a Spiritual Life—A Jewish Lights Companion
By the Editors at Jewish Lights; Foreword by Anita Diamant; Preface by Rabbi Sandy Eisenberg Sasso
A spiritual keepsake that will be treasured for generations. More than just a memory book, *shows you how—and why it's important*—to create a Jewish home and a Jewish life. 8 x 10, 64 pp, Deluxe Padded HC, Full-color illus., 978-1-58023-138-1 **$19.95**

The Jewish Pregnancy Book: A Resource for the Soul, Body & Mind during Pregnancy, Birth & the First Three Months *By Sandy Falk, MD, and Rabbi Daniel Judson, with Steven A. Rapp* Medical information, prayers and rituals for each stage of pregnancy. 7 x 10, 208 pp, b/w photos, Quality PB, 978-1-58023-178-7 **$16.95**

Celebrating Your New Jewish Daughter: Creating Jewish Ways to Welcome Baby Girls into the Covenant—New and Traditional Ceremonies *By Debra Nussbaum Cohen; Foreword by Rabbi Sandy Eisenberg Sasso* 6 x 9, 272 pp, Quality PB, 978-1-58023-090-2 **$18.95**

The New Jewish Baby Book, 2nd Edition: Names, Ceremonies & Customs—A Guide for Today's Families *By Anita Diamant* 6 x 9, 320 pp, Quality PB, 978-1-58023-251-7 **$19.99**

Parenting as a Spiritual Journey: Deepening Ordinary and Extraordinary Events into Sacred Occasions *By Rabbi Nancy Fuchs-Kreimer, PhD* 6 x 9, 224 pp, Quality PB, 978-1-58023-016-2 **$17.99**

Parenting Jewish Teens: A Guide for the Perplexed
By Joanne Doades Explores the questions and issues that shape the world in which today's Jewish teenagers live and offers constructive advice to parents. 6 x 9, 176 pp, Quality PB, 978-1-58023-305-7 **$16.99**

Judaism for Two: A Spiritual Guide for Strengthening and Celebrating Your Loving Relationship *By Rabbi Nancy Fuchs-Kreimer, PhD, and Rabbi Nancy H. Wiener, DMin; Foreword by Rabbi Elliot N. Dorff, PhD*
Addresses the ways Jewish teachings can enhance and strengthen committed relationships. 6 x 9, 224 pp, Quality PB, 978-1-58023-254-8 **$16.99**

The Creative Jewish Wedding Book, 2nd Edition: A Hands-On Guide to New & Old Traditions, Ceremonies & Celebrations *By Gabrielle Kaplan-Mayer* 9 x 9, 288 pp, b/w photos, Quality PB, 978-1-58023-398-9 **$19.99**

Divorce Is a Mitzvah: A Practical Guide to Finding Wholeness and Holiness When Your Marriage Dies *By Rabbi Perry Netter; Afterword by Rabbi Laura Geller* 6 x 9, 224 pp, Quality PB, 978-1-58023-172-5 **$16.95**

Embracing the Covenant: Converts to Judaism Talk About Why & How
By Rabbi Allan Berkowitz and Patti Moskovitz 6 x 9, 192 pp, Quality PB, 978-1-879045-50-7 **$16.95**

The Guide to Jewish Interfaith Family Life: An InterfaithFamily.com Handbook
Edited by Ronnie Friedland and Edmund Case
6 x 9, 384 pp, Quality PB, 978-1-58023-153-4 **$18.95**

A Heart of Wisdom: Making the Jewish Journey from Midlife through the Elder Years
Edited by Susan Berrin; Foreword by Rabbi Harold Kushner
6 x 9, 384 pp, Quality PB, 978-1-58023-051-3 **$18.95**

Introducing My Faith and My Community: The Jewish Outreach Institute Guide for the Christian in a Jewish Interfaith Relationship
By Rabbi Kerry M. Olitzky 6 x 9, 176 pp, Quality PB, 978-1-58023-192-3 **$16.99**

Making a Successful Jewish Interfaith Marriage: The Jewish Outreach Institute Guide to Opportunities, Challenges and Resources *By Rabbi Kerry M. Olitzky with Joan Peterson Littman*
6 x 9, 176 pp, Quality PB, 978-1-58023-170-1 **$16.95**

A Man's Responsibility: A Jewish Guide to Being a Son, a Partner in Marriage, a Father and a Community Leader *By Rabbi Joseph B. Meszler*
6 x 9, 192 pp, Quality PB, 978-1-58023-435-1 **$16.99**; HC, 978-1-58023-362-0 **$21.99**

So That Your Values Live On: Ethical Wills and How to Prepare Them
Edited by Rabbi Jack Riemer and Rabbi Nathaniel Stampfer
6 x 9, 272 pp, Quality PB, 978-1-879045-34-7 **$18.99**

Spirituality/Prayer

Making Prayer Real: Leading Jewish Spiritual Voices on Why Prayer Is Difficult and What to Do about It *By Rabbi Mike Comins*
A new and different response to the challenges of Jewish prayer, with "best prayer practices" from Jewish spiritual leaders of all denominations.
6 x 9, 320 pp, Quality PB, 978-1-58023-417-7 **$18.99**

Witnesses to the One: The Spiritual History of the *Sh'ma*
By Rabbi Joseph B. Meszler; Foreword by Rabbi Elyse Goldstein
6 x 9, 176 pp, Quality PB, 978-1-58023-400-9 **$16.99**; HC, 978-1-58023-309-5 **$19.99**

My People's Prayer Book Series: Traditional Prayers, Modern Commentaries *Edited by Rabbi Lawrence A. Hoffman, PhD*
Provides diverse and exciting commentary to the traditional liturgy. Will help you find new wisdom in Jewish prayer, and bring liturgy into your life. Each book includes Hebrew text, modern translations and commentaries from all perspectives of the Jewish world.

Vol. 1—The *Sh'ma* and Its Blessings
    7 x 10, 168 pp, HC, 978-1-879045-79-8 **$29.99**
Vol. 2—The *Amidah* 7 x 10, 240 pp, HC, 978-1-879045-80-4 **$24.95**
Vol. 3—*P'sukei D'zimrah* (Morning Psalms)
    7 x 10, 240 pp, HC, 978-1-879045-81-1 **$29.99**
Vol. 4—*Seder K'riat Hatorah* (The Torah Service)
    7 x 10, 264 pp, HC, 978-1-879045-82-8 **$29.99**
Vol. 5—*Birkhot Hashachar* (Morning Blessings)
    7 x 10, 240 pp, HC, 978-1-879045-83-5 **$24.95**
Vol. 6—*Tachanun* and Concluding Prayers
    7 x 10, 240 pp, HC, 978-1-879045-84-2 **$24.95**
Vol. 7—Shabbat at Home 7 x 10, 240 pp, HC, 978-1-879045-85-9 **$24.95**
Vol. 8—*Kabbalat Shabbat* (Welcoming Shabbat in the Synagogue)
    7 x 10, 240 pp, HC, 978-1-58023-121-3 **$24.99**
Vol. 9—Welcoming the Night: *Minchah* and *Ma'ariv* (Afternoon and
    Evening Prayer) 7 x 10, 272 pp, HC, 978-1-58023-262-3 **$24.99**
Vol. 10—Shabbat Morning: *Shacharit* and *Musaf* (Morning and
    Additional Services) 7 x 10, 240 pp, HC, 978-1-58023-240-1 **$29.99**

Spirituality/Lawrence Kushner

I'm God; You're Not: Observations on Organized Religion & Other Disguises of the Ego
6 x 9, 256 pp, Quality PB, 978-1-58023-513-6 **$18.99**; HC, 978-1-58023-441-2 **$21.99**

The Book of Letters: A Mystical Hebrew Alphabet
Popular HC Edition, 6 x 9, 80 pp, 2-color text, 978-1-879045-00-2 **$24.95**
Collector's Limited Edition, 9 x 12, 80 pp, gold-foil-embossed pages, w/ limited-edition silkscreened print, 978-1-879045-04-0 **$349.00**

The Book of Miracles: A Young Person's Guide to Jewish Spiritual Awareness
6 x 9, 96 pp, 2-color illus., HC, 978-1-879045-78-1 **$16.95** *For ages 9–13*

The Book of Words: Talking Spiritual Life, Living Spiritual Talk
6 x 9, 160 pp, Quality PB, 978-1-58023-020-9 **$18.99**

Eyes Remade for Wonder: A Lawrence Kushner Reader *Introduction by Thomas Moore*
6 x 9, 240 pp, Quality PB, 978-1-58023-042-1 **$18.95**

God Was in This Place & I, i Did Not Know: Finding Self, Spirituality and Ultimate Meaning 6 x 9, 192 pp, Quality PB, 978-1-879045-33-0 **$16.95**

Honey from the Rock: An Introduction to Jewish Mysticism
6 x 9, 176 pp, Quality PB, 978-1-58023-073-5 **$16.95**

Invisible Lines of Connection: Sacred Stories of the Ordinary
5½ x 8½, 160 pp, Quality PB, 978-1-879045-98-9 **$15.95**

Jewish Spirituality: A Brief Introduction for Christians
5½ x 8½, 112 pp, Quality PB, 978-1-58023-150-3 **$12.95**

The River of Light: Jewish Mystical Awareness
6 x 9, 192 pp, Quality PB, 978-1-58023-096-4 **$16.95**

The Way Into Jewish Mystical Tradition
6 x 9, 224 pp, Quality PB, 978-1-58023-200-5 **$18.99**; HC, 978-1-58023-029-2 **$21.95**

Inspiration

God of Me: Imagining God throughout Your Lifetime
By Rabbi David Lyon Helps you cut through preconceived ideas of God and dogmas that stifle your creativity when thinking about your personal relationship with God. 6 x 9, 176 pp, Quality PB, 978-1-58023-452-8 **$16.99**

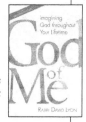

The God Upgrade: Finding Your 21st-Century Spirituality in Judaism's 5,000-Year-Old Tradition *By Rabbi Jamie Korngold; Foreword by Rabbi Harold M. Schulweis* A provocative look at how our changing God concepts have shaped every aspect of Judaism. 6 x 9, 176 pp, Quality PB, 978-1-58023-443-6 **$15.99**

The Seven Questions You're Asked in Heaven: Reviewing and Renewing Your Life on Earth *By Dr. Ron Wolfson* An intriguing and entertaining resource for living a life that matters. 6 x 9, 176 pp, Quality PB, 978-1-58023-407-8 **$16.99**

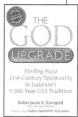

Happiness and the Human Spirit: The Spirituality of Becoming the Best You Can Be *By Rabbi Abraham J. Twerski, MD*
Shows you that true happiness is attainable once you stop looking outside yourself for the source. 6 x 9, 176 pp, Quality PB, 978-1-58023-404-7 **$16.99**; HC, 978-1-58023-343-9 **$19.99**

A Formula for Proper Living: Practical Lessons from Life and Torah
By Rabbi Abraham J. Twerski, MD 6 x 9, 144 pp, HC, 978-1-58023-402-3 **$19.99**

The Bridge to Forgiveness: Stories and Prayers for Finding God and Restoring Wholeness *By Rabbi Karyn D. Kedar* 6 x 9, 176 pp, Quality PB, 978-1-58023-451-1 **$16.99**

The Empty Chair: Finding Hope and Joy—Timeless Wisdom from a Hasidic Master, Rebbe Nachman of Breslov *Adapted by Moshe Mykoff and the Breslov Research Institute* 4 x 6, 128 pp, Deluxe PB w/ flaps, 978-1-879045-67-5 **$9.99**

The Gentle Weapon: Prayers for Everyday and Not-So-Everyday Moments— Timeless Wisdom from the Teachings of the Hasidic Master, Rebbe Nachman of Breslov *Adapted by Moshe Mykoff and S. C. Mizrahi, together with the Breslov Research Institute* 4 x 6, 144 pp, Deluxe PB w/ flaps, 978-1-58023-022-3 **$9.99**

God Whispers: Stories of the Soul, Lessons of the Heart *By Rabbi Karyn D. Kedar* 6 x 9, 176 pp, Quality PB, 978-1-58023-088-9 **$15.95**

God's To-Do List: 103 Ways to Be an Angel and Do God's Work on Earth
By Dr. Ron Wolfson 6 x 9, 144 pp, Quality PB, 978-1-58023-301-9 **$16.99**

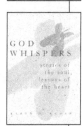

Jewish Stories from Heaven and Earth: Inspiring Tales to Nourish the Heart and Soul *Edited by Rabbi Dov Peretz Elkins* 6 x 9, 304 pp, Quality PB, 978-1-58023-363-7 **$16.99**

Life's Daily Blessings: Inspiring Reflections on Gratitude and Joy for Every Day, Based on Jewish Wisdom *By Rabbi Kerry M. Olitzky* 4½ x 6½, 368 pp, Quality PB, 978-1-58023-396-5 **$16.99**

Restful Reflections: Nighttime Inspiration to Calm the Soul, Based on Jewish Wisdom *By Rabbi Kerry M. Olitzky and Rabbi Lori Forman-Jacobi* 4½ x 6½, 448 pp, Quality PB, 978-1-58023-091-9 **$16.99**

Sacred Intentions: Morning Inspiration to Strengthen the Spirit, Based on Jewish Wisdom *By Rabbi Kerry M. Olitzky and Rabbi Lori Forman-Jacobi* 4½ x 6½, 448 pp, Quality PB, 978-1-58023-061-2 **$16.99**

Kabbalah/Mysticism

Jewish Mysticism and the Spiritual Life: Classical Texts, Contemporary Reflections *Edited by Dr. Lawrence Fine, Dr. Eitan Fishbane and Rabbi Or N. Rose* Inspirational and thought-provoking materials for contemplation, discussion and action. 6 x 9, 256 pp, HC, 978-1-58023-434-4 **$24.99**

Ehyeh: A Kabbalah for Tomorrow
By Rabbi Arthur Green, PhD 6 x 9, 224 pp, Quality PB, 978-1-58023-213-5 **$18.99**

The Gift of Kabbalah: Discovering the Secrets of Heaven, Renewing Your Life on Earth
By Tamar Frankiel, PhD 6 x 9, 256 pp, Quality PB, 978-1-58023-141-1 **$16.95**

Seek My Face: A Jewish Mystical Theology *By Rabbi Arthur Green, PhD*
6 x 9, 304 pp, Quality PB, 978-1-58023-130-5 **$19.95**

Zohar: Annotated & Explained *Translation & Annotation by Dr. Daniel C. Matt; Foreword by Andrew Harvey* 5½ x 8½, 176 pp, Quality PB, 978-1-893361-51-5 **$15.99**
(A book from SkyLight Paths, Jewish Lights' sister imprint)

Ecology/Environment

A Wild Faith: Jewish Ways into Wilderness, Wilderness Ways into Judaism
By Rabbi Mike Comins; Foreword by Nigel Savage 6 x 9, 240 pp, Quality PB, 978-1-58023-316-3 **$16.99**

Ecology & the Jewish Spirit: Where Nature & the Sacred Meet
Edited by Ellen Bernstein 6 x 9, 288 pp, Quality PB, 978-1-58023-082-7 **$18.99**

Torah of the Earth: Exploring 4,000 Years of Ecology in Jewish Thought
Vol. 1: Biblical Israel & Rabbinic Judaism; Vol. 2: Zionism & Eco-Judaism
Edited by Rabbi Arthur Waskow Vol. 1: 6 x 9, 272 pp, Quality PB, 978-1-58023-086-5 **$19.95**
Vol. 2: 6 x 9, 336 pp, Quality PB, 978-1-58023-087-2 **$19.95**

The Way Into Judaism and the Environment *By Jeremy Benstein, PhD*
6 x 9, 288 pp, Quality PB, 978-1-58023-368-2 **$18.99**; HC, 978-1-58023-268-5 **$24.99**

Graphic Novels/Graphic History

The Adventures of Rabbi Harvey: A Graphic Novel of Jewish Wisdom and Wit in the
Wild West *By Steve Sheinkin* 6 x 9, 144 pp, Full-color illus., Quality PB, 978-1-58023-310-1 **$16.99**

Rabbi Harvey Rides Again: A Graphic Novel of Jewish Folktales Let Loose in the
Wild West *By Steve Sheinkin* 6 x 9, 144 pp, Full-color illus., Quality PB, 978-1-58023-347-7 **$16.99**

Rabbi Harvey vs. the Wisdom Kid: A Graphic Novel of Dueling
Jewish Folktales in the Wild West *By Steve Sheinkin*
Rabbi Harvey's first book-length adventure—and toughest challenge.
6 x 9, 144 pp, Full-color illus., Quality PB, 978-1-58023-422-1 **$16.99**

The Story of the Jews: A 4,000-Year Adventure—A Graphic History Book
By Stan Mack 6 x 9, 288 pp, Illus., Quality PB, 978-1-58023-155-8 **$16.99**

Grief/Healing

Facing Illness, Finding God: How Judaism Can Help You and
Caregivers Cope When Body or Spirit Fails *By Rabbi Joseph B. Meszler*
Will help you find spiritual strength for healing amid the fear, pain and chaos of
illness. 6 x 9, 208 pp, Quality PB, 978-1-58023-423-8 **$16.99**

Midrash & Medicine: Healing Body and Soul in the Jewish Interpretive
Tradition *Edited by Rabbi William Cutter, PhD; Foreword by Michele F. Prince, LCSW, MAJCS*
Explores how midrash can help you see beyond the physical aspects of healing to
tune in to your spiritual source.
6 x 9, 352 pp, Quality PB, 978-1-58023-484-9 **$21.99**

Healing from Despair: Choosing Wholeness in a Broken World
By Rabbi Elie Kaplan Spitz with Erica Shapiro Taylor; Foreword by Abraham J. Twerski, MD
5½ x 8½, 208 pp, Quality PB, 978-1-58023-436-8 **$16.99**

Healing and the Jewish Imagination: Spiritual and Practical Perspectives on
Judaism and Health *Edited by Rabbi William Cutter, PhD*
6 x 9, 240 pp, Quality PB, 978-1-58023-373-6 **$19.99**

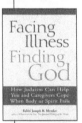

Grief in Our Seasons: A Mourner's Kaddish Companion *By Rabbi Kerry M. Olitzky*
4½ x 6½, 448 pp, Quality PB, 978-1-879045-55-2 **$15.95**

Healing of Soul, Healing of Body: Spiritual Leaders Unfold the Strength & Solace
in Psalms *Edited by Rabbi Simkha Y. Weintraub, LCSW*
6 x 9, 128 pp, 2-color illus. text, Quality PB, 978-1-879045-31-6 **$16.99**

Mourning & Mitzvah, 2nd Edition: A Guided Journal for Walking the Mourner's
Path through Grief to Healing *By Rabbi Anne Brener, LCSW*
7½ x 9, 304 pp, Quality PB, 978-1-58023-113-8 **$19.99**

Tears of Sorrow, Seeds of Hope, 2nd Edition: A Jewish Spiritual Companion
for Infertility and Pregnancy Loss *By Rabbi Nina Beth Cardin*
6 x 9, 208 pp, Quality PB, 978-1-58023-233-3 **$18.99**

A Time to Mourn, a Time to Comfort, 2nd Edition: A Guide to Jewish
Bereavement *By Dr. Ron Wolfson; Foreword by Rabbi David J. Wolpe*
7 x 9, 384 pp, Quality PB, 978-1-58023-253-1 **$21.99**

When a Grandparent Dies: A Kid's Own Remembering Workbook for Dealing
with Shiva and the Year Beyond *By Nechama Liss-Levinson, PhD*
8 x 10, 48 pp, 2-color text, HC, 978-1-879045-44-6 **$15.95** *For ages 7–13*

Meditation

Jewish Meditation Practices for Everyday Life
Awakening Your Heart, Connecting with God
By Rabbi Jeff Roth
Offers a fresh take on meditation that draws on life experience and living life with greater clarity as opposed to the traditional method of rigorous study.
6 x 9, 224 pp, Quality PB, 978-1-58023-397-2 **$18.99**

The Handbook of Jewish Meditation Practices
A Guide for Enriching the Sabbath and Other Days of Your Life
By Rabbi David A. Cooper Easy-to-learn meditation techniques.
6 x 9, 208 pp, Quality PB, 978-1-58023-102-2 **$16.95**

Discovering Jewish Meditation, 2nd Edition
Instruction & Guidance for Learning an Ancient Spiritual Practice
By Nan Fink Gefen, PhD 6 x 9, 208 pp, Quality PB, 978-1-58023-462-7 **$16.99**

Meditation from the Heart of Judaism
Today's Teachers Share Their Practices, Techniques, and Faith
Edited by Avram Davis 6 x 9, 256 pp, Quality PB, 978-1-58023-049-0 **$16.95**

Ritual/Sacred Practices

The Jewish Dream Book: The Key to Opening the Inner Meaning of
Your Dreams *By Vanessa L. Ochs, PhD, with Elizabeth Ochs; Illus. by Kristina Swarner*
Instructions for how modern people can perform ancient Jewish dream practices and dream interpretations drawn from the Jewish wisdom tradition.
8 x 8, 128 pp, Full-color illus., Deluxe PB w/ flaps, 978-1-58023-132-9 **$16.95**

God in Your Body: Kabbalah, Mindfulness and Embodied Spiritual Practice
By Jay Michaelson
The first comprehensive treatment of the body in Jewish spiritual practice and an essential guide to the sacred.
6 x 9, 272 pp, Quality PB, 978-1-58023-304-0 **$18.99**

The Book of Jewish Sacred Practices: CLAL's Guide to Everyday &
Holiday Rituals & Blessings *Edited by Rabbi Irwin Kula and Vanessa L. Ochs, PhD*
6 x 9, 368 pp, Quality PB, 978-1-58023-152-7 **$18.95**

Jewish Ritual: A Brief Introduction for Christians
By Rabbi Kerry M. Olitzky and Rabbi Daniel Judson
5½ x 8½, 144 pp, Quality PB, 978-1-58023-210-4 **$14.99**

The Rituals & Practices of a Jewish Life: A Handbook for Personal Spiritual
Renewal *Edited by Rabbi Kerry M. Olitzky and Rabbi Daniel Judson*
6 x 9, 272 pp, Illus., Quality PB, 978-1-58023-169-5 **$18.95**

The Sacred Art of Lovingkindness: Preparing to Practice
By Rabbi Rami Shapiro 5½ x 8½, 176 pp, Quality PB, 978-1-59473-151-8 **$16.99**
(A book from SkyLight Paths, Jewish Lights' sister imprint)

Science Fiction/Mystery & Detective Fiction

Criminal Kabbalah: An Intriguing Anthology of Jewish Mystery &
Detective Fiction *Edited by Lawrence W. Raphael; Foreword by Laurie R. King*
All-new stories from twelve of today's masters of mystery and detective fiction—sure to delight mystery buffs of all faith traditions.
6 x 9, 256 pp, Quality PB, 978-1-58023-109-1 **$16.95**

Mystery Midrash: An Anthology of Jewish Mystery & Detective Fiction
Edited by Lawrence W. Raphael; Preface by Joel Siegel
6 x 9, 304 pp, Quality PB, 978-1-58023-055-1 **$16.95**

Wandering Stars: An Anthology of Jewish Fantasy & Science Fiction
Edited by Jack Dann; Introduction by Isaac Asimov
6 x 9, 272 pp, Quality PB, 978-1-58023-005-6 **$18.99**

More Wandering Stars: An Anthology of Outstanding Stories of Jewish Fantasy and
Science Fiction *Edited by Jack Dann; Introduction by Isaac Asimov*
6 x 9, 192 pp, Quality PB, 978-1-58023-063-6 **$16.95**

Spirituality

The Jewish Lights Spirituality Handbook: A Guide to Understanding, Exploring & Living a Spiritual Life *Edited by Stuart M. Matlins*
What exactly is "Jewish" about spirituality? How do I make it a part of my life? Fifty of today's foremost spiritual leaders share their ideas and experience with us.
6 x 9, 456 pp, Quality PB, 978-1-58023-093-3 **$19.99**

The Sabbath Soul: Mystical Reflections on the Transformative Power of Holy Time *Selection, Translation and Commentary by Eitan Fishbane, PhD*
Explores the writings of mystical masters of Hasidism. Provides translations and interpretations of a wide range of Hasidic sources previously unavailable in English that reflect the spiritual transformation that takes place on the seventh day.
6 x 9, 208 pp, Quality PB, 978-1-58023-459-7 **$18.99**

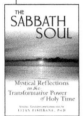

Repentance: The Meaning and Practice of *Teshuvah*
By Dr. Louis E. Newman; Foreword by Rabbi Harold M. Schulweis; Preface by Rabbi Karyn D. Kedar
Examines both the practical and philosophical dimensions of *teshuvah*, Judaism's core religious-moral teaching on repentance, and its value for us—Jews and non-Jews alike—today. 6 x 9, 256 pp, HC, 978-1-58023-426-9 **$24.99**

Aleph-Bet Yoga: Embodying the Hebrew Letters for Physical and Spiritual Well-Being
By Steven A. Rapp; Foreword by Tamar Frankiel, PhD, and Judy Greenfeld; Preface by Hart Lazer
7 x 10, 128 pp, b/w photos, Quality PB, Lay-flat binding, 978-1-58023-162-6 **$16.95**

A Book of Life: Embracing Judaism as a Spiritual Practice
By Rabbi Michael Strassfeld 6 x 9, 544 pp, Quality PB, 978-1-58023-247-0 **$19.99**

Bringing the Psalms to Life: How to Understand and Use the Book of Psalms
By Rabbi Daniel F. Polish, PhD 6 x 9, 208 pp, Quality PB, 978-1-58023-157-2 **$16.95**

Does the Soul Survive? A Jewish Journey to Belief in Afterlife, Past Lives & Living with Purpose *By Rabbi Elie Kaplan Spitz; Foreword by Brian L. Weiss, MD*
6 x 9, 288 pp, Quality PB, 978-1-58023-165-7 **$16.99**

Entering the Temple of Dreams: Jewish Prayers, Movements and Meditations for the End of the Day *By Tamar Frankiel, PhD, and Judy Greenfeld*
7 x 10, 192 pp, illus., Quality PB, 978-1-58023-079-7 **$16.95**

First Steps to a New Jewish Spirit: Reb Zalman's Guide to Recapturing the Intimacy & Ecstasy in Your Relationship with God *By Rabbi Zalman M. Schachter-Shalomi with Donald Gropman* 6 x 9, 144 pp, Quality PB, 978-1-58023-182-4 **$16.95**

Foundations of Sephardic Spirituality: The Inner Life of Jews of the Ottoman Empire
By Rabbi Marc D. Angel, PhD 6 x 9, 224 pp, Quality PB, 978-1-58023-341-5 **$18.99**

God & the Big Bang: Discovering Harmony between Science & Spirituality
By Dr. Daniel C. Matt 6 x 9, 216 pp, Quality PB, 978-1-879045-89-7 **$18.99**

God in Our Relationships: Spirituality between People from the Teachings of Martin Buber *By Rabbi Dennis S. Ross* 5½ x 8½, 160 pp, Quality PB, 978-1-58023-147-3 **$16.95**

Judaism, Physics and God: Searching for Sacred Metaphors in a Post-Einstein World
By Rabbi David W. Nelson 6 x 9, 352 pp, Quality PB, inc. reader's discussion guide,
978-1-58023-306-4 **$18.99**; HC, 352 pp, 978-1-58023-252-4 **$24.99**

Meaning & Mitzvah: Daily Practices for Reclaiming Judaism through Prayer, God, Torah, Hebrew, Mitzvot and Peoplehood *By Rabbi Goldie Milgram*
7 x 9, 336 pp, Quality PB, 978-1-58023-256-2 **$19.99**

Minding the Temple of the Soul: Balancing Body, Mind, and Spirit through Traditional Jewish Prayer, Movement, and Meditation *By Tamar Frankiel, PhD, and Judy Greenfeld*
7 x 10, 184 pp, Illus., Quality PB, 978-1-879045-64-4 **$18.99**

One God Clapping: The Spiritual Path of a Zen Rabbi *By Rabbi Alan Lew with Sherril Jaffe*
5½ x 8½, 336 pp, Quality PB, 978-1-58023-115-2 **$16.95**

The Soul of the Story: Meetings with Remarkable People
By Rabbi David Zeller 6 x 9, 288 pp, HC, 978-1-58023-272-2 **$21.99**

Tanya, the Masterpiece of Hasidic Wisdom: Selections Annotated & Explained
Translation & Annotation by Rabbi Rami Shapiro; Foreword by Rabbi Zalman M. Schachter-Shalomi
5½ x 8½, 240 pp, Quality PB, 978-1-59473-275-1 **$16.99**

These Are the Words, 2nd Edition: A Vocabulary of Jewish Spiritual Life
By Rabbi Arthur Green, PhD 6 x 9, 320 pp, Quality PB, 978-1-58023-494-8 **$19.99**

Social Justice

Where Justice Dwells
A Hands-On Guide to Doing Social Justice in Your Jewish Community
By Rabbi Jill Jacobs; Foreword by Rabbi David Saperstein
Provides ways to envision and act on your own ideals of social justice.
7 x 9, 288 pp, Quality PB Original, 978-1-58023-453-5 **$24.99**

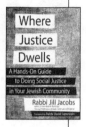

There Shall Be No Needy
Pursuing Social Justice through Jewish Law and Tradition
By Rabbi Jill Jacobs; Foreword by Rabbi Elliot N. Dorff, PhD; Preface by Simon Greer
Confronts the most pressing issues of twenty-first-century America from a deeply
Jewish perspective. 6 x 9, 288 pp, Quality PB, 978-1-58023-425-2 **$16.99**
There Shall Be No Needy Teacher's Guide 8½ x 11, 56 pp, PB, 978-1-58023-429-0 **$8.99**

Conscience
The Duty to Obey and the Duty to Disobey
By Rabbi Harold M. Schulweis
Examines the idea of conscience and the role conscience plays in our relationships
to government, law, ethics, religion, human nature, God—and to each other.
6 x 9, 160 pp, Quality PB, 978-1-58023-419-1 **$16.99**; HC, 978-1-58023-375-0 **$19.99**

Judaism and Justice
The Jewish Passion to Repair the World
By Rabbi Sidney Schwarz; Foreword by Ruth Messinger
Explores the relationship between Judaism, social justice and the Jewish identity
of American Jews. 6 x 9, 352 pp, Quality PB, 978-1-58023-353-8 **$19.99**

Spirituality/Women's Interest

New Jewish Feminism
Probing the Past, Forging the Future
Edited by Rabbi Elyse Goldstein; Foreword by Anita Diamant
Looks at the growth and accomplishments of Jewish feminism and what they
mean for Jewish women today and tomorrow.
6 x 9, 480 pp, HC, 978-1-58023-359-0 **$24.99**

The Divine Feminine in Biblical Wisdom Literature
Selections Annotated & Explained
Translation & Annotation by Rabbi Rami Shapiro
5½ x 8½, 240 pp, Quality PB, 978-1-59473-109-9 **$16.99**
(A book from SkyLight Paths, Jewish Lights' sister imprint)

The Quotable Jewish Woman
Wisdom, Inspiration & Humor from the Mind & Heart
Edited by Elaine Bernstein Partnow
6 x 9, 496 pp, Quality PB, 978-1-58023-236-4 **$19.99**

The Women's Haftarah Commentary
New Insights from Women Rabbis on the 54 Weekly Haftarah Portions,
the 5 Megillot & Special Shabbatot
Edited by Rabbi Elyse Goldstein
Illuminates the historical significance of female portrayals in the Haftarah and the
Five Megillot. 6 x 9, 560 pp, Quality PB, 978-1-58023-371-2 **$19.99**

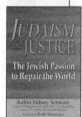

The Women's Torah Commentary
New Insights from Women Rabbis on the 54 Weekly Torah Portions
Edited by Rabbi Elyse Goldstein
Over fifty women rabbis offer inspiring insights on the Torah, in a week-by-week format.
6 x 9, 496 pp, Quality PB, 978-1-58023-370-5 **$19.99**; HC, 978-1-58023-076-6 **$34.95**

See Passover for *The Women's Passover Companion: Women's Reflections on
the Festival of Freedom* and *The Women's Seder Sourcebook: Rituals &
Readings for Use at the Passover Seder.*

About Jewish Lights

People of all faiths and backgrounds yearn for books that attract, engage, educate, and spiritually inspire.

Our principal goal is to stimulate thought and help all people learn about who the Jewish People are, where they come from, and what the future can be made to hold. While people of our diverse Jewish heritage are the primary audience, our books speak to people in the Christian world as well and will broaden their understanding of Judaism and the roots of their own faith.

We bring to you authors who are at the forefront of spiritual thought and experience. While each has something different to say, they all say it in a voice that you can hear.

Our books are designed to welcome you and then to engage, stimulate, and inspire. We judge our success not only by whether or not our books are beautiful and commercially successful, but by whether or not they make a difference in your life.

For your information and convenience, at the back of this book we have provided a list of other Jewish Lights books you might find interesting and useful. They cover all the categories of your life:

Bar/Bat Mitzvah	Life Cycle
Bible Study / Midrash	Meditation
Children's Books	Men's Interest
Congregation Resources	Parenting
Current Events / History	Prayer / Ritual / Sacred Practice
Ecology / Environment	Social Justice
Fiction: Mystery, Science Fiction	Spirituality
Grief / Healing	Theology / Philosophy
Holidays / Holy Days	Travel
Inspiration	Twelve Steps
Kabbalah / Mysticism / Enneagram	Women's Interest

Stuart M. Matlins, Publisher

Or phone, fax, mail or e-mail to: **JEWISH LIGHTS Publishing**
An imprint of Turner Publishing Company
4507 Charlotte Avenue • Suite 100 • Nashville, Tennessee 37209
Tel: (615) 255-2665 • www.jewishlights.com
Prices subject to change.

For more information about each book, visit our website at www.jewishlights.com

Printed in the USA
CPSIA information can be obtained
at www.ICGtesting.com
JSHW022325140824
68134JS00019B/1291